A Person-Centered Approach and the Rogerian Tradition

A Handbook

Adam Quinn

FOR,

Joan

- and -

Stephen McConnell

CONTENTS

INTRODUCTION

This book is about a person-centered approach to counseling and psychotherapy as developed by the psychologist Carl Rogers (1902-1987) and his colleagues. As indicated by the subtitle, this book is also in some sense a handbook on the person-centered approach and the Rogerian tradition. However, the content from which this handbook is constructed comes from my point of view and in the end is an argument - though relying upon a large amount of scholarly evidence - in defense of my point of view.

My Point of View

In short, my point of view is composed of two parts. First, (a) if a person is to be of help to another, then no treatment planning, agenda-setting, techniques, or coaching is necessary; all that is necessary is for the helper to be a genuinely congruent person, with an intention toward unconditional acceptance and understanding, possessing an ability to convey this intention to another. And second, (b) the Rogerian tradition (ca. 1940 – 1975) provided a necessary and sufficient theoretical framework from which a helping professional could offer a growth-promoting environment, with near-limitless potential to be of help. However, this tradition was systematically dismissed and decommissioned, so to speak, by social, behavioral, and psychological scientists in favor of their own treatment paradigms that are ineffective at best and psychologically damaging at worst. But, these treatment paradigms are both commercial and nonspecific enough to guarantee a livelihood for each new generation of psychologist, social worker, and social engineer; a livelihood provided in the form of jobs, academic positions, book deals, for-profit measurement instruments, and collegial esteem. That is, unlike the Rogerian tradition, today's mainstream treatment approaches have yet to empirically discover specific mechanisms of change or specific common factors that may contribute to increased client well-being. Rather, as the literature suggests, we know that these mainstream treatments are applied behind closed doors and sometime later the client may improve, and this improvement may last for a while. Furthermore, in the process of addressing this problem of how therapeutic change occurs, nearly all mainstream journal articles provide few concrete answers beyond those that could also be interpreted as aberrations correlated with researcher allegiance bias. They conclude, as is the fashion, that "further research is needed." In this way, life is continually breathed back into a research field that, the literature suggests, tends to reinvent the wheel every twenty to thirty years, to begin again.

The Structure of This Book

This book contains both a new and previously unpublished manuscript as well as my previous writings on the person-centered approach - which were originally published in the *Journal of Humanistic Psychology* (*JHP*). Specifically, Chapter 1, entitled "A Person-Centered Approach and the Structure of Scientific Revolutions," provides support to much of what I have outlined in part (b) of my point of view above. Chapter 1 is previously unpublished and is comprehensive. Chapters 2 thru 4 provide support to part (a) of my point of view above. In particular, a version of Chapter 2, entitled "A Person-Centered Approach to Multicultural Counseling Competence," can be found in the April 2013 issue of the *JHP*. Likewise, a version of Chapter 3, entitled "A Person-Centered Approach to the Treatment of Borderline Personality Disorder," can be found in the October 2011 issue of the same journal, which was also the *JHP's* 50th anniversary issue. Finally, a version of Chapter 4, entitled "A Person-Centered Approach to the Treatment of Combat Veterans with Posttraumatic Stress Disorder," can be found in the October 2008 issue which was also the *JHP's* special issue on the life and work of Abraham Maslow.

I have organized the chapters in descending time, with my most recent thinking presented in Chapter 1. In this way, an interested reader can read this book from start to finish and witness, albeit backwards, the evolution of my thinking on this subject. However, each chapter is also self-contained and can be read in any order. I admit that there is some overlap in ideas from chapter to chapter. However, as one will see, ideas or assertions made in Chapter 4 are expanded upon, clarified, and supported with further evidence in Chapter 3. Likewise, Chapter 2 provides further support to certain ideas that I only touched upon in Chapter 3.

Finally, if I were to have a *magnum opus* on the subject of Carl Rogers and the person-centered approach, Chapter 1 would be this. If a critic or skeptic were to read this book starting from Chapter 4, he or she would arrive at Chapter 1 with doubts, questions, and dismissals of many of my ideas in Chapters 2 thru 4. This is the nature of publishing page-limited journal articles, where one is not able to expand in detail in order to support assertions that some may regard as controversial or questionable. Therefore, Chapter 1, though longer than what can be published in a scholarly journal, provides a great deal of background and support to much of my thinking in the subsequent chapters.

The Evolution of the Ideas in This Book

As I begin to draw this introductory chapter to a close, I would like to provide a few reflections on how the ideas contained herein materialized in print. In the early years of the 21st century I was an arduous "necessary and sufficient" proponent, which has not changed as my earlier remarks in this Introduction suggest. However, in earlier years I was guided, more so than now, by my youthful righteousness; Carl Rogers and person-centered therapy was simply the best way, and the social, behavioral, and psychological sciences were simply wrong. This attitude is exemplified most in Chapter 4, which was published in 2008. I provide few citations and a great deal of speculation; though the passion and naivety I possessed while formulating this paper makes me very fond of it. I also feel strongly that Chapter 4 continues to provide an important contribution to understanding the development of PTSD in combat veterans.

In a similar way, I also feel this fondness and pride with regard to Chapter 3, my "borderline" paper. My borderline paper represents a point in my evolution as a writer in which I was compelled to take the risk of describing in detail the way in which I worked with one of the hardest-to-serve, most controversial populations of clients. In my experience, clients who exhibit suicidal and parasuicidal behaviors tend to engender in treatment professionals a state of near-hysteria, whereby only the most rigid and controlling treatment modalities are considered for use. Certainly, safety is a primary issue with clients who engage in risk-taking behaviors, but what will these treatment professionals do for the other 45 minutes of the 50-minute session, I wonder; will they spend three-quarters of an hour shaming the client or will they get to know the client as a person? In some ways this question is what compelled me to take the risk to really say what I thought, and charge forward with a set of hypothesized mechanisms of change that challenged Marsha Linehan's ideas in particular. Of note, I owe Kirk Schneider (the editor of the *Journal of Humanistic Psychology* at the time) a great deal for his patience, as well as the reviewers who asked from me - as I had felt then - for monumental and impossible changes to be made.

Next, Chapter 2 demonstrates the writing and thinking skills I acquired from the above process. This chapter also represents the time period during which I discovered that the root of the problems within the mainstream helping professions were more complicated than simply an ignorance of Rogers's work. In other words, I decided to begin building a real argument against the mainstream, rather than continue to hang my hat upon the "I'm right, they're wrong" attitude that I had previously held. Chapter 2, or my "multicultural paper," was oriented toward describing an applicable treatment approach, as were Chapters 3 and 4. Although Chapter 2 provides comprehensive information on multicultural counseling competence as well as a detailed culturally-adapted person-centered approach, in the end I felt that I had only explored the tip of the iceberg, so to speak. Two years in the making, Chapter 1 plumbs the depths to find out how big is this iceberg, and to what extent is this iceberg on a collision course with what remains of the goodness and purity in this profession.

The Audience

I feel that this book can be of use to the beginning student and counselor-in-training, as well as to the experienced and veteran counselors, psychotherapists, and academics. Whether one agrees or disagrees with what I have written, I feel that this book can be facilitative for anyone who possesses an interest in the helping professions. However, this book is not intended to be a replacement for practice experience, but to be a guide toward developing as a professional and, possibly, as a person.

Conclusion

In conclusion, I feel the following quotation summarizes much of what has propelled me along my path of inquiry and, in the end, what I hope this book will convey. In the introduction to their well-known compilation, *Client-Centered Therapy and the Person-Centered Approach: New Directions in Theory, Research, and Practice*, Levant & Shlien (1984) remark:

Rogerians are not blind fools, but neither do they want to turn the world over to the cynics, who already have the advantage of appearing to be more realistic. Why so? That advantage is all too easy. Cynicism takes its scornful ease at the expense of idealism's efforts. Pessimists can't be disappointed or accused of bad judgment in case of failure. They hold a defensive position [...] cynicism comes from weakness, not realism. It is weakness in the face of pain, and since realism is a "survival concept," pain is wrongly credited with more realism than is pleasure. To take the cynic's position is to feed on that wrong-headedness. In short, the world hangs together, as much as it does, because of what good there is in human nature. (Levant & Shlien, 1984, pp. 1-2)

1

A PERSON-CENTERED APPROACH AND THE STRUCTURE OF SCIENTIFIC REVOLUTIONS

Intuition suggests that scientific inquiry, particularly in the psychological sciences, shares little resemblance to a linear, straight-line progression of discoveries. Rather, the path of discovery may follow peaks and valleys or, perhaps, cyclical forms whereby fully developed ideas from decades earlier reemerge later to begin again under different names and after sufficient time has ushered those original ideas into the amnesia, in this case, of the psychological sciences.

For example, as inferred from the use of a word such as "timeline" to describe the passage of time, scientific progress is thought to follow a timeline, such that with each passing unit of time, improvement occurs with regard to methods of collecting and analyzing data and, as a result, increasingly valid and reliable inferences are expected to emerge. This characterization of time as a straight line - with a starting point prior to the present and with an end running into the distant horizon of the future - while convenient for reducing experience into understandable forms, seems to solely exist as a symbolic tool to carry out a required function. However, this action of symbolic abstraction on the part of the scientific community, in which raw experience must be reduced into a useful symbolic form, may easily be forgotten as having occurred, whereby the abstraction is accepted as reality. That is, similar to mistaking a family member's picture for the actual flesh-and-blood person, a similar mistake in confusing symbol with experience seems to be consistently made in the psychological sciences and, as a result, scientific inquiry is mistakenly thought to be "proceeding forward." Again, these assertions are supported only by an intuitive sense and, outside of philosophical argument and precarious speculation, may be difficult to prove. Moreover, these assertions may only be relevant if scientific discovery does, in fact, occur cyclically; repeating itself again and again as new generations of scientists replace the old. However, by examining the historical path through which the psychological sciences have engaged in the pursuit of evidence-based treatments, this article attempts to transform the above assertions from simple speculation into a viable reality using the evolution of Carl Rogers's person-centered approach as a specific case of the general trend.

As of the second decade of the 21st century, the evidence base in psychological science research, particularly counseling and psychotherapy research, has confirmed through the use of the scientific method that problems of a psychological nature can be alleviated under the direction of a mental health professional, such as a social worker, psychologist, or psychiatrist. In other words, seeking guidance from a counselor or therapist has been found to help a person. A mental health professional is trained in such methods of direction as providing evidence-based psychoeducation, advice, and behavioral guidance with a goal in mind that includes sufficient symptom reduction of a client's problem. Furthermore, in addition to relying upon a combination of treatment manuals, clinical supervision, and practice experience - through which a mental health professional hones his or her evidence-based methods - the mental health professional is also assisted in definition, diagnosis, and treatment by the American Psychiatric Association's (2013) Diagnostic and Statistical Manual of Mental Disorders (DSM).

The DSM, first published in the 1950s, provides the standard classification of mental disorders for use by mental health professionals in the United States. In 2013, the American Psychiatric Association published the 5th edition of the DSM (DSM-V; American Psychiatric

Association, 2013). In particular, the publication of the DSM-V confirmed that scientific inquiry in the psychological sciences was alive and well, so to speak, and was proceeding forward. That is, beginning with the 1952 edition, a scholar can examine the DSM's evolutionary timeline, discovering an ordered and systematic evidence base progressively supporting and refining the quality and reliability of the psychological/helping professions. Similar to an archaeologist charged with studying the layers of the Earth's crust, the scholar studying the DSM's evolution would likely discover that a linear timeline of increasingly complex yet refined layers of psychological guidance can be found across the DSM's periodic publications.

Likewise, a study of the evolutionary layers of Carl Rogers's person-centered approach could be carried out; and in some ways, this article is similar to an archaeological dig. The main question being: what will we find as we begin to brush away fifty years of scholarly sediment, examining each layer of sediment in detail as we go? In short, this article attempts to provide a more complete picture regarding the Rogerian tradition, only briefly mentioned in Quinn (2013). Specifically, in Quinn (2013) the suggestion was made that the Rogerian traditions of research and evidence-based practice had come to an abrupt end in the 1970s as a result of "unfounded claims made by a group of social scientists who held significant professional interest in seeing through the dismantling of the person-centered approach" (Quinn, 2013, p. 219).

In summary, the first half of this article examines modern and historical evidence regarding Rogers's facilitative conditions, including the events in the 1960s and 1970s that may have influenced the decline of PCT in the United States. Next, PCT is defined against the background of its process-direction counterparts, referred to in this article as "PCT plus process-direction" (PCT-plus). Furthermore, in the second half of this article, the events alluded to in Quinn (2013) are examined, providing strong evidence that a systematic dismantling process of the Rogerian tradition had occurred in the 1970s. In this respect, conclusions are drawn regarding the accuracy and validity of the interpretations of the research evidence during this period; a period dominated by a group of behavioral and psychoanalytic mental health professionals who, history suggests, benefitted considerably from the disappearance of the Rogerian psychotherapy tradition. In the final section of this article modern person-centered research evidence is reported, including the 2013 update to Elliott et al.'s (2004) well-known meta-analytic review of humanistic-existential outcome studies (Elliott et al., 2013).

The Person-Centered Approach, In Brief

Evidence from scholarly publications suggests that the Rogerian traditions of theory, research, and practice emerged, stabilized and receded during a 40-year period (ca. 1940-1980). In brief, Rogers and colleagues (a) began a process of describing a hypothetical therapeutic approach originally called "nondirective therapy" (Rogers, 1942), (b) broadened this approach with theory and initial research, changing the name to "client-centered therapy" (Rogers, 1951), (c) rigorously tested and confirmed their theory (Cartwright, 1957; Rogers & Dymond, 1954), (d) further clarified a complete theory of therapy and predicted symptom reduction by hypothesizing specific mechanisms-of-change, called "the necessary and sufficient conditions" (Rogers, 1957; 1959b), and (e) replicated these empirical studies, examining the effects of - what came to be known as - the "facilitative conditions" among difficult–to–serve and underserved client populations (Banks, Berenson, & Carkhuff, 1967; Redfering,1975; Rogers, Gendlin, Keisler, & Truax, 1967; Truax et al., 1966).

For over 20 years the research findings greatly favored Rogers's assertion that therapist-provided conditions of genuineness, warmth, and empathy - or, congruence, unconditional positive regard (UCPR), and empathic understanding - were related to outcome as perceived by clients (e.g., Gurman, 1977) as well as observers (i.e., trained raters of audio recordings; Truax & Mitchell, 1971). However, in the late 1960s, the validity and reliability of Charles Truax's observer measurement instruments were placed under scrutiny by a group of predominantly behavioral and psychoanalytic social scientists who, at the time, had carried out very little methodologically-sound research of their own (e.g., Bergin & Jasper, 1969; Chinsky & Rappaport, 1970; Gurman, 1973b; Mintz & Luborsky, 1971; Caracena & Vicory, 1969). Furthermore, despite substantial evidence that supported the validity and reliability of Rogers's and Truax's research methodologies, by the mid-1970s the Rogerian evidence base was summarily "invalidated" (Bergin & Suinn, 1975; Patterson, 1984).

By 1980, nearly a half-century of theory and research, which had provided considerable guidance to the helping professions, had been systematically removed from consideration as an evidence-based therapeutic treatment (e.g., Phillips & Bierman, 1981). This scientific revolution, which had begun in the late 1960s, was supported by a small but remarkably influential collection of articles that discredited over twenty years of Rogerian research findings. As the revolution grew, it rapidly ballooned into a general belief that PCT was ineffective, despite the absence of credible evidence. As a result, PCT rapidly declined in both the spheres of empirical and clinical influence (Quinn, 2013). While the next 20 years (ca. 1975-1995) witnessed the rise of cognitive, behavior, and psychodynamic evidence-based research traditions (e.g., Crits-Christoph, Cooper, & Luborsky, 1988; Emmelkamp, 1994; Hollon & Beck, 1986), PCT became regarded by scholars as a partial treatment paradigm at best; and, at worst, had become a historical footnote, if noted at all (e.g., Beutler, Crago, & Arizmendi, 1986; Parloff, London, & Wolfe, 1986).

After reviewing hundreds of articles and book chapters spanning 40 years (ca. 1945-1985), many of which are referenced in the subsequent sections of this article, a conservative conclusion may be stated as the following: the evidence consistently suggests that PCT was effective when provided by PCT therapists and ineffective or insufficient when provided by non-PCT therapists, such as behavior and psychoanalytic therapists. This disparity has been shown to continue into the 21st-century (Quinn, 2011; 2013).

Furthermore, in the United States the relative number of therapists possessing an "allegiance" to PCT and the Rogerian tradition has declined since 1975, with a limited number of training institutions remaining (Schneider, 1999). Moreover, since the turn-of-the-century, European and Asian PCT practitioners – once thought to have kept the torch lit, so to speak - have been engaged in a general process of diluting Rogers's necessary and sufficient therapeutic framework, promoting a "pluralistic" practice perspective instead. In short, the European PCT group appears to be integrating positive psychology with Rogers's so-called "classical" approach, using peculiar phrases, such as "fuzzy circles" when describing the types of Rogerian-influenced therapies (e.g., Bohart, 2012; Cooper & McLeod, 2012; Joseph & Murphy, 2013). Paralleling this "anything goes" approach to person-centered practice, the policies of European governments, aiming to achieve a unified technique-based mental health treatment system - much like the United States has done - is nearing completion (e.g., American Psychiatric Association, 2013; Elliott, Greenberg, Watson, Timulak, & Freire, 2013; Sommerbeck, 2012).

Rogers's Facilitative Mechanisms of Change: Definition and Measurement

Though open for debate, few psychotherapy traditions have been more misrepresented or misunderstood than Carl Rogers's person-centered therapy (PCT). Particularly misconstrued have been the six "necessary and sufficient" conditions, three of which typically referred to as the "core" or "facilitative" conditions. Moreover, the full set of conditions has also been described within a framework of "facilitative mechanisms of change" (Quinn, 2011). Rogers (1957; 1959b) hypothesized that the following six conditions would compose an effective therapeutic treatment system: (1) psychological contact exists between the therapist and client, (2) the client is experiencing anxiety or a vulnerability, (3) the therapist is congruent in the relationship, (4) the therapist experiences unconditional positive regard (UCPR) toward the client, (5) the therapist experiences and communicates an empathic understanding toward the client, and (6) therapist communication and client perception of UCPR and understanding is minimally achieved.

Observer ratings

To measure these conditions, a young Charles Truax (e.g., Truax, 1963; Truax & Carkhuff, 1967) developed and refined Likert scales to measure accurate empathy, UCPR/nonpossessive warmth, and congruence/genuineness constructs for use while trained raters listened to audio segments of therapy sessions. In this way, the primary mechanisms of change in Rogers's hypothesis could be measured by an outside observer, which was argued to minimize much of the nuance or interactional effects thought to inherently influence client and therapist perspectives of treatment effectiveness. Of particular importance, Truax's observer-rating scales satisfied the measurement of the first requirement of condition (6) above: that therapist communication of these conditions had occurred.

Client ratings

Similarly, Godfrey Barrett-Lennard (1962) developed the Relationship Inventory to measure client-perceived facilitative conditions by surveying the client at points in time during therapy, thereby satisfying the latter requirement of condition (6) above. Notably, attempts to measure the therapist's own perceived facilitative conditions were discarded early in the research efforts because the therapist's perspective was found unrelated to the two other perspectives (Rogers et al., 1967), and was likely biased by the therapist's own view of his or her own idealized therapeutic competencies (Fuertes et al., 2006).

Disagreement between observer and client ratings

During the 1960s Truax and Barrett-Lennard each argued that rating Rogers's facilitative conditions using their particular instrument (i.e., observer versus client perspective) was the most accurate way of measuring Rogers's (1957; 1959b) facilitative conditions. Not surprisingly, Truax (1966) and Barrett-Lennard's (1981; 1985) respective instruments did not always correlate when both measures were used in a particular study (Kurtz & Grummon, 1972; Rogers et al., 1967, Ch. 8; Truax, 1966), suggesting that observer and client perspectives were somewhat different when it came to measuring psychotherapy phenomena; for this reason, many researchers resorted to counting the number of words spoken as a way to assess the therapist's contribution to therapy effectiveness. Moreover, Truax and colleagues (Truax, 1966; Burstein & Carkhuff, 1968) demonstrated that the degree of a client's perceptual distortion (e.g., neurosis vs. psychosis) could adversely affect client-perceived measures of the therapist, leading to inaccurate measurement of Rogers's facilitative conditions. Despite this concern the client rating scale continued to be used, and both Truax's observer rating scales and Barrett-Lennard's client questionnaire were found to consistently predict client outcome across a range of client populations (Truax & Mitchell, 1971; Gurman, 1977).

However, by the early 1970s many researchers, particularly those social scientists previously suggested to have possessed a "researcher allegiance bias comparable to 'necessary, *not* sufficient'" (Quinn, 2013, p. 217), chose to overlook the substantial amount of evidence demonstrating the validity of Truax's observer rating scales, in particular, as well as the consistent positive relationship found in general between Rogers's facilitative conditions and client outcome. Moreover, when these social scientists carried out their own psychotherapy research using Truax's observer-rating scales, they failed to accurately replicate the typical research methodologies implemented and described in detail by Rogers, Truax, and colleagues (e.g., Rogers et al., 1967; Truax et al., 1966). Not surprisingly, these "replications" did not detect a positive relationship between therapist facilitative conditions and client outcome. Sources of this loss of statistical power to detect a relationship may have stemmed from these researchers' frequent attempts to replicate Rogers and Truax's work using analogue clients, such as college students (e.g., Bergin & Jasper, 1969; Kurtz & Grummon, 1972), rather than actual client samples typically used by the Rogers and Truax groups (e.g., persons with anxiety, depression, schizophrenia, or adolescents with mental health problems; Rogers & Dymond, 1954; Truax, 1971). Furthermore, the choice of raters may have substantially biased the findings; Rogers and Truax's groups used trained lay observers, while this competing group of social scientists tended to use expert psychotherapists to rate the facilitative conditions, or the researchers themselves acted as raters. Therefore, an argument could be made that there was less likelihood to detect a predictive relationship between the facilitative conditions and client outcome when these latter research methods were implemented, due to the considerable potential for rater bias. Despite the methodological oversights in the few studies carried out by this group of behavioral and psychoanalytic researchers, these social scientists, relying primarily upon speculation, concluded that Truax's measurement scales were flawed. Therefore, the social scientists argued, that because Truax's scales were predominantly used by the Rogers and Truax research groups from 1960 to 1974, much of the findings supporting Rogers's (1957) hypothesis were necessarily discarded.

Remarkably, throughout the decade-long process of this apparent systematic dismantling of the Rogerian evidence base (ca. 1969 to 1979) these behavioral and psychoanalytic researchers failed to acknowledge their "inattention" to reliably implementing standard replication procedures and, in addition to other sources of bias, these researchers failed to account for substantial threats to the validity and reliability of their reported findings. The literature suggests that this inattention was likely due to the particular motivations possessed by this group of behavioral and psychoanalytic researchers involved during this period, who brazenly reported less than favorable findings in an attempt to discredit Rogers's and Truax's considerable empirical evidence base. As will be shown in subsequent sections of this article, this particular motivation (i.e., researcher allegiance bias) would have likely extended to the attitudes of the therapists who participated in the studies as well. Moreover, since this same group of researchers was also intimately involved in writing the subsequent late-1970s literature reviews which effectively discredited PCT, it would not be difficult to imagine that researcher allegiance bias existed within the realms of psychotherapy research, practice, and the dissemination of findings during this "revolutionary period" within the helping professions (Quinn, 2013).

In summary, the research findings relied upon by these late-

1970s scholars in writing their reviews (e.g., Bergin & Suinn, 1975; Gomes-Schwartz, Hadley, & Strupp, 1978; Parloff, Waskow, & Wolfe, 1978) was rooted in only a few studies carried out by non-PCT researchers in the late-1960s and early-1970s (e.g., Bergin & Jasper, 1969; Gurman, 1973b; Mintz, Luborsky, & Auerbach, 1971). Moreover, the late-1970s psychotherapy literature in general suggests that these few, allegedly biased, studies conducted in the early-1970s were frequently and *unquestioningly* cited in the mainstream psychotherapy literature. As a result, the validity of Truax's observer-rating scales, and therefore Rogers's life's work was effectively discredited and for the most part forgotten. In support of this latter point, the arguments, the evidence, and the solutions are briefly reviewed in the next section.

A brief examination of the main problem with Truax's observer-rated measurement scales

Aggregating multiple observer ratings of audio-taped, randomly selected segments of psychotherapy sessions was a common method of measuring a therapist's accurate empathy, nonpossessive warmth (i.e., UCPR), and genuineness (i.e., congruence) during psychotherapeutic treatment. For example, by using Truax's observer-rating scales to obtain the average value of multiple observers' ratings of empathy using a 7-point Likert scale, the researcher could assess the degree to which therapist-provided empathy was related to client improvement.

However, if multiple observers' ratings did not possess a reasonable amount of positive correlation (i.e., inter-rater reliability; see Tinsley & Weiss, 1975; Tinsley & Weiss, 2000), this would indicate that empathy, congruence, and UCPR had not been accurately measured. Therefore, if these constructs were not being accurately measured, that is, inter-rater reliability was poor, then to suggest confirmation of Rogers's (1957) hypothesis would be scientifically irresponsible.

The argument and the evidence. In brief, Chinsky and Rappaport (1970) argued in support of the following: the Rogerian research tradition's method of assessing inter-rater reliability was flawed, producing spuriously inflated inter-rater reliabilities, and thus Rogerian research had failed to accurately and reliably measure the facilitative conditions. Therefore, any conclusions regarding Rogers's facilitative conditions related to client improvement were irrelevant. In addition, Chinsky and Rappaport (1970) suggested that rather than Rogers's hypothesized conditions, the psychotherapy phenomena being measured was simply the number of words the therapist spoke, or observer recognition of a particular therapists' voice in the audio-taped recordings. Furthermore, Chinsky and Rappaport (1970) argued, the Rogers/Truax research groups were introducing a substantial amount of systematic error into the data by failing to control for the "nonindependence" of measurements. In short, a fundamental statistical assumption rests in the assurance that measurement error is statistically independent and identically distributed (i.i.d.) in research studies; though a relaxation of this assumption may not necessarily impact the findings to such a degree as was previously thought (Kutner, Nachtsheim, Neter, & Li, 2005). Chinsky and Rappaport (1970) also argued that raters were recognizing the therapist's voice tone across sessions and, therefore, could be responding to the memory of previously hearing a particular therapist's voice. Though the authors failed to distinguish the latter from the former, this latter accusation fell under the domain of methodological, rather than statistical, independence (Beutler, Johnson, Neville, & Workman, 1973; Rappaport & Chinsky, 1972). In other words, the raters would become habituated to rating a therapist at a certain level of empathy, for instance, simply based on voice recognition alone – a problem previously noted by the Rogers group and substantially controlled for in their rater-training protocol (e.g., Rogers et al., 1967, ch. 8). Beutler et al. (1973), removing the influence of the therapist's voice by asking observers to rate transcribed segments of therapy sessions, demonstrated that this latter methodological nonindependence issue was not a problem.

However, Chinsky and Rappaport's (1970) primary concern was the statistical independence argument, which is more difficult to demonstrate outside of theoretical and mathematical means. The authors suggested that each rater was repeatedly rating each unique client-therapist dyad numerous times, and therefore statistically nonindependent and nonidentically-distributed events were being measured. While i.i.d. events are mathematically and probabilistically assumed, they rarely if ever are achieved in social science research (Stiles, 2009). Guided by the early work of Donald Campbell (Campbell, 1957; Campbell & Stanley, 1963), Rogers, Truax, and colleagues anticipated these inherent problems in social science research (Rogers et al., 1967, ch. 8) and developed a research design to minimize the theoretical threats to statistical independence, consisting of: (a) randomly selected segments within the session to maximize within-session variability, (b) randomly assigned segments to raters across all client-therapist dyads for all therapy sessions in order minimize the potential error caused by observers systematically assigning ratings by listening to a series of the same client-therapist dyad, and (c) during the rater training Rogers and colleagues instructed the raters to attempt, "as much as possible," to provide ratings based upon the therapist' responses heard in the audio segments. In this way, the Rogers group was well aware of and documented their efforts to control for these and other threats to internal validity.

But Chinsky and Rappaport (1970; Rappaport & Chinsky, 1972) argued that allowing each observer to hear the same client-therapist dyad more than once (i.e., multiple segments from different sessions, but from the same client-therapist pair) was the same as allowing the observer to rate the same audio segment repeatedly, which can result in a problem commonly called multicollinearity (Kutner et al., 2005). In other words, if a rater listens to a segment from each therapy session involving the same therapist and client, and the rater scores the level of therapist empathy for each audio segment using Truax's Accurate Empathy scale, then this violates the i.i.d. assumption that measurements are being independently collected. Again, in theory only, Chinsky and Rappaport (1970) suggested that the above problem would artificially inflate inter-rater reliability estimates (Maxwell, 1968), and therefore the findings would appear more accurate than they actually were.

For example, the unknown measurement error inherent in naturalistic research is assumed to be uncorrelated, and when added up, is assumed to equal zero. Simply speaking, this theoretical ideal suggests that systematic bias will then be minimized. In practice, this ideal can be more or less achieved when the psychotherapy researcher collects independent observations from a randomized sample of clients, resulting in i.i.d. events. Moreover, if the inter-rater reliability correlation coefficient is high (e.g., $r > 0.7$) for, say, multiple observer ratings of accurate empathy from the same audio segments, then the researcher is likely to conclude that empathy, to some degree, was provided by the therapist because multiple listeners' ratings were found to be similar, or positively correlated. Next, if the inter-rater correlation is found to be consistently high across all the audio segments, the researcher can conclude that, (a) accurate empathy was measured reliably, (b) he or she can then average each segment's empathy score for each particular client-therapist dyad, (c) subsequently examine descriptive statistics regarding the overall level of accurate empathy provided by a particular therapist with a particular client, and (d) using statistical analysis infer the impact of therapist empathy upon client improvement. As a result, if empathy is found to "positively predict" client outcome, then Rogers's (1957) hypothesis that empathy is a necessary condition is provided further support; because low levels of therapist empathy would be related to low levels of client outcome and vice versa. In addition, the researcher can perform the same procedures to assess the impact of congruence and UCPR upon client outcome. Consequently, if the researcher finds that clients tend to improve in the presence of a therapeutic environment high in empathy, congruence, and UCPR, then the researcher can suggest that Rogers's "necessary and sufficient" hypothesis was supported by the research findings. Guided by the scientific method, the researcher can then move forward with further replications of the study in order to build an evidence base that supports the necessity and sufficiency of Rogers's facilitative conditions. Though oversimplified, this is the course that psychotherapy research might take when testing Rogers's hypothesis.

However, as the reader may infer, the above research, like all rigorously implemented psychotherapy research, is complicated to carry out well. All that is needed is a seed of doubt inserted into a vulnerable location within the research methodology, and the findings may quickly transition from "empirically valid" to "highly suspect." In this way, Chinsky and Rappaport (1970; Rappaport & Chinsky, 1972) found their seed of doubt, developed their speculative argument regarding statistical nonindependence, and then simply asserted that empathy, congruence, and UCPR were not actually being measured; and therefore PCT research findings in general were dubious at best. Rather, argued Chinsky and Rappaport (1970), a more plausible explanation for the success of the Rogerian research tradition was that the number of therapists' words spoken, or possibly the extent to which the client was "likeable," was impairing the raters' judgments. Therefore, Rogers's (1957) hypothesis was simply describing a "good therapist" or a successful therapist, by virtue of working with an "easy client." Thus, after twenty years of evidence-based support, PCT, as of 1970, was positioned to be subsequently "invalidated" - initially, and most forcefully - by the well-known psychologists Allen Bergin (Bergin & Suinn, 1975), and Hans Strupp (1978a).

The solution. Interestingly, the solution to the problem described above would have put the Rogerian researchers in a double bind, so to speak. First, in order to demonstrate that each audio segment from different sessions of the same client-therapist dyad were statistically independent, researchers would be required to demonstrate that observer-rated facilitative conditions were not *solely* a therapist-provided measure, but that client factors contributed to the level of empathy provided by the therapist. One could then argue that the measurement of multiple segments from the same client-therapist dyad but coming from different therapy sessions were independent events, and therefore, theoretically uncorrelated. However (and here begins the double-bind), if levels of therapist facilitative conditions were influenced by client characteristics, then the argument could be made that therapists were only responding to and providing effective levels of Rogers's facilitative conditions in the presence of certain client types, such as the easiest or most likeable clients. This would also confirm the charges leveled by Chinsky and Rappaport (1970).

Second, if the above "client likeability" argument was accurate, then therapists would be assumed to provide different levels of empathy for different clients depending on the clients' likeability; but, for the same client, the therapist would be expected to provide stable levels of empathy within sessions *and* across sessions (i.e., Chinsky, Rappaport, and others naively assumed that client likeability was a stable trait for a given client). Therefore, if this were the case, then the problem has returned to one of statistical independence: due to the assumption of client likeability being stable for each client, when multiple audio segments of the same client-therapist dyad were rated, the observations were again measuring the same event multiple times, violating the i.i.d. assumption, inflating inter-rater reliability correlations, and again confirming Chinsky and Rappaport's (1970) argument.

In summary, this double bind suggested the following: if the therapist is found to provide varying levels of the facilitative conditions for the same client *within* and *between sessions* - as would happen if both sides of the double bind were occurring - then, suggested the critics, how can these conditions conform to Rogers's (1957) hypothesis and, more importantly, be related to outcome? Therefore, PCT researchers were required to demonstrate that two near-mutually exclusive phenomena were simultaneously occurring in psychotherapy treatment; hence the double bind.

"Both sides of the coin." Looking back half-a-century, Chinsky and Rappaport's (1970) argument was elegant. One side of the proverbial coin provided the criticism suggesting that Rogers, Truax, and colleagues had *failed* to actually measure Rogers's facilitative conditions and, as a result, the Rogerian evidence base could be subject to scientific impeachment, so to speak, and could be subsequently removed from the psychotherapy evidence base. The other side of the coin suggested that if the facilitative conditions were *accurately* being measured, then the research community could still conclude that Rogers's facilitative conditions only reached high levels in the presence of likeable clients and were generally low for difficult ones. Therefore, Rogers's (1957) hypothesis was simply describing a "good" therapy session, and this was far from a novel treatment approach (Auerbach & Luborsky, 1968). In other words, once flipped, the psychotherapy research community need not have concerned themselves as to which side of the coin landed face-up, both sides would lead to the conclusion that no actual evidence base had ever existed in support of Rogers's (1957) hypothesis.

Remarkably, a review of the research evidence suggests that Rogers's and Truax's research methodology did in fact control against threats from "both sides of the coin," in a manner of speaking. First, research had shown that a particular client influences therapist-provided facilitative conditions (Truax, 1966; van der Veen, 1965). However, studies also demonstrated that (a) skilled therapists (i.e., therapists that are skilled at providing Rogers's facilitative conditions) contributed substantially to the provision of this therapeutic climate, *partially* independent of unique client characteristics (Gurman, 1973a; Truax & Carkhuff, 1965), and (b) therapist facilitative conditions were found to stabilize at a consistent level across both therapy sessions and different types of clients (Anthony, 1971; Truax et al., 1966; Rogers et al., 1967). Furthermore, findings suggested that despite some overlap between observer-rated empathy and ratings of a "likeable" therapist, when this likeable-therapist rating was controlled, the level of client likeability and observer-rated empathy were not significantly related. Thus empathy was shown to be a separate and valid construct (Bozarth & Krauft, 1972; Gormally & Hill, 1974), *as opposed to*, (a) a component of a good therapy hour, (b) the result of observers targeting their favorite therapists for higher ratings, and (c) the result of likeable clients receiving higher levels of therapist empathy.

Furthermore, Beutler et al. (1973) confirmed, in part, the above evidence in support of the accuracy of Truax's facilitative conditions scales. Specifically, Beutler et al. (1973) demonstrated that inter-rater reliabilities for therapist-provided empathy were not significantly different when only one rating per client-therapist dyad was compared to repeatedly rating multiple segments of the same client-therapist dyad across different sessions. Therefore, statistical independence was partially confirmed – which is a substantial achievement in social science research in general.

Moreover, evidence also demonstrated that, despite some fluctuation of therapist facilitative levels within a session, the Truax scales were consistently able to discriminate between high and low facilitative therapists (Gurman, 1973b). That is, much of the fluctuation or variability within sessions was constricted within a narrow range along Truax's Likert scales for both high and low facilitative conditions. In light of his findings, Gurman (1973b) stated that "high-facilitative therapists tended to function at minimally facilitative or facilitative levels on the whole, and low-facilitative therapists tended to function at nonfacilitative or minimally facilitative levels" (Gurman, 1973b, p. 17). For example, if a therapist, on average, provided high levels of accurate empathy, according to Gurman's (1973b) data a particular therapist's facilitative conditions would vary, but only modestly, and, for a given therapy session, remained clustered around the therapist's average score. Taken directly from Truax's scale for empathy, a therapist providing high levels of empathy was operationalized as conveying,

> the message 'I am *with* you' is unmistakably clear - the therapist's
> remarks fit in just right with the client's mood and content...and
> [the therapist] can shift his own responses to correct for language
> or content errors in his own communications when his is not

'with' the client." (Truax, 1967a, p. 556)

Similarly, Gurman's (1973b) findings demonstrated that across time low-facilitative therapists could be predictably discriminated. Truax's scale operationalized low levels of empathy in the following way,

> at a *low* level…the therapist may be off on a tangent of his own or may have misrepresented what the patient is feeling, and, at a very low level, may be so preoccupied and interested in his own intellectual interpretations that he is scarcely aware of the client's 'being'…indeed, he may be accurately describing psychodynamics to the patient - but in a language not that of the client, or at a time when these dynamics are far removed from the current feelings of the client, so that it takes on the flavor of a teacher-pupil interaction. (Truax, 1967a, p. 556)

In summary, the evidence indicated that skilled therapists could provide consistently high levels of facilitative conditions despite the level of likeability or difficulty of the client. And Chinsky and Rappaport's (1970) arguments were provocative in theory, but in practice their arguments did not hold. However, despite evidence to the contrary, most psychotherapy reviews published in the mid- to late-1970s omitted and/or misinterpreted the findings described above. Had the writers of these late-1970s reviews accurately interpreted *all* of the available evidence, the majority of criticisms leveled against the Rogerian research tradition would have likely never taken place. Moreover, an emerging paradigm in psychotherapy research favoring specific-techniques for specific-diagnoses had gained sufficient momentum to drown out any voices of moderation that had remained, such as Gormally and Hill (1974) which will be reviewed later in this article. Leading the way in this "revolt" against the Rogerian paradigm, the literature suggests, were Allen Bergin and Hans Strupp, guiding the helping professions toward a new brand of psychotherapy and behavior change.

The Emergence of Allegiance-Guided Scientific Inquiry in Psychotherapy Research

The late 1950s marked substantial theoretical and empirical contributions to psychotherapy, the bulk of which had emerged from the previous decade of studies carried out by Rogers and colleagues at the University of Chicago (Cartwright, 1957). In 1997, John Shlien (1997) described this period: "as the artist historian Ewa Kuryluk said, 'sometimes history hibernates; at times it runs like a gazelle.' This was the time of the gazelle" (p. 68). However, in 1957, the year after receiving his 1956 APA scientific contribution award and the year that Rogers departed Chicago for Wisconsin, he published his renowned "necessary and sufficient" article (Rogers, 1957), effectively removing much of the common ground between himself and the psychological professions (Rogers, 1974).

Two years following Rogers's (1957) article, Albert Ellis - having recently departed from his psychoanalytic roots to found rational-emotive behavior therapy - disputed the logic behind Rogers's (1957) premise in three pages (Ellis, 1959). Ellis's argument contained three significant contributions, (a) Ellis reflected the general attitude toward PCT at the time, that is: are Rogers's facilitative conditions effective with psychotic clients?, (b) Ellis advertised his new and innovative "rational psychotherapy," as he referred to it at the time, and (c) Ellis foreshadowed the coming two decades of turmoil and uncertainty in the psychotherapy profession in his concluding paragraph:

> all that seems to be necessary is that the individual *somehow* come up against significant life experiences *or* learn about others' experiences *or* sit down and think for himself *or* enter a relationship with a therapist who is *preferably* congruent, accepting, empathic, rational, forceful, etc. Either/or rather than this-and-that seems to be the only realistic description of necessary conditions for basic personality change that can be made at the present time (Ellis, 1959, p. 540).

Notably, Ellis's statement, though somewhat less dramatic, prophesied Gordon Paul's well-known question which would be posed a decade later: "the question towards which all outcome research should ultimately be directed is the following: *What* treatment, by *whom*, is most effective for *this* individual with *that* specific problem, and under *which* set of circumstances?" (Paul, 1967, p. 111).

Going forward, the uncertainty of the 1960s marked by the

turmoil and unrest in the U.S. and overseas can also be found in person-centered theory, research, and practice as well. For instance, Rogers's tumultuous tenure at the University of Wisconsin (ca. 1957-1963) was substantially shorter than his previous time at Chicago (ca. 1945-1957). During the "Wisconsin years," Rogers and colleagues, including Eugene Gendlin, Charles Truax, and Donald Kiesler, carried out a large-scale research project attempting to investigate relationships between the facilitative conditions, client process, and therapeutic change among schizophrenic clients at a psychiatric hospital. This study marked the beginning of widespread use of the newly created therapist facilitative conditions scales as well as client process measurement scales (e.g., Rogers et al., 1967; Truax, 1963; van der Veen, 1965).

Later, evidence of considerable interpersonal conflict among the primary investigators of the Wisconsin project became public when Rogers's biography, *On Becoming Carl Rogers,* was published (Kirschenbaum, 1979). In the early 1970s, Rogers had given his biographer, Howard Kirschenbaum, full access to his notes and correspondence that he had accumulated throughout his career. Set within Kirschenbaum's (1979) well-known biography, the many problems that had arisen during the Wisconsin years were described in striking detail in a series of 1966 correspondence letters between Rogers, Gendlin, and the young Donald Kiesler. Initially, the mail-based correspondence was begun in order to discuss the questionable behaviors of Charles Truax during the early stages of the Wisconsin research project, in which Truax was alleged to have withheld the final results of the research project from the research team, and then lost the documents containing these results; the original data would subsequently need to be reanalyzed at great cost to the project. However, subsequent letters were exchanged due to discrepancies between Rogers's, Gendlin's, and Kiesler's opinions regarding how editorship and authorship credit would be given when the group's long-awaited book *The Therapeutic Relationship and Its Impact: A Study of Psychotherapy with Schizophrenics* would be eventually published (Rogers et al., 1967). However, the letters, which were reprinted verbatim in Kirschenbaum (1979), suggest that the correspondence quickly degenerated into personal attacks and insults, evidenced by the following excerpt of a letter that Rogers sent to Gendlin and Kiesler:

> it makes me regret that one of the scales we never developed was one for self-righteousness. The correspondence we have had on this topic of authorship could then be submitted to a group of bright undergraduates for a 'blind' rating as to who is the most righteous of the three – Charlie, Gene, or Don. I had always thought Charlie would win hands down, but I have had increasing doubts. I seem to be the only one who has made mistakes, but since those are glaringly evident to both of you I do not need to go into them (Kirschenbaum, 1979, p. 286).

The beginning of the end of the Rogerian tradition

The post-Chicago research years in Wisconsin witnessed a wavering of resolve within the person-centered therapy community. Surprisingly, circa 1964, Rogers's resolve toward the adequacy and effectiveness of his facilitative conditions may have begun to falter as well (Rogers, 1989; Shlien, 1992). Alluded to above, Rogers's biography illustrates the seeds of a turning point in PCT theory, research, and practice traditions that had taken root in the early 1960s, related specifically to the alleged actions of Charles Truax (Gendlin, 1988; Kirschenbaum, 1979).

In brief, Truax received his doctorate in psychology in 1960 from Wisconsin, for which Rogers was Truax's doctoral committee chair (Truax, 1960). Truax, for better or worse, contributed substantially to psychotherapy research from 1963 until his death in 1974 (Quinn, 2013; Truax & Mitchell, 1971). Though Truax's alleged actions are not condoned here to be appropriate scholarly behavior, Truax's actions appear to have unearthed distinctly divergent personalities and agendas possessed by the leaders of the Wisconsin project: namely, Rogers, Gendlin, and Donald Kiesler (i.e., Truax's 1963 replacement).

Kiesler (1997), who died in 2007 (Nowicki, 2008), received his doctorate in 1963 from the University of Illinois, and was immediately recruited to fill the gap left by Truax as Research Director from 1963 to 1964 for the Wisconsin schizophrenia project (Rogers et al., 1967).

Kiesler would later become a prominent advocate for the emerging "specific-techniques-for-specific-client-symptoms" movement, championed by Kiesler's well-known and frequently cited paper, "Some Myths of Psychotherapy Research and the Search for a Paradigm" (Kiesler, 1966), and other contributions (e.g., Kiesler, 1971; Kiesler, 1996).

As suggested by the tone of the 1966 correspondence letters (Kirschenbaum, 1979), the Wisconsin years may have marked a permanent split between Rogers and his colleagues Gendlin and Kiesler; both of whom would later become influential leaders in the helping professions. Exemplifying this fissure, particularly between Rogers and Gendlin, the Kirschenbaum (1979) biography documents actions taken by Gendlin's lawyer who wrote to Rogers in the mid-1960s, "our client may be irreparably damaged…" (that is, if Gendlin's suggested changes in author- and editorship of the Rogers et al. [1967] book failed to be honored, which included removal of Truax's name from editorship; Kirschenbaum, 1979, p. 284). However, a previously signed contract had protected the removal of Truax's name from editorship, and Kiesler, while not allying with Rogers, also disagreed with Gendlin on other points of editor and authorship. Moreover, compared to Gendlin's strategy of moderating his communications to Rogers through a third-party, Kiesler acted with less restraint, writing strongly worded letters to Rogers, for example: "our basic problem, as I see it, is that good men sometimes castrate themselves by not acting at the proper time…," continuing, "…you're squirming, sliding, and slipping again […] I will not let [the Wisconsin book] come out, *ever*, if you change your stand on the *four* major authors'" (Kirschenbaum, 1979, pp. 284-285). In a response letter sent both to Gendlin and Kiesler, Rogers too conveyed his growing anger and frustration:

> I also think of, and this is not intended as a criticism, but just as a fact of life, my enormous depression when I first read some of Don's [Kiesler] chapters. They were so dull!...my own optimistic estimate is that out of every million people who might hear of the book, possibly 500 might buy it or start to read it, and five would complete the reading of Don's chapters. I hope I am wrong but only time will tell. (Kirschenbaum, 1979, p. 286)

In reaction, Kiesler responded, "Congratulations, again! For the first time you are being congruent in our interaction. That dull, righteous Kiesler! In the moment of truth, the great White Father is able to say to himself: 'Piss on Unconditional Positive Regard! That Kiesler is a pain in the ass!' (Kirschenbaum, 1979, p. 287). Rogers would later express regret for his choices during this period:

> one of my serious mistakes was not firing Charlie immediately. By the time that I was really convinced that he was a scoundrel and presented the case against him through the Psychiatric Institute and stated my determination to fire him, they not only would not concur in the action but would not even permit me to

take the action, which was a very humiliating situation. (Kirschenbaum, 1979, p. 283)

Furthermore, during his well-known interviews with David Russell (ca. 1985 to 1986) which were published posthumously (Rogers & Russell, 2002), Rogers elaborated further regarding his feelings toward his former doctoral student:

> Charlie Truax was a brilliant person and one of the most brilliant researchers I've ever encountered. Very keen. But unfortunately, for a lot of deep reasons, he felt he needed to be better than he was, so he did some things that were dubiously ethical [...] at that time, I think, there was a real question in my mind: was Truax right and I wrong? But later he went from bad to worse and finally committed suicide. I feel there was only one time when I ever really knew Charlie, and that was when he was facing the matriculation exams at Wisconsin [...] I think that was the real Truax - that he was a frightened person who put up a tremendous front. If he'd been able to accept himself as he was...he had loads of ability and talent to face life very adequately, but he kept having to put up just a stiffer and stiffer shell. It was a real tragedy. (Rogers & Russell, 2002, pp. 177-178)

Allegiances forming: Gendlin, Kiesler, Bergin, and Strupp

By the late-1960s distinct allegiances had begun forming among various groups within the psychotherapeutic disciplines. Shlien (1966) provides a glimpse into the state of the field midway through the 1960s: "results [of psychotherapy evaluation studies] are usually received with a great deal of skepticism and often vigorously attacked by fellow professionals [...] often based on issues which are technical, and even petty for that matter...." (p. 125). Moreover, the literature suggests that by the late-1960s these allegiances were becoming less and less in favor of Rogers's (1957) hypothesized conditions of therapeutic change.

The downward turn for Rogerian research and practice may formally have begun in 1967, which was a significant year for publications in the psychotherapy profession. Three substantial works were published that arguably shaped the coming decade: (a) Rogers et al.'s (1967) book, which was belatedly published, reported positive and negative results from the Wisconsin schizophrenia project, with rather pessimistic chapters contributed by Kiesler and colleagues describing the results and limitations (Rogers et al., 1967, ch. 8-12), (b) Paul's (1967) well-known article "Strategy of Outcome Research in Psychotherapy," in which he posed his famous question, quoted earlier, articulating the growing "mechanisms-of-change" movement, and (c) Truax and Carkhuff's (1967) widely influential book *Toward Effective Counseling and Psychotherapy* in which the authors provided substantial evidence that Rogers's facilitative conditions *were in fact* effective across a range of settings and client populations. In addition, by the late-1960s Allen Bergin had emerged as the primary steward of collective opinion regarding psychotherapy theory, research, and practice within the profession; Bergin's influence continues to reverberate into the 21st century as well (e.g., Bergin, 1966; Bergin & Garfield, 1971; Garfield & Bergin, 1978; Lambert, 2013). Furthermore, by the late-1960s, Bergin - who had been a student at the University of Wisconsin during the years that Truax worked on the schizophrenia research project (Lambert, Bergin, & Collins, 1977) - had become a primary opponent of Rogers's and Truax's research foundation (Bergin & Suinn, 1975; Quinn, 2013).

More specifically, the literature strongly suggests that those researchers who had reason to ally against the Rogerian research and practice traditions (i.e., proponents of behavior, psychoanalytic, and eclectic therapies) consistently reported unfavorable findings relying upon the small handful of studies conducted by non-PCT researchers, referred to earlier in this article. Again, these negative findings were particularly focused on the inadequacy of the facilitative conditions when measured using Truax's observer-rated scales (e.g., Bergin & Jasper, 1969; Bergin & Strupp, 1970; Bergin & Suinn, 1975; Gomes-Schwartz et al., 1978; Mintz & Luborsky, 1971; Parloff, Waskow, & Wolfe, 1978).

Though subject to debate, those series of negative findings - reported by non-PCT researchers in the late-1960s and early-1970s - also paralleled a distinct paradigm shift away from the once prevailing post-WWII attitude that placed client autonomy in the forefront of ethical and effective psychotherapy treatment; needless to say, an attitude such as what the Rogerian psychotherapy tradition had possessed and promoted with an empirical evidence based begun in 1945 (Cartwright, 1957). In exchange, a new paradigm, intertwined with an increasingly technological worldview, was being constructed and disseminated by behaviorally- and psychoanalytically-oriented scholars. This paradigm, buttressed by behavior theory and supported by applied learning techniques, offered the young, "booming," late-1960s space-aged generation a roadmap toward their modern-day Utopia:

> the influence of behavioristic therapies has become an important phenomenon of the 1960s and cannot be overlooked in stating conclusions about the status of the field […] the number of new journals, research studies, and young people opting for this approach is impressive [however] there are exaggerated claims and a certain zealousness or tendency to rigidify ideas and techniques; but in spite of these signs, which are held in common with most innovations, there appears to be more substance to this movement than is typical of fads." (Bergin & Strupp, 1970, pp. 17-18)

Later in the same article, Bergin and Strupp, two of the most highly influential psychologists of the latter half of the 20th-century, provide a further glimpse into this envisioned future:

> we are in a phase of our history in which we are moving rapidly

away from the gross, placebo-laden [...] influence of therapy. We are moving more rapidly toward an understanding of the mechanisms of change and toward a more explicit technology of behavior and personality modification [...] it seems that these efforts should be encouraged. (Bergin & Strupp, 1970, p. 19)

Remarkably, as of the second decade of the 21st century, and after more than forty years, the empirical discovery of these mechanisms-of-change in psychotherapy continue to elude social scientists (Barlow, Bullis, Comer, & Ametaj, 2013; Kazdin, 2011).

Taken together, Gendlin's (1969) philosophically-grounded process-direction techniques (which will be examined later in this article); Kiesler's considerable pessimism, particularly regarding the results related to Truax's scales (Rogers et al., 1967); and the substantial influence exerted by Allen Bergin's and Hans Strupp's blossoming leadership (e.g., Bergin & Strupp, 1970; Bergin & Garfield, 1971) may have provided the necessary scholarly momentum to jumpstart the then-latent behavior therapy movement and revive the floundering psychoanalytic profession. However, an academic vacuum would be a necessary condition into which behavior and psychoanalytic research could enter. The literature suggests that the process of systematically dismantling the Rogerian research tradition, would soon take root so that Gendlin, Kiesler, Bergin, and Strupp's scientific revolution could begin.

Notably, the literature suggests that Strupp's early, though modest, leadership in the psychoanalytic movement (e.g., Strupp, 1955; 1956) surged forward in the late-1960s when he paired with Bergin, 15 years Strupp's junior, to write a number of influential works that substantially changed the course of psychotherapy research and practice (e.g., Strupp & Bergin, 1969; Strupp, 1978a). To be clear, early in the 1970s behavioral and psychoanalytic research was in its infancy and had only just begun building an empirical evidence base, composed mainly of quasi-experimental and analogue studies (Bergin & Strupp, 1970; Di Loreto, 1971; Kernberg, 1973; Luborsky & Spence, 1978; Mintz, Luborsky, & Auerbach, 1971). In particular, it would not be until 1975, when Sloane, Staples, Cristol, Yorkston, and Whipple's (1975) well-known research volume was published, that the behavior and psychoanalytic-oriented therapies would demonstrate findings sufficient for consideration as empirically-validated treatments (Quinn, 2013).

Charles Truax and Allen Bergin

Though debatable, at the time of his death in 1974 Charles Truax was likely the most influential proponent of the Rogerian research and practice traditions in North America. In a 10-year period, Truax had published and co-published nearly 70 articles, as well as his well-known treatment manual *Toward Effective Counseling and Psychotherapy* (Truax & Carkhuff, 1967). In short, Truax and colleagues' research provided strong evidence supporting the therapeutic effectiveness of Roger's facilitative conditions, measured using Truax's scales. Basing their conclusions on a substantial amount of evidence assembled during

Truax's tenure at the University of Kentucky, Truax and colleagues emphasized that psychotherapy could be "for better or for worse," primarily contingent upon the therapist-provided levels of Rogers's facilitative conditions (Truax, 1963; 1967b; Truax & Mitchell, 1971).

Noteworthy was a similar construct called "the deterioration effect" in psychotherapy, for which Allen Bergin became known (Barlow, 2010; Bergin, 1963; 1966; Lambert, Bergin, & Collins, 1977; Quinn, 2013). However, the difference between Truax's and Bergin's constructs is evident at face value: while Truax suggested a bidirectional relationship (i.e., "for better or for worse"), Bergin perceived only those unidirectional therapy characteristics that inhibited client growth (i.e., "deterioration"). For Bergin, the literature suggests, characteristics of a growth-promoting therapeutic environment remained a mystery to him, yet to be unraveled, despite 20-years of Rogerian research findings that validated certain necessary and sufficient therapy conditions, possibly *the* Rosetta Stone of psychotherapy (Bergin & Suinn, 1975). Furthermore, despite his early emphasis on mechanisms-of-change research, Bergin would later alter his views substantially, spending the majority of his career in search of a particular growth-promoting, eclectic approach that - he envisioned - would transcend psychotherapy technique and orientation (Bergin, 1980; Bergin & Garfield, 1994; Lambert, Garfield, & Bergin, 2004). A 1997 article entitled "Neglect of the Therapist and the Human Dimensions of Change," provides an example of Bergin's evolution from his allegiance to behaviorism early on (Bergin & Strupp,

1970), to the eclectic approach he had come to feel was therapeutically necessary (Bergin, 1997): "future research needs to take into account humanistic, phenomenological, agentive, and postmodern perspectives as opposed to the present overemphasis on mechanistic/naturalistic conceptions of causality and therapeutic change processes" (Bergin, 1997, p. 83). As such, over a 30-year period, Bergin's method of allegiance-guided scientific inquiry had changed course considerably. Bergin will be returned to in subsequent sections of this article.

Gendlin and Rogers

Despite Truax's questionable actions in Wisconsin, and until his untimely death, Truax had provided substantial evidence in support of Rogers's facilitative conditions and the effectiveness of a person-centered approach. In contrast, Gendlin's and Kiesler's post-Wisconsin work diverged substantially from the Rogerian tradition; Gendlin developed focusing-oriented psychotherapy (i.e., PCT-plus), and Kiesler emerged as a prominent critic of psychotherapy research methodology while developing his own theory of "interpersonal complementarity" (Kiesler, 1966; 1971; 1996; 2004). Furthermore, though debatable, the series of problems in Wisconsin between Rogers, Gendlin, Kiesler and Truax, as well as Rogers's subsequent departure from academia, had left over twenty years of accumulated evidence perilously vulnerable to criticism - legitimate or otherwise. That is, while Truax continued his research in support of the Rogerian facilitative conditions, his time was cut short; and while Kiesler demonstrated strong disfavor towards the Rogerian tradition, Gendlin - with his existential philosophy background as well as becoming the founding editor of the journal *Psychotherapy* in 1963 - remained a highly influential figure in the person-centered world. Remarkably, the literature suggests that Gendlin (Gendlin, 1962; Gendlin & Lietaer, 1983) was in fact promoting a treatment paradigm substantially different in philosophy and practice as compared to Rogers's yet to be disproved necessary and sufficient theory of psychotherapy (Rogers, 1957; 1959b).

In brief, Eugene Gendlin was trained as a person-centered therapist by Rogers and his colleagues at the University of Chicago's Counseling Center in the early 1950s, and received his PhD in philosophy, rather than psychology (Gendlin, 1992). After overseeing the research project in Wisconsin (Rogers et al., 1967), Gendlin would return to the University of Chicago where his faculty tenure would extend until 1995. Gendlin is an esteemed and well-known figure in the humanistic-existential professions, and has won many awards and honors.

In addition, Gendlin (1988) wrote a prominent obituary for Rogers following Rogers's death in 1987, which was published in the *American Psychologist*. The obituary suggests great respect for his former mentor and clinical supervisor. However, the problems from the Wisconsin years clearly remained salient for Gendlin, as evidenced in his writing:

in Wisconsin [...] this organizational model [which was used by Rogers successfully in Chicago] could not cope with even one deliberately unethical person [i.e., Truax], (who removed the data, tried to publish it, and then destroyed it so that much work had to be done again) [...] some said that in not expressing anger, he forced those around him to express it by fighting each other [...] in giving up control, he gave up all of it [...] but it is little to criticize, amid so many contributions and so much novelty, honesty, and courage. (Gendlin, 1988, p. 128)

Five years earlier, in 1983, Gendlin had also hinted at feelings of resentment toward Rogers. During an interview, Gendlin suggested that Rogers may have taken undue credit for Gendlin's work on the original conceptualization of the client experiencing construct that was developed in the 1950s:

my main [...] influence on Carl Rogers was during the period of the Process Scale [...] he took mostly from the work that I did together with Zimring, in the years just preceding '55, '57, '59 [...] and so he took much of our work and put it in the form of the Process Scale [...] I then also continued to take that again and developed it further and it became the Experiencing Scale [...] and in that whole period much of what Rogers was saying was taking some of my things....(Gendlin & Lietaer, 1983, p. 81)

Rogers himself corroborates Gendlin's statements in the above excerpt. That is, the literature suggests that Rogers consistently deferred to Gendlin regarding the Experiencing construct. For example:

> here I have been much stimulated and helped by the thinking of many of my colleagues, but I would like to mention my special indebtedness to Eugene Gendlin, William Kirtner, and Fred Zimring, whose demonstrated ability to think in new ways about these matters has been particularly helpful and from whom I have borrowed heavily. (Rogers, 1958, p. 142)

Moreover, in outlining the seven "strands" of his Process Scale, Rogers (1959a) gives special citation to Gendlin regarding the "Manner of Experiencing" strand of this Scale:

> Gendlin's development of this concept of experiencing is one which I believe will bear significance over the next decade or two [...] for this reason the discussion by Gendlin of the relationship of subjective experiencing to the logical positivism of psychology [...] is refreshing indeed. (p. 100)

Throughout the remainder of Rogers's career until his death, he frequently returned to Gendlin's work when speaking of the therapeutic process (e.g., Rogers, 1975; 1980).

However, despite Rogers's deference a further examination of the literature suggests a different interpretation of the facts. Gendlin's assertions in 1983 (Gendlin & Lietaer, 1983) appear to contradict his earlier writings related to when and who developed the ideas for what would come to famously be known as Gendlin's Experiencing construct (e.g., Goldman, Greenberg, & Pos, 2005; Kiesler, 1971; Wiser & Goldfried's, 1998). In other words, the literature suggests that Rogers had fully-formulated his theory of client process prior to 1955, and independent of Gendlin. Despite this, in his later years Rogers appears to have continued to considerably down-play his own work until his death in 1987.

As is now widely known, in the late 1950s Rogers developed a complete interpersonal theory of psychotherapy, presented most fully and succinctly in a book chapter entitled "A Theory of Therapy, Personality, and Interpersonal Relationships, as Developed in the Client-Centered Framework" (Rogers, 1959b), which was alluded to earlier in this article. Despite Gendlin's (Gendlin & Lietaer, 1983) assertion that much of Rogers's process formulations had emerged following Gendlin and colleagues' 1955 work, in 1967 Gendlin stated that Rogers's client process conceptions had been fully formulated and subsequently written by Rogers in 1953 - the same year that Gendlin began working with Rogers and colleagues (Gendlin & Tomlinson, 1967; Gendlin & Lietaer, 1983). "From the formal theory statement written in 1953 [i.e., what became Rogers, 1959b] this statement represents the starting point from which our thinking about process in therapy has gone forward [...] Gendlin and Zimring (1955) took the next step" (Gendlin & Tomlinson,

1967, pp. 112-113). In other words, Rogers had completed his 1959 book chapter (Rogers, 1959b) prior to having met the young Gendlin. Rogers (1974) also alludes to this time frame in his later article, "In Retrospect: Forty-Six Years."

To the point, although Gendlin's work was substantial, his contributions to the process conceptualization of client experiencing was just a fraction of Rogers's larger vision, which he had nearly fully formulated prior to Gendlin's contributions. Despite these discrepancies, Rogers continued to extend olive branches, so to speak, to Gendlin in his later writing: "to formulate a current description I would want to draw on the concept of experiencing as formulated by Gendlin [Gendlin, 1962] this concept has enriched our thinking in various ways as will be evident in this paper" (Rogers, 1975, p. 3). However, in spite of Rogers's interest in reconciliation, Gendlin's writings as well as his 1983 interview suggests that Rogers's peaceful overtures were rather cold comfort for the post-Wisconsin Gendlin.

Kiesler and the person-centered approach: A case study on allegiance effects

Suggested earlier, Donald Kiesler had demonstrated substantial dislike for the Rogerian research and practice traditions, but quickly came and went from the person-centered world following his brief time in Wisconsin. However, following the Wisconsin years, Kiesler's attitudes toward the Rogerian tradition and PCT provide a case study of the process through which allegiance-guided psychotherapy research may function.

In contrast to Gendlin, who continued to indirectly support the person-centered approach as the foundation for his PCT-plus, focusing-oriented therapy (Gendlin, 1992), Kiesler was likely not trained as a person-centered therapist, nor did he hold allegiance to the PCT tradition; having been recruited by the Wisconsin group to replace Truax in the early 1960s. Moreover, Kiesler (1996), in recounting his disappointment with the decisions made during the Wisconsin years, implied having developed a negative attitude toward Rogers and his work after Kiesler left Wisconsin. Comparing his experience with the Wisconsin project to an earlier research position with the Kaiser Permanente Research Project in the 1950s, Kiesler's terse mention of his Wisconsin experience demonstrates this particular disappointment:

> ...the 'real book' describing what transcribed [*sic*] during the Kaiser Permanente project [will not likely] ever see the light of day. That, of course, should not be surprising to many veterans in the field. It especially is not surprising to me, in light of my own earlier experience with a large scale research project, both as first summarized officially [Rogers et al., 1967] and then recounted biographically [Kirschenbaum, 1979]. (Kiesler, 1996, p. 269)

By no fault of his own, Kiesler failed to "buy-into" PCT or, in other words, had not been sufficiently inspired and trained by a "bona fide" PCT practitioner. As a result, Kiesler likely found PCT either insufficient for client change or ineffective as a therapeutic treatment system. That is, Kiesler did not develop a sufficient allegiance to Rogers's paradigm. Thus, similar to Gendlin's (1969) departure from Rogers, as evidenced by his focusing-oriented approach, Kiesler also did not hold allegiance to Rogers's hypothesis of "necessary and sufficient," which is evident in Kiesler's interpersonal complementarity treatment model (Kiesler, 1966; 1996). Therefore, Kiesler was likely guided by his allegiance to *any approach but PCT* due to his experiences during and after Wisconsin, and as evidenced in his well-known 1966 critique of psychotherapy research (Kiesler, 1966).

Allegiance-guided scientific inquiry. In short, allegiance-guided scientific inquiry, specific to a particular therapeutic paradigm, is an underemphasized concept in psychotherapy literature. However, researcher allegiance has been suggested to be a salient explanatory factor for why different "bona fide" therapies tend to consistently be found equivalent across decades of psychotherapy comparison studies and meta-analyses (McLeod, 2009; Wampold et al., 1997; 2010). In addition, allegiance-guided research has been suggested to consistently explain why "showcased" treatments are found to be superior to "watered-down" treatments. Though the previous statement may seem like tautological rhetoric, this type of psychotherapy research appears to frequently occur, and researchers soberly ignore these methodological discrepancies.

Then, in their final report of findings the lack of treatment fidelity and/or treatment equality given to the non-showcased treatment consistently fails to be recognized by the research authors (Quinn, 2011; 2013). So the question remains: would Kiesler's (1966) critique and recommendations for psychotherapy research, and would his chapters reporting the results of the Wisconsin project (Rogers et al., 1967) have been less pessimistic if he had had the opportunity to develop a positive allegiance toward the Rogerian research tradition? Or, were the choices made by Gendlin and Kiesler, and Bergin and Strupp, those of pragmatic, sober, and objective social scientists?

Using the literature as our guide, the evidence suggests that within and without, the person-centered Rogerian psychotherapy tradition was discarded; not as a result of overwhelming evidence suggesting a lack of effectiveness, but as a result of the personal and professional beliefs held by a group of young social scientists - Gendlin, Kiesler, Bergin, and Strupp in the forefront. Not surprisingly, these social scientists were the same who would go forward to lead the next generation of helping professionals into the last decades of the 20th century and beyond.

Coda: The end of the Rogerian tradition

In 1967 John Shlien moved to Boston where he became a professor at Harvard University until his retirement in 1984 (Shlien, 2003). Though debatable, Shlien's move to Harvard in 1967 represented the departure of the last "bona fide" person-centered Rogerian influence at the University of Chicago. Moreover, following Shlien's departure, the literature suggests that two prominent scientist-practitioners from the Rogerian lineage remained at Chicago: Eugene Gendlin (ca. 1963-1995) and Laura Rice (ca. 1955-1970), respectively the "grandfather" and "grandmother" of the emerging process-direction, PCT-plus movement.

In brief, during the 1960s, Rice (Rice, 1965; Watson & Wiseman, 2010) was the director of and obtained her research data from the Counseling Center that Rogers and colleagues had built two decades earlier (Kirschenbaum, 1979). Leaving Chicago for Toronto in 1970, Rice would become a professor at York University, as well as a mentor to a young Leslie Greenberg, the founder of emotion-focused therapy (Watson & Wiseman, 2010; Greenberg & Rice, 1981; Greenberg, & Watson, 1998). As a result, one could hypothesize that by 1975 the majority of person-centered therapists remaining at the University of Chicago, arguably charged with the responsibility of being the last, best group of Rogerian-based PCT trainers in the United States, had likely adopted a policy of relaxation or "détente," so to speak - as was the fashion of the times (Garthoff, 1994). Embracing this new, space-aged era of "innovation" within PCT (e.g., Wexler & Rice, 1974), Rice and Gendlin had ushered in a new way of thinking, and the PCT-plus movement was born.

Not surprisingly, by the 1970s Rogers's so-called "classical" PCT approach had become a diluted form of his former evidence-based "necessary and sufficient" treatment framework. Not without irony, PCT had become just that: a "classic," antiquated and ineffective. Moreover, Marge Witty (2004) provides support to the above assertions in her article on nondirectiveness. Witty (2004) provides a glimpse into the state of Rogers's Counseling Center at the University of Chicago in the early 1970s:

> if Barbara T. Brodley had not raised the issue of the distinctions between experiential and client-centered therapy [Brodley, 1990], it is unclear to me whether a genuinely non-directive school of client-centered therapy would have survived [...] at the time I took the practicum at the Chicago Counseling and Psychotherapy Center in 1972, client-centered therapy was taught in a highly oversimplified, shallow way as a kind of active listening. None of the staff at the time transmitted what I now understand to be client-centered therapy. (p. 22)

PCT versus PCT-plus in the Coming Decades

Alluded to above, in the early 1990s a renewal of interest arose in reappraising and clarifying the fundamental theoretical and practical components of PCT; that is the original "necessary and sufficient" approach. Moreover, some advocates of the necessary and sufficient person-centered approach argued that by adding directive techniques to PCT (e.g., process-experiential therapies), these latter approaches had evolved away from the original formulations by Rogers (e.g., 1951; 1959b). Hinted at in the previous section, these PCT-plus approaches have historically been grounded in two primary frameworks: (a) Eugene Gendlin's experiential or focusing-oriented therapy, which relies upon guiding the client's process toward discovering the inner referent, or felt sense, of his or her experiencing (Gendlin, 1962; 1969), and (b) Laura Rice and Leslie Greenberg's process-experiential and emotion-focused therapies (EFT) that, moving beyond Gendlin's philosophy, further asserted the therapist's position as a process-guide by attempting to shape the client's in-session process behaviors, for example, by encouraging the resolution of "unfinished business" (Greenberg & Rice, 1981; Greenberg, Rice, & Elliott, 1993; Rice, 1965; Rice, 1974; Watson, Goldman, & Greenberg, 2011).

In particular, Barbara Brodley (1990) was largely responsible for laying the groundwork which would subsequently lead to definitive discrepancies between PCT and PCT-plus. In her 1990 chapter, "Client-Centered and Experiential: Two Different Therapies" Brodley articulated a mutual exclusivity between PCT and PCT-plus, drawing a line in the sand, as it were, between the philosophical underpinnings of the two approaches. During this period, a series of "nondirective dialogues" had begun to emerge in person-centered and humanistic-oriented journals; some scholars calling for a return to Rogers's nondirective-oriented therapy, and others arguing the premise - potentially, the moral imperative - that integrating "mainstream" therapeutic techniques into a Rogerian, person-centered approach was the only choice left.

In brief, these dialogues (see Patterson, 2000 for an overview), which began in the *Personal Centered Review* in the early 1990s (e.g., Cain, 1989; Grant, 1990) and carried over into the *Journal of Humanistic Psychology* early in the 21st century (e.g., Bozarth, 2002; Kahn, 1999; Merry & Brodley, 2002), suggested distinct disparities between the various "tribes" of the person-centered tradition (Warner, 2000). In the context of an emerging age of treatment plans, managed care organizations, and technique-driven practice, for better or for worse, a general trend toward refitting the theory, research, and practice of PCT had become apparent. Later, these non-directive dialogues were given new life in the Europe-based *Person-Centered and Experiential Psychotherapies* journal (Freire, 2012).

PCT integration and pluralistic practice

Until her death in 2007 Barbara Brodley continued to defend the theory and practice of PCT as it was "originally intended," alongside Jerold Bozarth and a small group of colleagues (e.g., Bozarth, 2002; 2012; Brodley, 2006a; 2006b; Merry & Brodley, 2002; Sommerbeck, 2002; 2012). This latter point of "originally intended" has been disputed by a number of authors who have cited Rogers's later publications (e.g., Holdstock & Rogers, 1983) as evidence that he had come to possess an "anything goes" mentality toward PCT practice (Cooper & McLeod,

2011; Bohart, 2012). For example, Bohart (2012) cites Rogers as endorsing the premise that expertise, if not forced upon the client, is welcomed in PCT.

Briefly, the practice recommendations frequently found in modern PCT scholarship seem to suggest that the therapist should use agenda-making behaviors (e.g., "metacommunication", formal goal-setting), rather than allowing the process of therapy to unfold in an environment of trusting the client's own process. In addition, the concept of a "pluralistic practice," marshaled forth by integrative and PCT-plus adherents such as Mick Cooper (Cooper & McLeod, 2012) and Stephen Joseph (Joseph & Murphy, 2013) directly lends to an agenda-based form of PCT. Furthermore, as the emphasis of pluralistic practice increasingly drowns out other perspectives, as the literature suggests, a given person-centered therapist is left to follow the guidance of these technique-laden approaches; the essence of which suggests to the therapist to develop a set of replicable behaviors or wooden techniques with which to provide the client in therapy. To the point, the danger lays in what is missing in current PCT scholarship. Rarely do discussions focus on specifying a therapist's way of being with a client. Rather, a growth-promoting therapist way of being is presupposed, and PCT-plus techniques are seldom questioned regarding their potential to distract from, rather than enhance, the PCT therapist's primary goal: to monitor his or her provision of a congruent personality structure when in the presence of a client (Quinn, 2008).

In contrast, the question can be asked: does therapist provision of a congruent personality structure possess relevance in the second decade of the 21st century and in the future? That is, is it worth distinguishing between genuine and utilitarian congruence as possessed by a therapist? Likewise, does the job description of the helping professional include becoming a meaningful and healthy personality who is integrated into a client's life - as experienced in the therapy session; or, is the helping professional simply a behavioral engineer with "provision of meaning" included as a checkbox amongst a list of weekly treatment plan criteria?

Person-centered scholars (e.g., Cooper & McCleod, 2011) contend that pluralistic practice is highly consistent with the principles of a person-centered approach as originally articulated by Rogers, and the authors provide two primary strategies in the practice of integrative PCT:

> the first is to specifically orientate the therapeutic work around the client's goals, and the second is to develop the degree of negotiation, metacommunication and collaboration in the therapeutic relationship. (Cooper & McLeod, 2011, p. 216)

The authors proceed to delineate methods that, more likely than not, will disrupt the process of therapy. For example, Cooper and McLeod (2011) suggest that "different clients are likely to benefit from different therapeutic methods at different points in time, and that therapists should work collaboratively with clients to help them identify what they want from therapy and how they might achieve it" (Cooper & McLeod, 2011, pp. 7-8 as cited in Cooper & McLeod, 2011, p. 215).

From a standpoint of PCT-as-originally-intended, the above recommendations will likely be distractions to practice, but may be necessary for use in PCT-plus frameworks where the therapist is arguably less integrated into the relationship, focusing more on what behavioral modifications that he or she will provide next (Watson, Goldman, & Greenberg, 2011). However, Cooper and other PCT-plus colleagues have consistently failed to delineate between PCT and PCT-plus, and therefore, in the absence of a definition, Cooper in particular has failed to consider the impact of pluralistic practice recommendations upon a therapist's ability to provide a congruent personality structure to the client throughout therapy. In support of Cooper, Bohart (2012) may be colluding with the general trend of blurring definitions by including Gendlin's focusing-oriented, Greenberg's emotion-focused, and Cooper's pluralistic approaches in his operational definition of "a fuzzy circle named 'person-centered psychotherapy'," (Bohart, 2012, pp. 3-4). In this way, in the absence of definition, a general attitude is suggested in PCT literature which conveys the belief that PCT, as originally intended, is a classical approach and, ironically by this definition, obsolete and ineffective.

Therefore, as PCT-plus scholars appear to imply, the use of a pluralistic therapeutic treatment system is subject less to debate than to a question of common sense. Somewhat incongruously, the "fuzziness," as it were, has arisen, not from Rogers's failure to describe or operationalize PCT in exhaustive detail throughout his professional career, but from a choice by the majority of person-centered and experiential therapy scholars since the 1970s to persistently ignore the sufficiency criterion. In short the sufficiency criterion may be defined in the following way:

> the therapist wants to understand for no other reason but to understand. If the therapist is motivated to understand solely to be a change agent for the client, then the facilitative [conditions] may not be sufficient because a tendency toward unconditional acceptance will not effectively emerge. When the therapist presents an agenda (of change), already undue and ill-needed conditions have been placed on the relationship, and trust in the client's natural tendencies toward change have been discarded. (Quinn, 2011, p. 482)

Ignoring the growth-promoting influence provided by the above way of being, PCT-plus adherents seem to be confined to a tunnel in which simple common sense suggests to them that the Rogerian therapeutic system *must* be lacking and therefore insufficient. Meanwhile, the status of the therapist's personality structure (i.e., congruence or genuineness) continues to be overlooked, and consequently continues to remain the true "'dark continent' for psychology" (Freud, 1926/1978, p. 38 - which Freud famously stated about another psychological phenomena that was causing great threat to the status quo of his profession (i.e., the female gender).

From PCT to PCT-plus: Anatomy of the therapist's choice

If, as suggested by Rogers's (1957) hypothesis, the therapist's personality structure, or degree of genuine congruence, is the factor that separates sufficient PCT treatment from insufficient treatment, then the need for a therapist to provide direction such as agenda-setting, advice-giving, or coaching becomes a question of individual therapist characteristics, rather than the particular therapeutic needs of the client. In other words: (a) why must some helping professionals assist the client in focusing on his or her inner referent or felt sense, such as in experiential psychotherapy (Gendlin, 1969)?; (b) why must other helping professionals systematically raise or lower his or her voice tone, vary his or her emotional affect in the client's presence, or systematically plan a gestalt technique in order to "change what clients attend to," such as consistently employed in EFT (Greenberg & Safran, 1981; Rice, 1974)?; and last, (c) why do other helping professionals advocate for eclectic integration and treatment plurality within the person-centered community (Joseph & Murphy, 2013)? Is it because different clients require different techniques, or has the profession lost trust in the client's process? These efforts to move PCT toward mainstream therapy practice seems not a path toward the future, but as David Elkins (2010) stated, "a road to nowhere" (p. 262).

To be clear, when a therapist transforms a set of attitudes, for example, genuine congruence, into a set of prescriptive and replicable behaviors (e.g., utilitarian congruence), the therapist's attitudinal intention toward becoming "genuinely unconditional" in relating to the client will likely be diluted, and PCT will become an insufficient treatment system (Quinn, 2008; 2011). This is the therapist's choice. Again, rather than a specific therapeutic technique or intervention, here the therapist's personality structure is argued to be the active ingredient in the sufficiency of the Rogerian PCT approach. In this way, if the therapist does not primarily value a "genuinely unconditional way of being" as the primary mechanism of change in a person-centered approach, then the effectiveness of PCT will likely be lost (Quinn, 2011). The therapist must then resort to behaviors, external to his or her personality structure, in order to affect or impose client change. Choosing, then, not to trust his or her own growth-promoting personality structure, the therapist's trust in the client's process deteriorates. Next a choice to integrate guidelines for implementing specific strategies, methods, techniques, and treatment plans becomes necessary. Consequently as the therapist continues to choose movement away from Rogers's therapy, his or her clinical skills will likely devolve into mechanically repeated behaviors. In this way, the more the helping professions attempt to disseminate an "individually-tailored" paradigm which views each client as different, paradoxically the less unique will become the client and the more dissociated from the client's experiences will become the therapist. This appears to be the general path that mainstream psychology has chosen, and the specific path that influential PCT theorists such as Cooper and Joseph appear to be following as well (Cooper, 2007; Cooper & McLeod, 2007; Joseph, 2006; Joseph & Murphy, 2013).

An appeal to reason and virtue

Stated earlier, a review of the literature from the first decade of the 21st century suggests that pluralistic and integrative perspectives among person-centered scholars (e.g., Cain, 2010; Cooper & McCleod, 2007; Joseph & Linley, 2006; Rennie, 2007) have increasingly become more the norm than the exception, threatening to transmute the practice of PCT into a diffuse eclecticism. A substantial threat to Rogerian PCT – as it was originally intended - is found within the seemingly benign arguments that support PCT-plus and pluralist practice.

First, the arguments have a superficially virtuous appeal. Joseph and colleagues (e.g., Joseph, 2006; Joseph & Linley, 2006; Joseph & Murphy, 2013) possess an "it's not so much what you do, but how you do it" attitude that, at face value, appears equivalent to Rogers's (1980) "way of being" concept. For example, "terms like coaching, counseling, and psychotherapy are interchangeable in person-centred practice because they all refer to the practice of respecting the self-determination of others" (Joseph, 2006, p. 49). Joseph continues:

the person-centred approach does not prescribe techniques of

> practice, but allows for a diversity of practice methods, insofar as practice is securely grounded in the metatheoretical assumption that people have an inherent tendency toward growth [...] thus, the person-centred coaching psychologist can draw on various cognitive-behavioural, multi-model, solution-focused and systems theory approaches [...] there is no prohibition of the use of techniques *per se*". (Joseph, 2006, p. 52)

Next, PCT-plus scholars tend to use a distinct rhetorical style in arguing for the integration of techniques in the person-centered approach. For instance, the literature suggests that PCT-plus scholars first blunt the debate by suggesting that their "classical" PCT counterparts (i.e., Brodley, Bozarth, and colleagues) are "dogmatic", advising their classical counterparts to take theory and practice "lightly" (Cooper & McLeod, 2011). Continuing this seemingly reasonable and linear path of logic, Cooper and McLeod (2011), in particular, argue that a pluralistic perspective dispels:

> the belief that person-centered and experiential theories or methods are in some, generic way superior to other therapeutic practices and understandings. Rather [pluralistic practice] invites members of the person-centered community [...] to be open to challenges and different viewpoints from both within, and outside of, the person-centered field. At this level, it invites us to be 'person-centered' about person-centered therapy:

nondefensive, open to a range of experiences, and willing to be 'in process' rather than hold a fixed and rigid concept of self. (Cooper & McLeod, 2011, p. 220)

Likewise, other PCT-plus proponents have called for an end to the "contentious" tone between the PCT and PCT-plus groups (Bohart, 2012).

In summary, these PCT-plus adherents appear to be repeatedly staking their claim as the new stewards of the person-centered approach in the 21st century by arguing that integrating technique and directive methods into PCT, (a) is necessary, though no convincing empirical evidence is provided, (b) encourages the client's "free will," in contrast to the dogmatic, classical-PCT approach that is argued to stifle the client, (c) is at times considered a moral imperative, in spite of the client (Rennie, 2007), and (d) Rogers would have wanted it that way (Bohart, 2012). As this pluralistic PCT-plus movement continues to gain momentum, the so-called "fuzzy circle" of person-centered therapies will likely become more rather than less diffuse, threatening to engulf humanistic-existential practice in general. As a result, to identify distinct contrasts between mainstream cognitive and behavior therapies and humanistic-existential ones may become increasingly difficult. Or, said another way, "twelve voices were shouting [...] and they were all alike. No question, now, what had happened [...] already it was impossible to say which was which..." (Orwell, 1946/1996, p. 139). When this happens, humanistic-existential psychology will truly have lost its way (Elkins, 2009).

The Structure of a Scientific Revolution in the Helping Professions

The literature suggests that the division described in the above section between PCT and PCT-plus, which had begun in the early 1990s, was a special case of a more general trend that had developed momentum in the early 1960s, during the time of Rogers et al.'s (1967) Wisconsin schizophrenia study. Examination of the literature from this period suggests that - for the first time within a Rogers-led research group - the attitude of "necessary, not sufficient" had emerged among Rogers's colleagues. Eugene Gendlin (1988), in the obituary he wrote following Rogers's death in 1987, provides support for the existence of this emerging fissure and the beginning of conflict in late-1960s between what Gendlin referred to as "the pure client-centered method and those who integrate it with other methods" (Gendlin, 1988, p. 128). As a result, by the 1970s a sequence of events had taken place, including academic isolation between PCT colleagues, deaths of influential person-centered researchers, and Rogers's withdrawal from academia, all weakening the structure of the Rogerian research and evidence-based practice traditions in the United States (Quinn, 2013). Alluded to earlier in this article, in the late 1970s there emerged a small but influential cluster of literature reviews (e.g., Gomes-Schwartz et al., 1978; Lambert,

DeJulio, & Stein, 1978; Parloff et al., 1978; Strupp, 1978b) that effectively discredited the practice of PCT, while also removing PCT's previous status as an evidence-based treatment approach (Phillips & Bierman, 1981). Remarkably, the literature suggests that the seeds from which this process of amnesia had sprung in the helping professions had been planted decades earlier in the 1940s when PCT was known only as "Rogers's nondirective approach" (Kirschenbaum, 1979).

Historical misunderstandings of the person-centered approach

Despite Rogers's early accolades, and even prior to Rogers's (1957) formal definition of the facilitative conditions as outlined earlier in this article, Rogers and colleagues' evidence-based treatment approach (Rogers, 1951; Rogers & Dymond, 1954) had weathered nearly twenty years of negative regard. For example, as early as 1940 Rogers described strong reactions from his colleagues following a presentation he gave to the counseling program at the University of Minnesota on his "nondirective, relationship therapy" (Ellingham, 2011). Years later, Rogers would write about the Minnesota experience: "I was criticized, I was praised, I was attacked, I was looked on with puzzlement" (Wexler & Rice, 1974, p. 8). In many ways, this description summarizes his overall experience across his 23-year academic career (ca. 1940 to 1963; Kirschenbaum, 1979; 2004):

at different times and places psychologists, counselors, and educators have been moved to great wrath, scorn and criticism by my views. As this furore [uproar, craze, fad] has tended to die down in these fields it has in recent years been renewed among psychiatrists, some of which sense [...] a deep threat to many of their most cherished and unquestioned principles. And perhaps the storms of criticisms are more than matched by the damage done by uncritical and unquestioning 'disciples' [...] using as weapons both inaccurate and accurate understandings of me and my work. I have found it difficult to know, at times, whether I have been hurt more by my 'friends' or my enemies" (Rogers, 1961, p. 15).

A particular example of the scorn directed towards Rogers is described in the Kirschenbaum (1979) biography. In brief, during the 1940s an informal caricature of Rogers's nondirective therapy had begun to circulate which likely became an effective device for ridiculing Rogers's approach. The caricature described a suicidal client meeting with Rogers during a therapy session, and proceeding to communicate his plan and intent to kill himself by jumping out the window of Rogers's office. From the client's initial statement of feeling suicidal to the client's departure through the window, Rogers is satirized as parroting back the client's statements using his "nondirective technique," even while the client jumps to his death (Kirschenbaum, 1979; 2004). Not surprisingly, three decades later, Rogers would write, this tendency to focus on the therapist's responses had consequences which appalled me. I had met hostility, but these reactions were worse. The whole approach came, in a few years, to be known as a technique. 'Nondirective therapy,' it was said, 'is the technique of reflecting the client's feelings.' Or an even worse caricature was simply that, 'In nondirective therapy you repeat the last words the client has said.' I was so shocked by these complete distortions of our approach that for a number of years I said almost nothing about empathic listening. (Rogers, 1975, p. 2)

In contrast, Rogers was also highly esteemed within the psychological profession. Rogers served as the American Psychological Association's (APA) president during the 1946-1947 term (Rogers, Marquis, & Hilgard, 1950), he later received the APA's scientific award in 1956, and the APA's professional award in 1972 (Kirschenbaum, 2004). Moreover, suggested by his 1956 award, Rogers appears to have somewhat legitimized PCT, or at least legitimized the science of empirically testing the effects of psychotherapy (e.g., Rogers & Dymond, 1954; Cartwright, 1957). During this period (ca. 1945-1957), Rogers (1951) published his well-known practice manual *Client-Centered Therapy*, and developed his 72-page formal theory of PCT (Rogers, 1959b), discussed earlier in this article. Regarding the latter, Rogers (1974) remarked years later that, "I worked harder on this theoretical formulation than on anything I have written before or since"; adding that the chapter was "the most thoroughly ignored of anything I have written..." (pp. 119-120).

Modern misunderstandings of the person-centered approach

From the time of Rogers's departure from academia in 1963 to the second decade of the 21st century, the literature suggests that a general misunderstanding or misrepresentation of Rogers's work continued. The literature suggests that since the early 1980s prominent scholars have failed to acknowledge the existence of Rogers's (1959b) full theoretical work and have interpreted inaccurately much of the content they have chosen to cite. An examination of the seminal work of the well-known psychologist, Charles Gelso (pronounced "Jelso"; Hill, 2010), provides a representative example of post-1970s scholarship.

Gelso and Carter's (1985; 1994) well-known set of works entitled respectively, "The Relationship in Counseling and Psychotherapy: Components, Consequences, and Theoretical Antecedents," and, "Components of the Psychotherapy Relationship: Their Interaction and Unfolding During Treatment" provide a clear case study of modern misrepresentations of Rogers's work. First, Gelso and Carter (1985; 1994) appear to have only performed a minimal review of Rogers's theoretical work before categorically dismissing Rogers's theory in favor of their own remarkably similar one:

Rogers [and colleagues] seemed to offer a definition when they equated the relationship with certain therapist-offered conditions

74

[…] upon reflection, it is clear that these conditions, however important, do not define the relationship […] and say nothing about the client-therapist interaction per se. (Gelso & Carter, 1994, pp. 296-297)

Without apology, formal justification, or defense, Gelso and Carter's (1985; 1994) theoretical formulation suggests that they engaged in a cursory and superficial review of the Rogers evidence base, concluding that Rogers's theory ignored the client-therapist interaction. However, in their earlier 1985 article, Gelso and Carter (1985) appear to contradict their later 1994 statements by stating that "Carl Rogers (1951, 1957), in particular, offered that the real relationship between counselor and client is the crucial vehicle for change" (Gelso & Carter, 1985, p. 194).

In brief, across the span of a decade, Gelso and Carter (1985;1994) proceeded to develop their tripartite model of the therapeutic relationship which was remarkably similar to Rogers's facilitative and process conditions as outlined in many publications (e.g., Barrett-Lennard, 1962; Gendlin, Jenney, & Shlien, 1960; Rogers, 1958; Rogers et al., 1967) but most fully in Rogers's (1959b) chapter. Specifically, Gelso and Carter's (1985;1994) framework was built upon (a) Bordin's (1979) working alliance/therapeutic relationship, (b) a nonspecific transference/countertransference relationship, and (c) the "real relationship," for which Gelso is primarily known (Hill, 2010). Upon closer examination, the major difference between Rogers's theory and Gelso and Carter's (1994) is accounted for by the existence of part (b) above; the transference relationship. Defined by the authors as "the feelings and attitudes that counseling participants have toward one another, and the manner in which these are expressed" (Gelso & Carter, 1985, p. 159), Gelso & Carter (1994) insisted that the transference relationship was the primary client mechanism of change.

To be clear, from Gelso and Carter's (1994) perspective, suggested by their 1994 statement, that Rogers's facilitative conditions "say nothing about the client-therapist interaction per se" (p. 297), is accurate only if (a) Rogers's theoretical framework failed to account for client process conditions and the client-therapist interaction (i.e., encounter), and (b) Rogers failed to include acknowledgement of the existence of the transference/countertransference phenomenon. However, Gelso and Carter (1985) acknowledged that Rogers did insist that the real relationship between the client and therapist was crucial, which is difficult to reconcile with their later statement that Rogers said nothing about the client-therapist interaction (Gelso & Carter, 1994). Moreover, the literature suggests that Rogers recognized that a substantial proportion of the helping profession believed in transference and countertransference, but Rogers did not endorse transference and countertransference as being other than a distraction from the client-therapist interaction (Rogers, 1961).

A new language for an old idea

When the variability introduced by Gelso and Carter's (1985; 1994) use of psychoanalytic language is controlled, so to speak, from a practice standpoint one is left with substantial difficulty in perceiving a marked difference between Rogers's (1959b) complete theory and the theory Gelso and Carter (1985; 1994) articulated 30 years later. Rather, a case can be made that in order to develop and disseminate a theoretical framework so similar to Rogers's (1957;1959b), Gelso and Carter (1985; 1994) were compelled to rely upon evidence which negatively showcased Rogers's research and practice traditions. Complete or partial, accurate or a canard, the literature suggests that Gelso and Carter (1985; 1994) also found refuge in those unfavorable reviews of PCT research published in the late-1970s and early 1980s. With the arguments already having been developed and refined by scholars such as Parloff et al. (1978), Bergin and Suinn (1975), and Strupp (1978), Gelso and Carter (1985; 1994) were tasked with little additional work prior to their rapid and succinct dismissal of Rogers's theory of psychotherapy and behavior change in favor of their own.

Deferring to Parloff et al.'s (1978) well-known review - the accuracy of which has earlier been questioned (Patterson, 1984; Quinn, 2013) - Gelso and Carter (1985) suggest that

> the conditions once postulated as necessary *and* sufficient for
> positive outcomes do not seem to account for all that much

outcome variance, even in client-centered interventions. To boot, it is unclear whether these conditions account for more than minor variance in therapies that are not client-centered. (Gelso & Carter, 1985, p. 156)

In support of these speculations, Gelso and Carter (1985) subsequently invoke Thomas Kuhn's (1962) eminent book, *The Structure of Scientific Revolutions*, to explain why the Rogerian research and practice traditions had disappeared:

in good Kuhnian tradition, the client-centered paradigm vis-à-vis the 'facilitative conditions' held sway for many years, attracted many disciples and intense advocates, showed great promise, and generated a wealth of theory and positive research findings [...] as skeptics began examining the propositions, and posing alternative formulations, things did not look so bright. At the same time, *or perhaps consequently* [emphasis added], research on the 'facilitative conditions' or the 'necessary and sufficient conditions' seems to have been markedly reduced or stopped. (Gelso & Carter, 1985, p. 156-157)

Notably, in the course of their above argument, Gelso and Carter (1985) seem to give the suggestion that scientific bias and researcher allegiance is an acceptable method of eliminating scientific paradigms that have held "sway" too long. In particular, Gelso and Carter (1985) appear to be suggesting that the Rogerian paradigm ended as a consequence of

78

"skeptics" who examined the Rogerian evidence base. Would not "neutral observers" have been a more appropriate term than "skeptic"; the latter term suggesting a type of scientist who possessed *a priori* allegiance in opposition to the object of their investigation?

Remarkably, Gelso (1979), six years earlier, had articulated a somewhat different application of Kuhn's theory, suggesting that to rely upon "good Kuhnian tradition" may not have been so useful for the helping professions:

> [Kuhn] suggests that the mature sciences have passed through the stage of disagreement among schools of thought, and have adhered to the unifying paradigm of one major school (which over the years is superceded by a new paradigm). *I suggest that this formulation may be neither useful nor accurate for psychology in general and counseling in particular* [emphasis added]. It is also not a 'valid' notion for methodological paradigms in counseling. It is not out of immaturity that the lack of a single paradigm should apply to counseling research. The lack of a unifying paradigm is a function, rather, of our highly complex subject matter […] the greater risk for counseling research […] would be for it to become enmeshed in 'paradigm fixation.'" (Gelso, 1979, p. 13)

Moving forward 33 years, Gelso appears to have changed course again, disregarding his 1979 indictment of "paradigm fixation." In an article in

Psychotherapy, Gelso and Bhatia (2012) suggest that the traditionally Freudian paradigm which guides the therapist's response to client transference may be important to integrate into all therapy frameworks:

> there is a great paucity of research on the effective ways of responding to positive and negative transference in nonanalytic therapies. We suspect that there are methods of responding to transference that are at once effective and consistent with the given nonanalytic approaches used by particular therapists; and yet there is little or no research on such differential methods of varying theoretical approaches with given patients. To our minds, this represents the growing edge of research on the use of transference in nonanalytic therapies. (Gelso & Bhatia, 2012, pp. 388-389)

In other words, Gelso appears to be suggesting that all therapies should become more rather than less similar to the psychoanalytic/dynamic treatment paradigms. Alluded to earlier, Rogers disagreed many years prior:

> [the relationship created in PCT] is something which is mutual and appropriate, where transference or countertransference are phenomena which are characteristically one-way and inappropriate to the realities of the situation. Certainly one reason why this phenomena is occurring more frequently in our experience is that as therapists we have become less afraid of our

positive (or negative) feelings toward the client. As therapy goes on the therapist's feeling of acceptance and respect for the client tends to change to something approaching awe.... (Rogers, 1961, p. 82)

Later, Rogers's colleague John Shlien would amplify this point:

'transference' is a fiction, invented and maintained by the therapist to protect himself from the consequences of his own behavior [...] it is not entirely new to consider transference as a defense. Even its proponents cast it among the defense mechanisms when they term it a 'projection'. But they mean that the defense is on the part of the patient. My assertion suggests a different type of defense; denial or distortion, and on the part of the therapist. (Shlien, 1984, p. 153)

In summary, Gelso and Carter's (1985; 1994) well-known work is a particular example of a general trend that had emerged in the early 1980s. Like many such instances in the psychotherapy literature, Gelso and Carter - relying upon the negative reviews from the late-1970s - were able to state a few cursory, but well-supported (by the mainsteam) remarks which effectively dismissed the Rogerian paradigm. Next, Gelso and Carter (1985; 1994), in "good Kuhnian tradition," replaced Rogers's ideas with their remarkably similar theory of psychotherapy and behavior change. In the second decade of the 21st century, the literature suggests that the Rogerian tradition continues to wither at the margins of the profession (e.g., Barlow et al., 2013; Lambert, 2013). However, Kuhn's perspective, though famous among social scientists, is only one of many perspectives on the topic of the structure of scientific revolutions. A lesser-known philosopher of science provides an alternative perspective on how these types of scientific revolutions come about:

> new subjects bring with themselves new languages. The new languages contain many terms of the original views and so they seem important, for the original views were, after all, 'great discoveries.' But the terms have been re-defined and are new idioms. The practitioners learn these idioms; they learn and absorb them to such an extent that they become incapable of understanding other ways of describing things [...] if they meet such other ways they either don't understand them (and can reject them as being 'insufficiently precise'), or they read them in their own simple-minded fashion (and, naturally, soon find faults). (Feyerabend, 1978, p. 50)

On Systematically Dismantling an Evidence-Based Paradigm

Stated several times in this article, by the 1980s PCT's status as an effective psychotherapy had become resolutely degraded. Considerable evidence in support of the above statement can be found in two influential and periodic sources for psychotherapy research and practice: the *Annual Review of Psychology* (*ARP*), and Bergin and

Garfield's *Handbook of Psychotherapy and Behavior Change* (*HPBC*).

As the Rogerian tradition entered the mid-1970s, PCT scholars, who had previously been asked to contribute to the *ARP* and *HPBC*, in particular (e.g., R. Cartwright, 1968; Patterson, 1966; Truax & Mitchell, 1971) had begun to recede from mainstream visibility. By 1975 a new generation of helping professionals - under the leadership of Allan Bergin and Hans Strupp - had assumed responsibility for disseminating psychotherapy research and practice guidelines to the helping professions at large. In particular, Bergin and Strupp exerted substantial influence within each recurring publication of *ARP* and *HPBC* (e.g., Bergin & Garfield, 1971; Bergin & Suinn, 1975; Garfield & Bergin, 1978; Gomes-Schwartz et al., 1978; Strupp, 1978a). In addition, Bergin and Strupp's influence extended to scholarly works other than *ARP* and *HPBC* (e.g., Lambert, Bergin, & Collins, 1977; Strupp, 1978b). However, the scholarship found in *ARP* and *HPBC*, two enduring and influential publications, provide specific examples of the general trend of bias favoring the growing behavior and psychoanalytic movements during this period (Patterson, 1984; Quinn, 2011; 2013).

Literature review: Process and methodology

Charged with a time-consuming and challenging task, prominent researchers and scholars in the 1970s were invited to review the psychotherapy literature in order to update the previous editions of *ARP* and *HPBC*, consequently formulating conclusions regarding "what works" in effective psychotherapy treatment. However, the invited scholars were asked only to review the years since the previous reviews' edition, allowing for a substantially easier task, and arguably reducing redundancy.

For example, Phillips and Bierman's (1981) edition of the clinical section of the *ARP*, took for granted research evidence prior to 1976. The authors began with a short note providing the reader with a reference to the previous *ARP* psychotherapy review: "the most recent review of individual therapies for adults appeared in Volume 29, by Gomes-Schwartz, Hadley, & Strupp (1978)" (Phillips & Bierman, 1981, p. 405). Similarly, Gomes-Schwartz et al. (1978) drew conclusions from their review of research spanning 1974 to 1976, and Gomes-Schwartz et al.'s (1978) predecessors, Bergin and Suinn (1975), drew their conclusions from research spanning the years 1971 to 1973, and so on. In sum, a clinical contribution to the *ARP* was published every three years, whereby the new authors would update and draw conclusions based upon the previous three years of psychotherapy research, beginning where their predecessors had ended.

Likewise, Bergin and Garfield's *HPBC* editions, begun in 1971, demonstrate a similar method for reviewing psychotherapy research. For example, the authors of the recurring chapter on therapist variables in psychotherapy - traditionally the flagship chapter on clinical practice - would begin their literature review at the point in time where their predecessors had ended; again, taking for granted that the previous authors had accurately captured the review of literature from the years prior. This continues to be the prescribed method in *HPBC* (e.g., Baldwin & Imel, 2013; Beutler, Crago, & Arizmendi, 1986; Beutler, Machado, & Neufeldt, 1994; Beutler et al., 2004; Parloff et al., 1978); save for one anomaly in 1978. Parloff et al.'s (1978) clinical chapter substantially discounted and ignored their predecessor's edition (i.e., Truax and Mitchell, 1971). Historically, within *ARP* and *HPBC* this event marked the single time in which the successors would substantially dismiss and revise their predecessor's conclusions; that is, Parloff et al.'s (1978) review methodology was novel to the standard review methodologies used in both *ARP* and *HPBC* both prior to and since 1978. In particular, Parloff et al. (1978) devoted eight pages specifically to refuting Truax and Mitchell's (1971) earlier evidence-based conclusions that psychotherapy, contingent upon levels of Rogers's facilitative conditions, could be "for better or for worse":

> the Truax and Mitchell (1971) review not only concluded that the evidence was directly supportive of Rogers' basic hypothesis, but pointed out a new and unanticipated confirmation implicit in the tendency for patients who receive low levels of the three prerequisite conditions not simply to fail to improve, but to become clinically worse […] this overall assessment of research evidence available to them, however, seems somewhat injudicious, for they failed to give sufficient weight to the

> obvious inconsistencies among the reports they cited. (Parloff et
> al., 1978, p. 245)

As will be shown, Parloff et al. (1978) subsequently go on to refute Truax and Mitchell's (1971) conclusions by engaging in, arguably, the same "injudicious process" by which Parloff et al. (1978) indicted their predecessors.

Systematic bias in reviews of the literature

At face value, from a standpoint of productivity and to avoid redundancy, the method of reviewing psychotherapy literature described above - that is, continuing from the point in time that the prior authors had ended their review - would appear to provide a substantial degree of efficiency and precision in assessing the evidence base of psychotherapy. However, this method of the successor taking for granted the accuracy of the predecessor, from one literature review to the next, violates an important requirement for methodological independence in scientific inquiry. In other words, using this "for-granted" method, save for the Parloff et al. (1978) anomaly, each subsequent edition of *ARP* and *HPBC* immediately became vulnerable to potential systematic error introduced, in this case, into the collective beliefs of the helping professions as to "what works" in psychotherapy. These types of systematic errors, which more than likely would be introduced by the authors' "less-than-independent" conclusions, would consequently increase the probability of the error becoming correlated.

Correlated error due to methodological bias violates the basic assumption of the scientific method which assumes independently and identically distributed (i.i.d.) events; that is, the assumption that error or inaccuracy introduced into a system is randomly distributed and (statistically) independent: "in the actual collection of the data the assumption of independence cannot be left to chance: a deliberate attempt to achieve it has to be made and this is met by randomization" (Maxwell, 1968, p. 805). In other words, the methods used in any scientifically-based inquiry will likely affect the degree to which each datum within the dataset is assigned an equal probability of occurring, and therefore assigned an equal probability of influencing the dataset's subsequent statistical estimates (e.g., mean, median, mode, standard deviation, regression coefficient). Said another way, the researcher must genuinely attempt to give each datum a "fair shake," so to speak; it is only later that so-called "outliers" must be addressed. However, if the data has been collected in a scientifically-rigorous fashion, an alleged outlier may not necessarily represent bias, and need not necessarily be discarded (Kutner et al., 2005).

Going forward, although randomization may be difficult or unrealistic in literature review methodology, the reviews under question here neither reassessed past conclusions - again, save for the Parloff et al. (1978) anomaly - nor performed a reasonably exhaustive review of the existing literature outside the narrow group of publications comprising the highest ranked journals of the time. Therefore, in terms of probability, the reviews in *ARP* and *HPBC* violated the basic assumption of scientific inquiry: the researcher must faithfully attempt to provide a climate conducive to i.i.d. events, while he or she performs the data collection. Furthermore, i.i.d. events in review methodology would increase the likelihood that all relevant literature had received an equal probability of review (i.e., equal and objective consideration). The well-known "file-drawer effect" is one way through which this violation may happen (Fanelli & Ioannidis, 2013). Remarkably, Rogers (1961) described an experience of this latter type:

> for more than a decade this problem has puzzled me. I know that I speak to only a fraction of psychologists. The majority [...] are so committed to seeing the individual solely as an object, that what I have to say often baffles if it does not annoy them [...] so when it comes to the publication of a particular paper, I have felt dissatisfied with presenting it to a professional journal [...] the majority of my writings in recent years have piled up as unpublished manuscripts, distributed privately in mimeographed form. They symbolize my uncertainty as to how to reach whatever audience it is I am addressing. (Rogers, 1961, pp. viii – ix)

To amplify the current argument: scientists, when conducting literature reviews, should not *leave to chance* that scientific rigor and objectivity will be met without engaging in sufficient effort toward this end (Maxwell,

1968); otherwise, conclusions of an empirical or observable sort may be spurious at best. However, from the 1970s onward, an examination of the reviews in *ARP* and *HPBC* suggests that both the authors and the editors failed to control for potential inaccuracy and bias, and consequently these reviews became vulnerable to systematic nonrandom error. As time went on, and the next editions of the *ARP* and *HPBC* were subsequently published, these inaccuracies would likely have become consolidated within mainstream psychotherapy doctrine, and gradually perceived as psychotherapy "fact." As a result, there is reasonable likelihood that the conclusions disseminated by these highly influential publications have been replicated repeatedly across more than four decades (e.g., Barlow et al., 2013; Bergin & Garfield, 1994; Goldfried, Greenberg, & Marmar, 1990; Hollon, Stewart, & Strunk, 2006; Kopta, Lueger, Saunders, & Howard, 1999; Lambert, 2004; Parloff, London, & Wolfe, 1986). While these reviews, which continue to be published (e.g., Barlow et al., 2013; Baldwin & Imel, 2013), demonstrate a great level of precision, the accuracy of these conclusions is uncertain. That is, the conclusions in *ARP* and *HPBC* have reliably hit the same place on the scientific "dartboard," so to speak, but for over forty years, the extent to which these reviews have accurately hit the "bull's-eye" on this dartboard is highly questionable. Due to their questionable validity, substantial difficulty exists in trusting these conclusions as they pertain to the practice of counseling and psychotherapy in the helping professions. And, as a result, the helping profession's perceptions about "what works" in counseling and psychotherapy have become - as of the second decade of the 21ˢᵗ century - fixed and immutable yet potentially invalid.

Given the above assertions, the negative conclusions regarding the ineffectiveness of Rogerian research and practice have also been perpetuated, and are more than likely irrelevant. However, these conclusions have been generally accepted by the helping professions since the time they were disseminated in the 1970s predominantly by Allen Bergin and Hans Strupp (e.g., Bergin & Suinn, 1975; Strupp, 1978a). A 2013 article in the Annual Review of Clinical Psychology, equivalent to the *ARP*'s past clinical sections, provides strong support for this argument. In a review entitled, "Evidence-Based Psychological Treatments: An Update and a Way Forward," Barlow et al. (2013) remark:

> one of the most sophisticated psychotherapy researchers of that era [pre-1970s], Carl Rogers, well known for his early work evaluating psychological treatments for schizophrenia, advocated abandoning formal research in psychotherapy altogether in 1969, since in his view it was yielding nothing of value and had no impact on practice (Bergin & Strupp, 1972). But another pioneer in our field, Gordon Paul, suggested that the question, is psychotherapy effective? was the wrong question to ask in the first place, since any test of a global treatment, such as

psychotherapy, was bound to fail [...] following Paul's guidelines, the early work of pioneers such as Joseph Wolpe and Isaac Marks [Marks, 1978], but also Allen Bergin and Hans Strupp, changed the landscape of research on psychological treatments. (Barlow et al., 2013, p. 3)

Barlow et al. (2013) continue:

also during the 1970s, conceptualizations of psychopathology became more empirical and specific, facilitating the development of reliable and valid dependent variables, and both behavioral and psychodynamic treatments were described in detail, paving the way for more systematic and objectively defined independent variables. (Barlow et al., 2013, p. 3)

"Winners" and "losers"

Allen Bergin's (Bergin & Suinn, 1975) conclusions, particularly in the 1975 edition of the *ARP,* regarding the quality of Rogers's and Truax's evidence base, have been previously questioned as to the degree of accuracy (Patterson, 1984; Quinn, 2013). Moreover, Bergin and Suinn's (1975) review has been suggested as marking the starting point of a new literature review methodology that possessed two distinct characteristics: (a) emphatic, immutable, and markedly positive conclusions regarding the effectiveness of a given authors' favored therapeutic paradigm (e.g., behavior or psychoanalytic therapy), and (b) quick, superficial, and negative reviews of the evidence regarding treatment paradigms not favored by a given group of authors (Quinn, 2013). In the case of Bergin's (Bergin & Suinn, 1975) review of PCT, this review overlooked substantial evidence that, at the time, refuted the ongoing criticism of the Rogerian evidence base (i.e., Chinsky & Rappaport, 1970). Bergin's review will be examined in detail in the next section.

However, literature reviews were not always conducted according to a "winner-loser" methodology. Stated earlier, prior to the 1970s, PCT was the only evidence-based treatment approach that possessed a large body of literature supporting its status as an "empirically-validated treatment", while behavior and psychoanalytic therapies possessed little empirical evidence in general (Luborsky & Spence, 1978; Marks, 1978). By the 1970s, initial behavior and psychoanalytic outcome studies had been reported by Di Loreto (1971), Kernberg (1973) and Sloane et al. (1975).

Not surprisingly, the transition from a pre-1970s balanced-review methodology to a post-1970s "winner-loser" review methodology coincides with an emergence of the competing evidence-bases of the behavioral and psychoanalytic groups. Nowhere was this competition more exemplified than in Luborsky, Singer, and Luborsky's (1975) well-known article, "Comparative Studies of Psychotherapies: Is it True that "Everyone has Won and All Must Have Prizes"?; where the authors allude to the Dodo bird's method of selecting "winners" following the

famous "race" in *Alice's Adventures in Wonderland* (Carroll, 1865/1997).
The Dodo bird:

> marked out a race-course, in a sort of circle, ("the exact shape
> doesn't matter," it said,) and then all the party were placed along
> the course, here and there [...] they began running when they
> liked, and left off when they liked, so that it was not easy to
> know when the race was over. However [...] the Dodo suddenly
> called out, "The race is over!" and they all crowded round it,
> panting, and asking, "But who has won?" [...] at last the Dodo
> said, "*Everybody* has won, and all must have prizes." "But who is
> to give the prizes?" [...] "Why, *she*, of course," said the Dodo,
> pointing to Alice with one finger; and the whole party at once
> crowded round her, calling out in a confused way, "Prizes!
> Prizes!" (Carroll, 1865/1997, pp. 33-34)

Furthermore, the literature suggests that in their early years
Allen Bergin's (Bergin, 1966; Bergin and Suinn, 1975) and Hans
Strupp's (1955; 1977) opinions toward PCT's effectiveness were
markedly different compared to later years, as is evident in the excerpts
that will be provided below. Whereas these eminent scholars once were
not as concerned with "prizes," by the 1970s Bergin and Strupp appear to
have designated themselves as the proverbial "Alice" in Carroll's
(1865/1997) story, seeking to become the stewards of awarding prizes to
the psychotherapy community. However, unlike Carroll's (1865/1997)

story, Bergin and Strupp demonstrated a distinct interest - not in "all must have prizes" – but, rather, in creating a highly competitive "winner-loser" dichotomy within the helping professions. Bergin's early attitudes are exemplified by the following:

> to date, the only school of interview-oriented psychotherapy which has consistently yielded positive outcomes in research studies is the client-centered approach (Rogers & Dymond, 1954; Shlien, Mosak, & Dreikurs, 1962; Truax & Carkhuff, 1964) [...] the fact that other schools have not subjected their methods to systematic study of this sort is important but it should not deter one from accepting the fact that client-centered treatment has some positive value when properly conducted according to Rogers' (1957) paradigm. (Bergin, 1966, p. 241)

Likewise, in the 1950s, Strupp (1955) wrote that:

> the research effort by Carl Rogers and his students to describe and elucidate the process of nondirective counseling has provided objective evidence in an area in which such evidence has been sorely lacking. Unfortunately, this impetus has not extended to other theories of psychotherapy, particularly those based more explicitly upon psychoanalytic principles.... (Strupp, 1955, p. 1)

However, by the mid- to late-1970s Bergin and Strupp had respectively changed their opinions toward PCT, basing their conclusions on a small, unfavorable, and biased body of research that likely possessed substantial methodological flaws. In his 1975 review of the clinical literature, Bergin stated the following:

> one of the most popular areas of research continues to be the analysis of empathy, warmth, and therapist genuineness or congruence and other therapist behaviors as they relate to process and outcome. In recent years, a number of studies have induced skepticism concerning the potency of these variables except in highly specific, client-centered type conditions [...] many critical questions concerning the nature of these therapeutic conditions, as rated by the currently popular scales [Truax's scales], have been raised by Chinsky & Rappaport [...] they show a number of psychometric defects in the nature of the scales and question the validity of the outcome studies [...] *these findings may invalidate much of this program of research* [emphasis added]. (Bergin and Suinn, 1975, p. 515)

Bergin, who wrote the individual psychotherapy portion of this particular *ARP* review, notes at the bottom of the page: "we note here with sadness the regrettable and untimely death of Dr. Truax in December 1973" (Bergin & Suinn, 1975, p. 515).

Similar to Bergin, by the late 1970s Strupp had changed his viewpoint considerably:

> the nature of the change desired or attempted may vary widely

depending upon circumstances, but unless the therapist views his task as that of a change agent he does not merit the appellation of therapist. The foregoing implies that *there is no such thing as 'nondirective' therapy, a term that is basically self-contradictory and has served largely propagandistic purposes (i.e., to castigate psychoanalysts)* [no emphasis added]." (Strupp, 1977, p. 4)

Two decades later, Wampold et al. (1997) summarized the state of psychotherapy research, particularly since Luborsky et al.'s (1975) famous article, and concluded that a "winner-loser" mentality had become the dominant paradigm in the field of psychotherapy research:

> so the race has been run over and over again. In fact and maybe because of the Dodo bird conclusion, psychotherapy research has become increasingly pragmatic, designed to detect winners and losers [...] lately, the races have been sanctioned by the psychotherapy community [...] in fact, 18 therapies have been identified as winners by the [APA] task force and consequently designated as empirically validated [...] clearly, to identify the winners and losers among the set of treatments, the race should be fair [...] to receive a prize that has meaning, the competitors must have a level playing field [...] occasionally individual races have produced winners [...] but the loser in any such race can always find conditions that put them at a disadvantage. (Wampold et al., 1997, p. 203)

The next section provides detailed support to the main argument under development in this article; that is, the Rogerian traditions of research and evidence-based practice ended as a result of "unfounded claims made by a group of social scientists who held significant professional interest in seeing through the dismantling of the person-centered approach" (Quinn, 2013, p. 219). And the final section briefly examines the status of evidence-based psychotherapy treatments as of the second decade of the 21st century, and subsequently summarizes Elliott et al.'s (2013) update to their previous meta-analytic review of humanistic-existential psychotherapy effectiveness (Elliott et al., 2004).

A "Review of The Reviews" from the 1970s

The conclusions arrived at by Bergin and Strupp in the 1970s, and cited frequently in this article, were distinctly negative regarding PCT. The literature suggests that Bergin and Strupp relied upon studies that either (a) reported no relationship between Rogers's facilitative conditions and client outcome, or (b) reported evidence which suggested the existence of major methodological flaws in the Rogerian research tradition.

A review of the evidence from this period suggests the following: Bergin, Strupp, and colleagues had begun a movement to discredit all PCT research findings, and by the early 1980s this movement proved to be a success. According to the literature, nearly 25 years of work by Rogers, Truax, and colleagues in testing Rogers's (1957) hypothesis was no longer considered valid; and, as if the proverbial champagne was thrown out with the cork, all previous research demonstrating the effectiveness of PCT was summarily disregarded (e.g., Rogers & Dymond, 1954). As a result, PCT was no longer mentioned in psychotherapy literature, except to lend further criticism when the need suited the scholar (e.g., Charles Gelso). In particular, Bergin's (Bergin & Suinn, 1975) review was a flagship article during this period that at once provided substantial momentum to the movement to discredit PCT, and exemplified the emerging winner-loser mentality in psychotherapy research, as described in the previous section.

Furthermore, Bergin's (Bergin & Suinn, 1975) conclusions in the 1975 clinical section of the *ARP* (i.e., *Annual Review of Psychology*) appear to have possessed substantial inaccuracy, primarily due to his failure to deliberate over all the evidence to which he plausibly would have had access (Quinn, 2013). In short, Bergin and Suinn (1975) cited some articles (i.e., Bozarth & Krauft,1972; Chinsky & Rappaport, 1970; Gurman, 1973b; Mintz & Luborsky, 1971; Rappaport & Chinsky, 1972; Truax, 1972), but overlooked other findings which would have provided empirical support to the validity and reliability of Rogers and Truax's methodology (i.e., Beutler, Johnson, Neville, & Workman, 1973; Gurman, 1973a; Wenegrat, 1974). In addition, the following points are relevant to the content later in this section: one year after Bergin and Suinn's (1975) review, Beutler's (1976) article provided further support to the validity of Truax's observer-rated measurement scales and, 13 years later, Friedlander et al. (1988) demonstrated that specific findings cited by Bergin & Suinn (1975), particularly, Mintz & Luborsky (1971), were unfounded. However, despite Bergin's (Bergin & Suinn, 1975) fragmented and unbalanced review, many late-1970s reviews of psychotherapy research relied substantially upon Bergin's conclusions, disregarding or minimizing newer or overlooked findings that would have unequivocally supported the Rogers/Truax evidence base.

In summary, these late-1970s reviews (e.g., Parloff et al., 1978; Lambert et al., 1978; Gomes-Schwartz et al., 1978; Strupp, 1978a; Strupp, 1978b) did not *exclusively* rely upon Bergin's review (Bergin & Suinn, 1975) but, if not directly, then indirectly these reviews cited other articles that had directly relied upon Bergin and Suinn (1975).

Strupp's contribution: Gomes-Schwartz, Hadley, and Strupp (1978)

Three years after Bergin and Suinn's (1975) *ARP* review, Hans Strupp and his Vanderbilt University research team contributed the subsequent *ARP* clinical review. Strupp and colleagues (Gomes-Schwartz et al., 1978) cited a dozen studies and/or reviews of findings within their brief, six-sentence paragraph, whereby the authors rapidly concluded that PCT research findings were universally flawed, and therefore the effectiveness of PCT as a psychotherapy treatment was questionable. The foundation of Strupp and colleagues' (Gomes-Schwartz et al., 1978) argument relied upon the conclusions of two earlier reviews: (a) their predecessor's review (Bergin & Suinn, 1975), and (b) Gormally and Hill (1974). However, the respective conclusions reported in Bergin and Suinn (1975) and Gormally and Hill (1974) conflicted substantially, particularly regarding the validity of Truax's measurement scales and, therefore, the subsequent status of the Rogerian research methodology. Due to the substantial discrepancies between these two primary reviews cited by Gomes-Schwartz et al. (1978) in support of their patently negative conclusions, each of these earlier reviews will briefly be examined beginning with the lesser-known review by Gormally and Hill (1974).

Gormally and Hill (1974). In contrast to Bergin and Suinn's (1975) review, which overlooked substantial evidence in support of Rogers's and Truax's research methods (Quinn, 2013), Gormally and Hill (1974) included one of three additional studies (Beutler, Johnson, Neville, & Workman, 1973) that Bergin and Suinn (1975) had failed to acknowledge, though this study may have exerted substantial impact upon Bergin's conclusions. That is, this additional study alone may have been the pivotal evidence that led to the marked discrepancies between Gormally and Hill (1974) and Bergin and Suinn (1975).

Cited by Gormally and Hill (1974), Beutler et al. (1973) reported findings suggesting that the theoretical criticisms leveled by Chinsky and Rappaport (1970) against Truax's observer-rating scales did not hold in practice. Thus, in contrast to Bergin and Suinn's (1975) definitive conclusion that the evidence "in recent years" invalidated the Rogerian research findings, Gormally and Hill (1974), drawing from the same available literature base, concluded that: "the traditional method for assessing reliabilities (many segments per counselor) seems justified" (Gormally & Hill, 1974, p. 544). That is, Chinsky and Rappaport's (1970) "statistical independence" criticism of Truax's measurement scales, outlined earlier in this article, was considered of little importance by Gormally and Hill (1974) in light of Beutler et al.'s (1973) findings, which overturned Chinsky and Rappaport's (1970) "armchair" theory, so to speak. Notably, Gormally and Hill (1974) had arrived at their conclusion - directly in conflict with Bergin's (Bergin & Suinn, 1975) - having only included one of the three pivotal studies listed earlier, that were overlooked in the Bergin and Suinn (1975) review. Therefore, would Bergin (Bergin & Suinn, 1975) have arrived at a conclusion similar to Gormally and Hill's (1974) if he had included even one of the three studies available at the time?

Bergin and Suinn (1975). One of the few empirically-based studies that Bergin (Bergin & Suinn, 1975) relied upon as a cornerstone of his final conclusions regarding Rogerian research was published by Bergin's doctoral student Alan Gurman (1973b). In particular, Gurman (1973b) suggested that therapists were unable to maintain consistent levels of the facilitative conditions within a session as well as across sessions (mentioned earlier in this article, this finding – if true - had direct consequences upon the validity of Truax's observer-rating scales). However, when Gurman's (1973b) report is closely examined, moderate to large exaggerations of the findings can be found. Moreover, Gurman had published a second, more sobering, article, (Gurman, 1973a), which was ignored by Bergin, yet remarkably suggested that skilled therapists were able to minimize within-session fluctuations of the facilitative conditions they provided - which further calls into question the strength of Gurman's (1973b) conclusions.

Despite the above contradictions between the findings reported in Gurman's two studies (i.e., Gurman, 1973a, 1973b) - studies that originated during his doctoral work under Bergin - Bergin (Bergin & Suinn, 1975) appears to have considered Gurman's (1973b) interpretation of *some* of the findings as indisputable evidence that substantiated Chinsky and Rappaport's (1970) criticism of Truax's rating scales. In addition, Bergin (Bergin & Suinn, 1975) connected Gurman's (1973b) findings to Mintz and Luborsky's (1971) lesser-known article in which these latter authors called into question the appropriate length of a sufficiently "ratable" audio-recorded segment of a psychotherapy session. In short, Mintz and Luborsky (1971) argued, based on their findings, that relatively short randomly selected segments from therapy sessions were less reliable compared to an expert therapist's overall rating after listening to a full, 50-minute audio-recorded therapy session.

As Bergin's (Bergin & Suinn, 1975) argument developed momentum, he relied heavily upon Gurman's (1973b) report as well as

Mintz and Luborsky's (1971). Moreover, in the final moments prior to the climax of Bergin's argument, in which he ultimately stated, "these findings may invalidate much of [Rogerian] research" (Bergin & Suinn, 1975, p. 515), Bergin exclaimed:

> in analyzing 4 min segments as opposed to whole sessions, [Mintz and Luborsky] discovered similar variables with much overlap in correlation except for the empathy variable, indicating that judgments of therapist empathy based on brief segments *cannot* be generalized to whole sessions! [*sic*] (Bergin & Suinn, 1975, p. 515)

However, and of particular importance, the Rogers research group (e.g., Rogers et al., 1967) had acknowledged within-session fluctuations of therapist facilitative conditions as a measurement problem, and chose to randomly select short segments of each session in an effort to control for potential measurement error (see Kiesler, Klein, & Mathieu, 1965; Truax, 1972). Moreover, mentioned earlier, 13 years later Friedlander et al. (1988) demonstrated that segments as short as 4 minutes can be generalized for the purposes of the research carried out by Rogers, Truax, and colleagues; too late for the Rogerian research tradition, but effectively discounting the Mintz and Luborsky (1971) study.

Furthermore, two additional methodological criticisms used by Bergin (Bergin & Suinn, 1975) to support his enthusiastic conclusions may also have been neutralized, if Bergin had included all the evidence available at the time (i.e., Beutler et al., 1973; Wenegrat, 1974): (a) the criticism that trained raters were responding to a therapist quality such as "likeability" or a "good therapy hour," which was discounted by Beutler et al. (1973) and, lamentably, too late by Hill and King (1976); and (b) the criticism that trained raters were responding to the number of words spoken by the therapist (Chinsky & Rappaport, 1970) was contradicted by Wenegrat (1974). However, the three pivotal articles to which Bergin presumably would have had access (i.e., Beutler et al., 1973; Gurman, 1973a; Wenegrat, 1974), were markedly absent from Bergin's review (Bergin & Suinn, 1975). Moreover, the literature suggests that these three studies also failed to be seriously regarded in the late-1970s reviews as well (e.g., Gomes-Schwartz et al., 1978; Parloff et al., 1978).

Consequently, by the end of the decade, the negative reviews of Rogers's and Truax's work had become a commonly held belief in the helping professions. Lambert et al. (1978) provide an example: "despite more than 20 years of research and some improvements in methodology, only a modest relationship between the so-called facilitative conditions and therapy outcome has been found" (Lambert et al., 1978, p. 486). Similar to other articles of the period, Lambert et al.'s (1978) conclusions failed to incorporate a complete picture of the issues in question (e.g., Beutler, 1976; Engram & Vandergoot, 1978; Hill & King, 1976; Tinsley & Weiss, 1975). Later, Michael Lambert would assume editorial leadership of Bergin's famous *HPBC* handbook (Lambert, 2004; Lambert, 2013).

In summary, Strupp's (Gomes-Schwartz et al., 1978) major contribution as the successor to Bergin and Suinn (1975) suggests that he and his Vanderbilt research group arrived at conclusions regarding the Rogerian research tradition that were supported by scholarship distinctly in disagreement (Bergin & Suinn, 1975; Gormally & Hill, 1974). This section will conclude below with an examination of the extent to which the critics of the Rogerian research base possessed understanding of the theoretical foundations of hypothesis testing in scientific research. The assertion here is that the critics did not understand the theory of hypothesis testing, and therefore their interpretations of the findings were seriously flawed.

PCT provided by person-centered therapists

Throughout the 1970s, few literature reviews argued that the facilitative conditions were unrelated to outcome *when provided by person-centered therapists*. For example, Bergin stated that "a number of studies have induced skepticism concerning the potency of these variables except in highly specific, client-centered type conditions" (Bergin & Suinn, 1975, p. 515). In other words, when provided by a PCT therapist who, arguably, held allegiance toward the sufficiency of the facilitative conditions, positive client outcome was found (Quinn, 2011). In contrast, among non-PCT therapists, or therapists who were unable to provide effective levels of these conditions, the facilitative conditions did not relate to client outcome (Lambert et al., 1978; Mitchell, Bozarth, &

Krauft, 1977). Therefore, if methodological flaws associated with Truax's rating scales existed, as first suggested by Chinsky and Rappaport (1970), one would expect that the levels of both PCT and non-PCT therapists' facilitative conditions would be spuriously inflated, assuming that the same methodological flaws would infiltrate any research using Truax's observer rating scales. That is, if measurement errors were favoring the outcomes reported by Rogers and Truax, then one would expect these measurement errors to impact non-PCT therapists' findings as well; and therefore significant correlations between facilitative conditions and client outcome would similarly be found among non-PCT studies. And, if non-PCT therapist-facilitative conditions were being measured using some other method, then this failure to replicate would be grounds for dismissing their findings as supporting Chinsky and Rappaport's (1970) "armchair" theory discussed earlier.

Counter to the expectation described above, researchers who carried out facilitative conditions studies using non-PCT therapists frequently failed to reject the null hypothesis, despite using the so-called "flawed" Rogers/Truax method of performing repeated observations of the same client-therapist dyad over the course of therapy. That is, no significant relationships were found between therapist conditions and client outcome. Parloff et al.'s review (1978) emphasized these studies in particular, but neglected to remind the reader that failure to reject the null hypothesis does not directly imply improved scientific rigor; rather, if anything, failure to reject (i.e., the decision to accept) the null hypothesis is more likely to occur in the presence of poorly planned and poorly executed experiments. In other words, the likelihood of poorly designed experiments to be significant beyond a 5% "alpha" level is substantially less when compared to well-designed experiments' odds. This is particularly due to an inability for poorly designed experiments to "detect" a significant effect (Kutner et al., 2005).

Weak methodology among non-PCT researchers. In

brief, the evidence supports the above assertions. In contrast to Rogers, Truax, and colleagues' use of trained lay raters, such as undergraduate students who were not associated with the research study (Rogers et al., 1967; Truax et al., 1966), many non-PCT studies utilized trained expert raters, such as clinical psychologists; or, in some cases, the study's primary investigators acted as the raters, listening to and rating the therapists' levels of the facilitative conditions (e.g., Auerbach & Luborsky, 1968; Bergin & Jasper, 1969; Mintz & Luborsky, 1971; Mintz, Luborsky, & Auerbach, 1971). Moreover, these non-PCT studies, rather than sampling all or nearly all therapy sessions, tended to rate the therapists' facilitative conditions from audio segments taken from an early session only, or an early and next-to-last session only (e.g., Kurtz & Grummon, 1972; Sloane et al., 1975). As a result, a reasonable argument can be made that non-PCT researchers were using substantially less rigorous research methodologies, and as a result, null findings (i.e., nothing significant happened) would more than likely be found; which confirms the theory of hypothesis testing (Hogg & Craig,

1978).

A brief theory of hypothesis testing. In a given experiment
if an unexpected finding occurs (i.e., the finding is significant), then the
finding is either, (a) due to chance or expected sampling variation, which
is set at the well-known 5% probability-level of occurrence (i.e., $p < .05$),
or (b) due to a treatment effect. Either way, if a finding from an
experiment falls below the 5% probability level, then grounds for
rejecting the null hypothesis is warranted. This 5% "cutoff" is purposely
chosen in social science research to ensure that when unexpected events
occur they will be taken seriously because they only have a 5 in 100 (or 1
in 20) chance of occurring.

The discipline of hypothesis testing is based upon decision-
making; the decision to accept or reject the null hypothesis. In other
words, the decision to accept the null hypothesis (i.e., failure to reject)
suggests that a finding from an experiment failed to be novel and under
normal conditions is expected and theoretically uninteresting. In
contrast, under the assumptions of a well-designed experiment (i.e.,
randomization, a large-enough sample size, a control-comparison group),
then when a finding is significant and the decision to reject the null
hypothesis is necessary, this suggests that the treatment likely exerted a
discernible effect on the group receiving it, and that this "treatment
group" was significantly unlike the null or control group since the
treatment group was exposed to the treatment. Time and financial

constraints typically allow only a few replications of an experiment, so when the findings fall in the 5%-or-less probability region (i.e., $p < .05$), then there is a strong indication that if the original experiment was carried out faithfully many times, one would frequently find significant results beyond chance or sampling variation. In other words, the planned treatment had an effect. One caveat dictates that if the number of observations (i.e., client sample size) were small, then many experiments would be required to verify that the rejection of the null hypothesis in the original experiment was not in error or simply due to chance. Similarly, if the scientific rigor was poor, then to ensure that the original study's findings were not due merely to chance, many studies would be required. In contrast to the small sample size problem, poor experimental design introduces many threats to the validity and reliability of the outcomes of the original experiment as well as future experiments. For example, poor design, inadequate measurement methods, and researcher bias will greatly obscure the future predictive ability of a single experiment in which the findings were significant.

As such, the implementation of rigorous methods of scientific inquiry (i.e., striving to collect data under independent and identically distributed [i.i.d.] conditions) as well as copious documentation of a researcher's methods - which is how the Rogers groups functioned - provides a strong case in favor of the significance of a treatment effect (e.g., the facilitative conditions were significantly related to client outcome). Under these research conditions, one could be confident that the findings did not happen by the 1 in 20 likelihood of chance but, rather, the findings happened due to the effect exerted by the treatment and would reliably occur in subsequent replications of the experiment.

The Rogerian research evidence base, to which Truax contributed greatly, possessed all the characteristics that would instill confidence in a group of objective scientists. First, despite some studies possessing small sample sizes, Rogers's and Truax's research were found to be statistically significant so frequently across independent studies that this small sample size problem would be neutralized in the long-term. In addition, Rogers's and Truax's research groups described their methodologies in such detail (i.e., Rogers & Dymond, 1954; Rogers et al., 1967) that if some articles failed to copiously report every bit of minutiae (i.e., usually due to journal space) the large number of statistically significant studies that did report the methods in detail would allay concerns of poor methodological rigor in the long term. This latter point is similar to the difference between a doctoral thesis and a journal article: the neophyte researcher must validate his or her research more so than the seasoned and trusted veteran researcher. Despite the problems during the Wisconsin years, as this article suggests, no evidence exists that Rogers and Truax were weak on research design, statistical analysis, or accurately reporting results. Remarkably, the eminent work by Donald Campbell and Julian Stanley references Rogers's work as exemplary in their section entitled "Three True Experimental Designs" (Campbell & Stanley, 1963). By 1971, Rogers,

Truax, and colleagues had built a large evidence base supporting PCT in general and Rogers's (1957) hypothesis in particular.

In contrast, the literature suggests that most non-PCT researchers in the 1970s failed to understand the difficulty that researchers, such as Rogers, Truax and colleagues, faced in order to achieve significant findings in psychotherapy research. This is not surprising given that the literature also suggests that the biggest critics of Rogers and Truax were non-PCT scholars who had little experience conducting naturalistic clinical research. Furthermore, the literature suggests that most non-PCT researchers in the 1970s also failed to understand the basic theory of hypothesis testing as briefly touched upon above (see Hogg & Craig, 1978).

To the point, Truax and Mitchell's (1971) flagship clinical chapter in *HPBC* (i.e., *Handbook of Psychotherapy and Behavior Change*) marked a major update and consolidation of PCT-based research conducted during the previous decade and, exemplified by the reaction from non-PCT researchers, their chapter also elicited a demonstration of a lack of general knowledge in the helping professions regarding the theory of statistical hypothesis testing. Truax and Mitchell's (1971) conclusions suggested that a significant relationship between the facilitative conditions and client outcome had been found throughout the majority of the hundreds of research studies conducted during the 1960s by the Rogers and Truax groups. In other words, as of 1971 the work of

Rogers, Truax, and colleagues during the past decade strongly suggested that their findings were not occurring by accident, but were systematically occurring because PCT and the facilitative conditions provided effective treatment for depressed, anxious, traumatized, schizophrenic, troubled-adolescent, and multicultural client populations. Moreover, Truax and Mitchell (1971) reported additional findings which strongly suggested that psychotherapy was predictably "for better or for worse," dependent upon the degree to which a therapist could provide Rogers's facilitative conditions in the presence of the client.

In summary, despite their many critics, Rogers's and Truax's adherence to methodological rigor and careful research designs suggests that the Truax and Mitchell (1971) report was accurate. However, Truax and Mitchell's (1971) remarkable report appears to have been too remarkable for non-PCT researchers to accept. In other words, Rogers's and Truax's research found PCT, as well as the facilitative conditions, to be significantly related to client outcome so often - well beyond long-term chance - that when Truax and Mitchell (1971) published their findings, instead of following the path suggested by the most rigorously obtained data of the time period, the stewards of psychotherapy research responded by generating numerous unfounded criticisms, conducted a handful of poorly designed experiments which generated unfavorable results and, by the late-1970s, Parloff et al. (1978) proceeded to rewrite Truax and Mitchell's (1971) chapter.

The late C.H. Patterson realized these problems early on (Patterson, 1984). After examining Parloff et al.'s (1978) widely-influential review, Patterson concluded that,

> they recognize that there are positive findings, but emphasize the negative, failing to note that there are more positive than negative studies, or to note that the negative studies are not without serious problems or flaws. They make the important point that Rogers's (1957) statement included as a necessary condition the client's perception of the therapist's empathy, warmth, and genuineness, and note that most studies do not involve measures of client perceptions of the conditions, but rather use observer's ratings of the conditions. They fail, however, to recognize that this would lead to attenuation [dilution] of the relationship between the conditions and outcomes, or to negative results in some cases where client ratings might produce positive results. Thus it is *significant* [emphasis added] that positive results are obtained where the conditions are measured from an observer's rather than from the client's viewpoint. (Patterson, 1984, p. 433)

'Good Kuhnian tradition', or researcher-allegiance bias?

In summary, the literature suggests that PCT, as a result of questionable conclusions arrived at by a group of social scientists in the 1970s, was discredited despite little empirical evidence supporting these actions. Of note, in reaction to the Truax methodology turmoil, Beutler (1976) provided cautionary guidance to the psychological research community during this period. However, a review of the literature suggests that his advice was ignored:

> in the absence of techniques that can provide such proof [that Rogers's and Truax's methods led to inflated observer ratings], and before abandoning an established procedure [of using Truax's observer-rating scales], the burden rests with the critic to demonstrate the lack of value in these procedures. (Beutler, 1976, p. 861)

However, no such proof by the critics emerged in the following years or decades. Rather, history has shown that the research methodology and statistical theory implemented by Rogers, Truax, and colleagues (e.g., Guilford, 1954; Campbell & Stanley, 1963; Rogers & Dymond, 1954; Rogers et al., 1967) have changed little in the ensuing half-century, and continue to be used in studies of psychotherapy outcome (e.g., Adelson & Owen, 2012; Friedlander et al., 1988; Tinsley & Weiss, 2000). Therefore, many years later it is difficult to determine whether or not the act of systematically dismantling over 40 years of Rogerian research conformed, as Charles Gelso put it, to "good Kuhnian tradition." Rather, was this simply a tragic version of Galileo's hard-won argument that the earth revolved around the sun (Feyerabend, 1975)?

The last section of this article examines findings which suggest that PCT is comparable in effectiveness to PCT-plus treatments as well as cognitive-behavioral and psychodynamic therapies.

Modern Person-Centered Research Evidence

In general, analyses of psychotherapy outcome studies comparing different therapies' effect sizes are consistently found to be equivocal (Bennish, Imel, and Wampold, 2008; Kliem, Kroger, & Kosfelder, 2010; Luborsky et al., 1975; Wampold et al., 1997). Moreover, little difference in effect size has been found between PCT, PCT-plus (e.g., emotion-focused therapy, focusing-oriented therapy, gestalt/humanistic therapies), cognitive, and behavior therapies. In particular, the meta-analysis of experiential psychotherapies reported by Elliott, Greenberg, and Lietaer (2004) cast doubt upon directive, technique-based therapies possessing superiority to PCT or other humanistic-existential treatments in terms of effectiveness. In addition, Elliott et al.'s (2004) findings suggested that researcher allegiance substantially influenced the differences between PCT and PCT-plus, CBT, and psychodynamic therapies.

Furthermore, Elliott et al.'s (2004) findings supported the work of Wampold and colleagues (1997) who concluded that winner-loser based psychotherapy research had answered few novel questions of use to the helping professions. As a result of their work, Wampold and colleagues (1997) suggested that all comparison studies should use "bona fide" treatments in order to reduce unwanted mediating and moderating effects (Shadish and Sweeney, 1991). In short, bona fide treatments were defined as "those that have ingredients common to all legitimate psychotherapies, including a cogent rationale for the disorder being treated, a treatment based on psychological principles, therapeutic actions consistent with the rationale, and active collaborative participation of both patient and therapies" (Wampold et al., 2010, p. 924).

Examples of dilution and constraint effects in PCT research

Despite Wampold and colleagues recommendations, comparison studies continue to demonstrate the practice of introducing researcher and therapist allegiance bias into the data by methods of comparing a "showcased" treatment with a non-bona fide, or watered-down, version of a legitimate treatment. In many studies, PCT has been provided in this diluted or non-bona fide format, while the comparative, or showcased, treatment in the study was afforded a considerable amount of attention related to training and preparing the therapists (Quinn, 2011; 2013). For example, among psychotherapy comparison studies, DBT and a family systems therapy (i.e., structural ecosystems therapy [SET]) have been reported to be superior to PCT. Moreover, despite considerable researcher allegiance favoring DBT and SET, upon examination, DBT and SET, respectively, were only slightly superior (Quinn, 2011; 2013). In particular, the researchers failed to provide PCT in a format, (a) consistent with Rogers's rationale (Rogers, 1951), (b) based on psychological principles (Rogers, 1959b), and (c) providing therapeutic actions consistent with the rationale (Rogers, 1957; Truax & Carkhuff, 1967). Remarkably, the respective founders of DBT and SET (i.e., Linehan, 1993; Szapocznik et al., 2004) would later cite these studies as evidence that their treatment approach was more effective than PCT (Quinn, 2011; 2013). Specifically, Linehan and colleagues (Lynch, Trost, Salsman, & Linehan, 2007) concluded that, "although subjects in both treatments tended to improve, the results strongly favored DBT over [PCT]" (p. 190). Likewise, Szapocznik et al., (2004) concluded that SET was "significantly more efficacious" (p. 301) than PCT. Furthermore, three years later Szapocznik cited his research as evidence that PCT was an iatrogenic or harmful family treatment approach (Szapocznik & Prado, 2007). Szapocznik et al.'s (2004) study provided a somewhat more bona fide version of PCT, but introduced constraints upon the PCT condition by directing those therapists to focus solely on client treatment, and to avoid family-related treatment. In contrast, the family therapy, SET, possessed a substantial family-oriented component. Not surprisingly, the primary measure that demonstrated SET's superiority was a family-related improvement measure that was sensitive to an increase in a client's problems related to his or her family.

Meta-analysis findings: No evidence for one superior treatment

If a particular treatment protocol does in fact possess effect-size superiority to other treatments, when the most competitive and bona fide psychotherapeutic treatments are compared, a meta-analysis will likely be sensitive to this effect difference (Wampold et al., 2010). However, meta-analyses have typically reported less than favorable evidence supporting, (a) the superiority of one treatment over another, (b) the "specific-techniques-for-specific-symptoms" paradigm, or (c) superior outcomes related to therapist adherence to and competence in providing a manualized treatment protocol. For example, bona fide treatments for borderline personality disorder and posttraumatic stress disorder, respectively, have been found to be comparable (BPD: Kliem, Kroger, & Kosfelder, 2010; PTSD: Bennish, Imel, and Wampold, 2008; Wampold et al., 2010). Moreover, little difference in treatment effectiveness has been found using the meta-analytic method to investigate the importance of therapist adherence and competence related to providing techniques specific to a particular treatment approach (Webb, DeRubeis, & Barber, 2010). In other words, Webb, DeRubeis, and Barber (2010) reported that therapists who adhered to the techniques prescribed in a treatment manual and who were competent in providing those techniques to the client were no more effective than therapists not adhering to a manual and not competent in providing the prescribed techniques.

However, despite an abundance of evidence to the contrary, psychotherapy research continues to invest time and money in studies which seek to confirm that treatment-specific techniques produce predicted therapeutic effects. As Wampold et al. (1997) suggested, individual studies may reject the null hypothesis, indicating that the treatment in general helped the clients, but little long-term evidence suggests that one treatment is superior to another; or that a client's alleviation of symptoms is induced by therapist-provided mechanisms of behavior change such as coaching, advice, or homework (Kazdin, 2011). In contrast, meta-analytic studies which have been accumulating since the early 1980s strongly suggest that a therapist's intention to help his or her clients, combined with genuinely believing in the effectiveness of his or her treatment-of-choice (i.e., the therapist's treatment allegiance) may account for much of the difference between treatments, and the difference between treatment and no-treatment. Moreover, the literature suggests that the long-held belief in the superiority of one bona fide therapy over another has become a less immutable attitude: "it may be that a more important set of factors are those that are common to most or all forms of psychotherapy, such as the quality of the therapeutic alliance" (Webb et al., 2010, p. 207).

Similarly, Benish, Quintana, and Wampold (2011) have demonstrated that a particular treatment's "illness myth" - that is, the therapist incorporates a culturally-congruent understanding and explanation of a racial/ethnic minority client's problem or illness - may account for the additional effect size found when culturally-adapted treatments have been compared to unadapted treatments. That is to say, if a therapist's perception of the client's "illness" (e.g., automatic thoughts, cognitive distortions) is congruent with the client's own perception of his or her illness, then culturally-adapted treatments are more effective than non-adapted treatments. However, few non-White, non-Western cultures perceive their problems to stem, for example, from Aaron Beck's cognitive theory of depression (Beck, Rush, Shaw, & Emery, 1979). Moreover, since Beck's cognitive theory of depression is arguably blended into most modern psychotherapy treatments, this places racial/ethnic minority clients, particularly in the United States, in a situation in which the majority of mainstream treatments are arguably inappropriate (Quinn, 2013).

This article concludes below with a brief summary of Elliott et al.'s (2013) meta-analytic update of treatment comparisons.

Elliott et al.'s (2013) meta-analysis

Elliott, Greenberg, and colleagues' (Elliott et al., 2013) updated meta-analysis suggests that humanistic-existential psychotherapies (HEP) in general, and PCT in particular, may be more potent than previously reported in the early years of the 21st century. With 77 additional studies not included in their 2004 analysis, Elliott et al. (2013) have confirmed and strengthened their earlier findings, which suggest equivalence between HEP, cognitive-behavioral therapies, and non-CBT treatments. Among the comparison studies, 100 different studies compared HEP to other treatments with 82 of these studies fitting the criteria for randomized control trials (RCTs). To test treatment equivalence, Elliott et al. (2013) used Elliott, Stiles and Shapiro's (1993) recommendations as a guide for discriminating between-treatment effect size (ES) differences. The criteria are the following: (a) "Equivalent"; the ES was within .1 standard deviation (SD) of zero; (b) "Trivially worse/better"; the ES was between .1 and .2 SD's of zero; (c) "Equivocally worse/better"; between .2 and .4 SD's of zero, and (d) "Clinically worse/better"; at least .4 SD's from zero. Using these cutoffs, Elliott et al. (2013) provide substantial evidence that HEP treatments are comparable to CBT.

Remarkably, *without* controlling for researcher allegiance bias, as was necessary in Elliott et al. (2004), the mean comparison effect size between PCT and PCT-plus treatments was only trivially in favor of PCT-plus (Total sample: n = 9; ES = .14; 95% CI [-.21, .5]; RCTs: n = 8; ES = .08; CI [-.30, .44]). Likewise, the comparative effect size between PCT and CBT treatments was only trivially in favor of CBT (Total sample: n = 22; ES = -.06; 95% CI [-.11, -.01]; RCTs: n = 17; ES = -.10; CI [-.23, -.02]).

In summary, the analyses indicate that among all studies, PCT-plus compared to PCT treatments were only trivially better, but among RCTs only, PCT-plus and PCT were found to possess equivalent effect sizes. In contrast, PCT was found to be equivalent to CBT among all studies included in the analysis. However, among RCTs-only, CBT was trivially better; in other words, "the facts are friendly" (Rogers, 1961, p. 25).

Conclusion

Many explanations can be suggested for the decline and disappearance of the person-centered approach within the spheres of theory, research, and practice in counseling and psychotherapy. As suggested in this article, the majority explanation appears to suggest a "survival-of-the-fittest" rationale for PCT's decline. That is, this perspective suggests that the psychological sciences move forward by subjecting the natural world to increasingly rigorous methods of evaluation, obtaining increasingly precise evidence and, consequently, any paradigm whose evidence fails the test is eliminated from the list of empirically-validated treatments.

In contrast, this article has developed an alternative explanation for the disappearance of the person-centered approach in mainstream psychology and psychotherapy: psychological scientific inquiry is not guided by groups of neutral and objective scientists and researchers who choose to go where the evidence leads them; rather, groups of social scientists cluster together based on shared values as well as allegiance to their beliefs regarding what works and what does not. The literature suggests this is particularly evident in the helping professions. As a result, systematic bias is introduced into all aspects of the research endeavor - from hypothesis formation to design; from provision of therapeutic treatment to the choice of statistical analyses. This procession of allegiance-guided scientific inquiry in psychotherapy is suggested to have been the primary mechanism through which a systematic dismantling of the Rogerian traditions of theory, research, and practice occurred. Moreover, this systematic dismantling, as the description implies, was not by accident but was carried out by a group of social scientists who possessed substantial professional interests in doing so. In summary, then, this article has provided two contrasting explanations, (a) the mainstream perspective, and (b) the allegiance-guided perspective; though other explanations may exist that are beyond the scope of the present article.

In conclusion, the evidence continues to suggest that if a therapist can provide Rogers's facilitative conditions (as operationalized by Rogers, Truax, Barrett-Lennard, and colleagues) and the client perceives these facilitative mechanisms, then a process is hypothesized to occur, described in detail in Quinn (2011). This process is suggested to be sufficient for facilitating the client's movement toward happiness and symptom-reduction; or, as intuition suggests, toward becoming one's own person.

References

Adelson, J. L., & Owen, J. (2012). Bringing the psychotherapist back: Basic concepts for reading articles examining therapist effects using multilevel modeling. *Psychotherapy: Theory, Research, Practice, Training*, 49(2), 152-162.

American Psychiatric Association (2013). *Diagnostic and statistical manual of mental disorders* (5th ed.). Arlington, VA: American

Psychiatric Publishing.

Anthony, W. A. (1971). A methodological investigation of the" minimally facilitative level of interpersonal functioning. *Journal of Clinical Psychology, 27*(1), 156-157.

Auerbach, A. & Luborsky, L. (1968). Accuracy of judgments of psychotherapy and the nature of the "good hour." In J. Shlien, H. F. Hunt, J. P. Matarazzo, & C. Savage (Eds.), *Research in psychotherapy* (pp. 155-168). Washington, D.C.: American Psychological Association.

Baldwin, S., & Imel, Z. (2013). Therapist effects: Findings and methods. *Bergin and Garfield's Handbook of Psychotherapy and Behavior Change* (6th ed.) (258–297). New York, NY: Wiley.

Banks, G., Berenson, B. G., & Carkhuff, R. R. (1967). The effects of counselor race   and training upon counseling process with Negro clients in initial interviews. *Journal of Clinical Psychology, 23*(1), 70-72.

Barlow, D. H. (2010). Negative effects from psychological treatments: A perspective. *American Psychologist, 65*(1), 13-20.

Barlow, D. H., Bullis, J. R., Comer, J. S., & Ametaj, A. A. (2013). Evidence-based psychological treatments: An update and a way forward. *Annual review of clinical psychology, 9*, 1-27.

Barrett-Lennard, G. T. (1962). Dimensions of therapist response as causal factors in therapeutic change. *Psychological Monographs, 76*(43), 1-36.

Barrett-Lennard, G. T. (1981). The empathy cycle: Refinement of a nuclear concept. *Journal of Counseling Psychology, 28*, 91-100.

Barrett-Lennard, G. T. (1985). The helping relationship: Crisis and advance in theory and research. *The Counseling Psychologist, 13*(2), 279–294.

Beck, A. T., Rush, A. J., Shaw, B. F., & Emery, G. (1979). *Cognitive therapy of depression*. New York: Guilford Press.

Benish, S. G., Imel, Z. E., & Wampold, B. E. (2008). The relative efficacy of bona fide psychotherapies for treating post-traumatic stress disorder: A meta-analysis of direct comparisons. *Clinical psychology review, 28*(5), 746-758.

Benish, S. G., Quintana, S., & Wampold, B. E. (2011). Culturally adapted psychotherapy and the legitimacy of myth: A direct-comparison meta-analysis. *Journal of Counseling Psychology, 58*(3), 279-289.

Bergin, A. E. (1963). The empirical emphasis in psychotherapy: A symposium. The effects of psychotherapy: Negative results revisited. *Journal of Counseling Psychology, 10*(3), 244-250.

Bergin, A. E. (1966). Some implications of psychotherapy research for therapeutic practice. *Journal of Abnormal Psychology, 71*(4), 235-246.

Bergin, A. E. (1980). Psychotherapy and religious values. *Journal of consulting and clinical psychology, 48*(1), 95-105.

Bergin, A. E. (1997). Neglect of the therapist and the human dimensions of change: A commentary. *Clinical Psychology: Science and Practice, 4*(1), 83-89.

Bergin, A. E., & Jasper, L. G. (1969). Correlates of empathy in psychotherapy: A replication. *Journal of Abnormal Psychology, 74*(4), 477-481.

Bergin, A. E. & Garfield, S. L. (Eds.). (1971). *Handbook of psychotherapy and behavior change: An empirical analysis* (1st ed.). New York, NY: Wiley.

Bergin, A. E. & Garfield, S. L. (1994). Overview, trends, and future issues. In A. E. Bergin & S.   L. Garfield (Eds.), *Handbook of psychotherapy and behavior change: An empirical analysis* (4th ed.) (pp. 821-830). New York, NY: Wiley.

Bergin, A. E., & Strupp, H. H. (1970). New directions in psychotherapy research. *Journal of Abnormal Psychology, 76*(1), 13-26.

Bergin, A. E., & Suinn, R. M. (1975). Individual psychotherapy and behavior therapy. *Annual Review of Psychology, 26*(1), 509-556.

Beutler, L. E. (1976). More sources of variance in accurate empathy ratings: A response. *Journal of Consulting and Clinical Psychology, 44*(5), 860-861.

Beutler, L. E., Johnson, D. T., Neville, C. W., & Workman, S. N. (1973). Some sources of variance in "accurate empathy" ratings. *Journal of Consulting and Clinical Psychology, 40*(2), 167-169.

Beutler, L. E., Crago, M., & Arizmendi, T. G. (1986). Therapist

variables in psychotherapy process and outcome. In S. L.
Garfield & A. E. Bergin (Eds.), *Handbook of psychotherapy and behavior change: An empirical analysis* (3rd ed.) (pp. 257-310).
New York, NY: Wiley.

Beutler, L. E., Machado, P. P., & Neufeldt, S. (1994). Therapist variables. In A. E. Bergin & S. L. Garfield (Eds.), *Handbook of Psychotherapy and Behavior Change* (4th ed.) (pp. 229 - 269). New York: John Wiley & Sons, Inc.

Beutler, L. E., Malik, M. L., Alimohamed, S., Harwood, T. M., Talebi, H., Noble, S., & Wong, E. (2004). Therapist variables. *Bergin and Garfield's Handbook of Psychotherapy and Behavior Change* (5th ed.) (pp. 227–306). New York, NY: Wiley.

Bohart, A. C. (2012). Can you be integrative and a person-centered therapist at the same time? *Person-Centered & Experiential Psychotherapies, 11*(1), 1-13.

Bordin, E. S. (1979). The generalizability of the psychoanalytic concept of the working alliance. *Psychotherapy: Theory, Research & Practice, 16*(3), 252-260.

Bozarth, J. D. (2002). Nondirectivity in the person-centered approach: Critique of Kahn's critique. *Journal of Humanistic Psychology, 42*(2), 78-83.

Bozarth, J. (2012). "Nondirectivity" in the theory of Carl R. Rogers: An unprecedented premise. *Person-Centered & Experiential Psychotherapies, 11*(4), 262-276.

Bozarth J. D., & Krauft C. C. (1972). Accurate empathy ratings: Some methodological considerations. *Journal of Clinical Psychology, 28*(3), 408-210.

Brodley, B. T. (1990). Client-centered and experiential: Two different therapies. In G. Lietaer, J. Rombauts, & R. Van Balen (Eds.), *Client-centered and experiential psychotherapy in the nineties* (pp. 87-107). Leuven, Belgium: Leuven University Press.

Brodley, B. T. (2006a). Client-initiated homework in client-centered therapy. *Journal of Psychotherapy Integration, 16*(2), 140-161.

Brodley, B. T. (2006b). Non-directivity in client-centered therapy. *Person-Centered & Experiential Psychotherapies, 5*(1), 36-52.

Burstein, J. W., & Carkhuff, R. R. (1968). Objective, therapist and client ratings of therapist-offered facilitative conditions of moderate to low functioning therapists. *Journal of clinical psychology, 24*(2), 240.

Cain, D. J. (1989). The paradox of nondirectiveness in the person-centered approach. *Person-Centered Review,4*, 123-131.

Cain, D. J. (2010). *Person-centered psychotherapies.* Washington, D.C.: American Psychological Association.

Campbell, D. T. (1957). Factors relevant to the validity of experiments in social settings. *Psychological bulletin, 54*(4), 297-312.

Campbell, D. T. & Stanley, J. C (1963). Experimental and quasi-experimental designs for research. In N. L. Gage (Ed.). *Handbook of Research on Teaching* (pp. 171-246). Chicago: Rand

McNally.

Caracena, P. F., & Vicory, J. R. (1969). Correlates of phenomenological and judged empathy. *Journal of Counseling Psychology, 16*(6), 510-515.

Carroll, L. (1865/1997). *Alice's adventures in wonderland.* Boston: Lee and Shepard.

Cartwright, D. S. (1957). Annotated bibliography of research and theory construction in client-centered therapy. *Journal of Counseling Psychology, 4*(1), 82-100.

Cartwright, R. D. (1968). Psychotherapeutic processes. *Annual review of psychology, 19*(1), 387-416.

Chinsky, J. M., & Rappaport, J. (1970). Brief critique of the meaning and reliability of "accurate empathy" ratings. *Psychological Bulletin, 73*(5), 379-382.

Cooper, M. (2007). Person-centred therapy: The growing edge. *Therapy Today, 18*(6), 33-36.

Cooper, M., & McLeod, J. (2007). A pluralistic framework for counselling and psychotherapy: Implications for research. *Counselling and Psychotherapy Research, 7*(3), 135-143.

Cooper, M., & McLeod, J. (2011). Person-centered therapy: A pluralistic perspective. *Person-Centered & Experiential Psychotherapies, 10*(3), 210-223.

Cooper, M., & McLeod, J. (2012). From either/or to both/and: Developing a pluralistic approach to counselling and psychotherapy. *European Journal of Psychotherapy & Counselling*, *14*(1), 5-17.

Crits-Christoph, P., Cooper, A., & Luborsky, L. (1988). The accuracy of therapists' interpretations and the outcome of dynamic psychotherapy. *Journal of Consulting and Clinical Psychology*, *56*(4), 490-495.

Di Loreto, A. O. (1971). *Comparative psychotherapy*. Chicago, IL: Aldine-Atherton.

Elkins, D. N. (2009). Why humanistic psychology lost its power and influence in American psychology: Implications for advancing humanistic psychology. *Journal of Humanistic Psychology*, *49*(3), 267-291.

Elkins, D. N. (2010). David Elkins responds. *Journal of Humanistic Psychology, 50*(2), 256-263.

Ellingham, I. (2011). Carl Rogers' fateful wrong move in the development of Rogerian relational therapy: Retitling "relationship therapy" "non-directive therapy". *Person-Centered & Experiential Psychotherapies*, *10*(3), 181-197.

Elliott, R. K., Greenberg, L. S., & Lietaer, G. (2004). Research on experiential psychotherapies. In M. J. Lambert (Ed.), *Bergin and Garfield's handbook of psychotherapy and behavior change* (5th ed.) (pp. 493-539). New York: Wiley.

Elliott, R., Stiles, W. B., & Shapiro, D. A. (1993). Are some psychotherapies more equivalent than others? In T. R. Giles

(Ed.), *Handbook of effective psychotherapy* (pp. 455-479). New York, NY: Plenum Press.

Elliott, R. K., Greenberg, L. S., Watson, J., Timulak, L., & Freire, E. (2013). Research on humanistic-experiential psychotherapies. In M. J. Lambert (Ed.), *Bergin and Garfield's handbook of psychotherapy and behavior change* (6th ed.) (pp. 495-538). New York: Wiley.

Ellis, A. (1959). Requisite conditions for basic personality change. *Journal of Consulting Psychology, 23*(6), 538-540.

Emmelkamp, P. M. G. (1994). Behavior therapy with adults. In A. E. Bergin & S. L. Garfield (Eds.), *Handbook of psychotherapy and behavior change* (4th ed.) (pp. 379-427). Oxford, England: John Wiley.

Engram, B. E., & Vandergoot, D. (1978). Correlation between the Truax and Carkhuff scales for measurement of empathy. *Journal of Counseling Psychology, 25*(4), 349-351.

Fanelli, D., & Ioannidis, J. P. A. (2013). US studies may overestimate effect sizes in softer research. *Proceedings of the National Academy of Sciences, 110*(37), 15031–15036.

Feyerabend, P. K. (1975). *Against method.* London: New Left Books.

Feyerabend, P. K. (1978). From incompetent professionalism to professionalized incompetence—The rise of a new breed of intellectuals. *Philosophy of the Social Sciences, 8*(1), 37-53.

Freire, E. (2012). Introduction to special issue on nondirectivity.

Person-Centered & Experiential Psychotherapies, 11(3), 171-172.

Freud, S. (1926/1978). *The question of lay analysis: Conversations with an impartial person.* W.W. Norton & Company.

Friedlander, M. L., Ellis, M. V., Siegel, S. M., Raymond, L., Haase, R. F., & Highlen, P. S. (1988). Generalizing from segments to sessions: Should it be done? *Journal of Counseling Psychology, 35*(3), 243-250.

Fuertes, J. N., Stracuzzi, T. I., Bennett, J., Scheinholtz, J., Mislowack, A., Hersh, M., & Cheng, D. (2006). Therapist multicultural competency: A study of therapy dyads. *Psychotherapy: Theory, Research, Practice, Training, 43*(4), 480-490.

Garfield, S. L. & Bergin, A. E. (Eds.). (1978). *Handbook of psychotherapy and behavior change: An empirical analysis* (2nd ed.). New York, NY: Wiley.

Garthoff, R. L. (1994). *Detente and confrontation: American-Soviet relations from Nixon to Reagan.* Washington, D.C.: Brookings Institution.

Gelso, C. J. (1979). Research in Counseling: Methodological and Professional Issues. *The Counseling Psychologist, 8*(3), 7-36.

Gelso, C. J., & Carter, J. A. (1985). The Relationship in Counseling and Psychotherapy: Components, Consequences, and Theoretical Antecedents. *The Counseling Psychologist, 13*(2), 155-243.

Gelso, C. J., & Carter, J. A. (1994). Components of the psychotherapy relationship: Their interaction and unfolding during treatment. *Journal of counseling psychology, 41*(3), 296-306.

Gelso, C. J., & Bhatia, A. (2012). Crossing theoretical lines: The role and effect of transference in nonanalytic psychotherapies. *Psychotherapy, 49*(3), 384-390.

Gendlin, E. T. (1962). *Experiencing and the creation of meaning: A philosophical and psychological approach to the subjective.* Glencoe, IL: The Free Press of Glencoe

Gendlin, E. T. (1969). Focusing. *Psychotherapy: Theory, Research & Practice, 6*(1), 4-15.

Gendlin, E. T. (1988). Carl Rogers (1902–1987). *American Psychologist, 43*(2), 127-128.

Gendlin, E. T. (1992). Celebrations and problems of humanistic psychology. *The Humanistic Psychologist, 20*(2-3), 447-460.

Gendlin, E.T. & Tomlinson, T. M. (1967). The process conception and its measurement. In C.R. Rogers, E.T. Gendlin, D.J. Kiesler, & C.B. Truax (Eds.) *The therapeutic relationship and its impact: A study of psychotherapy with schizophrenics* (pp. 109-131). Madison, WI: University of Wisconsin Press.

Gendlin, E.T. & Lietaer, G. (1983). On client-centered and experiential psychotherapy: An interview with Eugene Gendlin. In W.R. Minsel & W. Herff (Eds.), *Research on psychotherapeutic approaches. Proceedings of the 1st European conference on psychotherapy research, Trier, 1981, Vol. 2* (pp. 77-104). Frankfurt

am Main/Bern: Peter Lang. Retrieved from
http://www.focusing.org/gendlin/docs/gol_2102.html

Gendlin, E. T., Jenney, R. H., & Shlien, J. M. (1960). Counselor ratings of process and outcome in client-centered therapy. *Journal of Clinical Psychology, 16*, 210-213.

Goldman, R. N., Greenberg, L. S., & Pos, A. E. (2005). Depth of emotional experience and outcome. *Psychotherapy Research, 15*(3), 248-260.

Goldfried, M. R., Greenberg, L. S., & Marmar, C. (1990). Individual psychotherapy: Process and outcome. *Annual Review of Psychology, 41*(1), 659-688.

Gomes-Schwartz, B., Hadley, S. W., & Strupp, H. H. (1978). Individual psychotherapy and behavior therapy. *Annual Review of Psychology, 29*(1), 435-471.

Gormally, J., & Hill, C. E. (1974). Guidelines for research on Carkhuff's training model. *Journal of Counseling Psychology, 21*(6), 539-547.

Grant, B. (1990). Principled and instrumental nondirectiveness in person-centered and client-centered therapy. *Person-Centered Review, 5*, 77– 88.

Greenberg, L. S., & Rice, L. N. (1981). The specific effects of a Gestalt intervention. *Psychotherapy: Theory, Research & Practice, 18*(1), 31-37.

Greenberg, L. S., & Safran, J. D. (1981). Encoding and cognitive therapy: Changing what clients attend to. *Psychotherapy: Theory, Research & Practice, 18*(2), 163-169.

Greenberg, L. S., Rice, L. N., & Elliott, R. (1993). *Facilitating emotional change: The moment-by-moment process.* New York: Guilford Press.

Greenberg, L. S., & Watson, J. (1998). Experiential therapy of depression: Differential effects of client-centered relationship conditions and process experiential interventions. *Psychotherapy Research, 8*(2), 210-224.

Guilford, J. P. (1954). *Psychometric methods.* NewYork: McGraw-Hill.

Gurman, A. S. (1973a). Effects of therapist and patient mood on the therapeutic functioning of high- and low-facilitative therapists. *Journal of Consulting and Clinical Psychology, 40*(1), 48-58.

Gurman, A. S. (1973b). Instability of therapeutic conditions in psychotherapy. *Journal of Counseling Psychology, 20*(1), 16-24.

Gurman, A. S. (1977). The patient's perception of the therapeutic relationship. In A. S. Gurman & A. M. Razin (Eds.), *Effective psychotherapy: A Handbook of Research* (pp. 503-543). New York, NY: Pergamon Press.

Henry, W. P., Schacht, T. E., & Strupp, H. H. (1990). Patient and therapist introject, interpersonal process, and differential psychotherapy outcome. *Journal of Consulting and Clinical Psychology, 58*(6), 768-774.

Hill, C. E. (2010). Charles Gelso: The "Real" Person. *The Counseling*

Psychologist, 38(4), 567-599.

Hill, C. E. & King, J. (1976). Perceptions of empathy as a function of the measuring instrument. *Journal of Counseling Psychology, 23*(2), 155-157.

Hogg, R. V. & Craig, A. T. (1978). *Introduction to mathematical statistics.* New York: Macmillan Publishing Co.

Holdstock, T.L., & Rogers, C.R. (1983). Person-centered theory. In R.J. Corsini & A.J. Marsella (Eds.), *Personality theories, research, and assessment* (pp. 189–228). Itasca IL: F.E. Peacock.

Hollon, S. D., Stewart, M. O., & Strunk, D. (2006). Enduring effects for cognitive behavior therapy in the treatment of depression and anxiety. *Annual Review of Psychology, 57,* 285-315.

Hollon, S., & Beck, A. T. (1986). Research on cognitive therapy. In S. L. Garfield & A. E. Bergin (Eds.), *Handbook of psychotherapy and behavior change: An empirical analysis* (3rd ed.) (pp. 443-482). New York, NY: Wiley.

Joseph, S. (2006). Person-centred coaching psychology: A meta-theoretical perspective. *International Coaching Psychology Review, 1*(1), 47-54.

Joseph, S., & Linley, P. A. (2006). Growth following adversity: Theoretical perspectives and implications for clinical practice. *Clinical Psychology Review, 26*(8), 1041-1053.

Joseph, S. & Murphy, D. (2013). Person-centered approach, positive psychology, and relational helping: Building bridges. *Journal of*

Humanistic Psychology, *53*(1), 26-51.

Kahn, E. (1999). A critique of nondirectivity in the person-centered approach. *Journal of Humanistic Psychology*, *39*(4), 94-110.

Kahn, E. (2002). A way to help people by holding theory lightly: A response to Bozarth, Merry and Brodley, and Sommerbeck. *Journal of Humanistic Psychology*, *42*(2), 88-96.

Kazdin, A. E. (2011). Evidence-based treatment research: Advances, limitations, and next steps. *American Psychologist*, *66*(8), 685-698.

Kernberg, O. F. (1973). Summary and conclusions of "Psychotherapy and psychoanalysis: Final report of the Menninger Foundation's psychotherapy research project." *International Journal of Psychiatry*, *11*(1), 62-77.

Kiesler, D. J. (1966). Some myths of psychotherapy research and the search for a paradigm. *Psychological Bulletin*, *65*(2), 110-136.

Kiesler, D. J. (1971). Experimental designs in psychotherapy research. In A. E. Bergin & S. L. Garfield (Eds.), *Handbook of psychotherapy and behavior change: An empirical analysis* (1st ed.) (pp. 36-74). New York, NY: John Wiley.

Kiesler, D. J. (1971). Patient experiencing and successful outcome in individual psychotherapy of schizophrenics and psychoneurotics. *Journal of Consulting and Clinical Psychology*, *37*(3), 370-385.

Kiesler, D. J. (1996). From communications to interpersonal theory: A personal odyssey. *Journal of Personality Assessment*, *66*(2), 267-282.

Kiesler, D. J. (1997). *Curriculum vitae*. Retrieved
from http://www.people.vcu.edu/~dkiesler/doncv.html

Kiesler, D. J. (2004). Intrepid pursuit of the essential ingredients of
psychotherapy. *Clinical Psychology: Science and Practice, 11*(4),
391-395.

Kiesler, D. J., Klein, M. H., & Mathieu, P. L. (1965). Sampling from
the recorded therapy interview: The problem of segment
location. *Journal of Consulting Psychology, 29*(4), 337.

Kirschenbaum, H. (1979). *On becoming Carl Rogers*. New York, NY:
Delacorte Press.

Kirschenbaum, H. (2004). Carl Rogers's life and work: An assessment
on the 100th anniversary of his birth. *Journal of Counseling &
Development, 82*(1), 116-124.

Kliem, S., Kröger, C., & Kosfelder, J. (2010). Dialectical behavior
therapy for borderline personality disorder: A meta-analysis
using mixed-effects modeling. *Journal of Consulting and Clinical
Psychology, 78*(6), 936-951.

Kopta, S. M., Lueger, R. J., Saunders, S. M., & Howard, K. I. (1999).
Individual psychotherapy outcome and process research:
Challenges leading to greater turmoil or a positive transition?
Annual Review of Psychology, 50(1), 441-469.

Kuhn, T. S. (1962). *The structure of scientific revolutions*. University of
Chicago press.

Kurtz, R. R., & Grummon, D. L. (1972). Different approaches to the measurement of therapist empathy and their relationship to therapy outcomes. *Journal of Consulting and Clinical Psychology, 39*(1), 106-115.

Kutner, M. H., Nachtsheim, C. J., Neter, J., & Li, W. (2005). *Applied linear statistical models*. New York: McGraw-Hill.

Lambert, M. J. (Ed.) (2004). *Bergin and Garfield's handbook of psychotherapy and behavior change* (5th ed.). New York: Wiley.

Lambert, M. J. (Ed.) (2013). *Bergin and Garfield's handbook of psychotherapy and behavior change* (6th ed.). New York: Wiley.

Lambert, M. J., Bergin, A. E., & Collins, J. L. (1977). Therapist-induced deterioration in psychotherapy. In A. S. Gurman & A. M. Razin (Eds.), *Effective psychotherapy: A Handbook of Research* (pp. 452-481). New York, NY: Pergamon Press.

Lambert, M. J., DeJulio, S. S., & Stein, D. M. (1978). Therapist interpersonal skills: Process, outcome, methodological considerations, and recommendations for future research. *Psychological bulletin, 85*(3), 467.

Lambert, M. J., Garfield, S. L., & Bergin, A. E. (2004). Overview, trends, and future issues. In M. J. Lambert (Ed.), *Bergin and Garfield's handbook of psychotherapy and behavior change* (5th ed.) (pp. 805-821). New York: Wiley.

Levant, R. F. & Shlien, J. M. (Eds.). (1984). *Client-centered therapy and the person-centered approach: New directions in theory, research, and practice*. New York: Praeger.

Linehan, M. M. (1993). *Cognitive-behavioral treatment of borderline personality disorder*. New York, NY: Guilford Press.

Luborsky, L., Singer, B., & Luborsky, L. (1975). Comparative studies of psychotherapies: Is it true that "everyone has won and all must have prizes"?. *Archives of General Psychiatry, 32*(8), 995-1008.

Luborsky, L., & Spence, D. P. (1978). Quantitative research on psychoanalytic therapy. In S. L. Garfield & A. E. Bergin (Eds.), *Handbook of psychotherapy and behavior change: An empirical analysis* (2nd ed.) (pp. 331-368). New York, NY: Wiley.

Lynch, T. R., Trost, W. T., Salsman, N., & Linehan, M. M. (2007). Dialectical behavior therapy for borderline personality disorder. *Annual Review of Clinical Psychology, 3*, 181-205.

Marks, I. M. (1978). Behavioural psychotherapy of adult neurosis. In S. L. Garfield & A. E. Bergin (Eds.), *Handbook of psychotherapy and behavior change: An empirical analysis* (2nd ed.) (pp. 493-589). New York, NY: Wiley.

Maxwell, A. E. (1968). The effect of correlated errors on estimates of reliability coefficients. *Educational and Psychological Measurement, 28*, 803-811.

McLeod, B. D. (2009). Understanding why therapy allegiance is linked to clinical outcomes. *Clinical Psychology: Science and Practice, 16*(1), 69-72.

Merry, T. & Brodley, B. T. (2002). The nondirective attitude in client-centered therapy: A response to Kahn. *Journal of*

Humanistic Psychology, 42(2), 66-77.

Mintz, J., & Luborsky, L. (1971). Segments versus whole sessions: Which is the better unit for psychotherapy process research? *Journal of Abnormal Psychology, 78*(2), 180-191.

Mintz, J., Luborsky, L., & Auerbach, A. H. (1971). Dimensions of psychotherapy: A factor analytic study of ratings of psychotherapy sessions. *Journal of Consulting and Clinical Psychology, 36*(1), 106-120.

Mitchell, K., Bozarth, J., & Krauft, C. (1977). Reappraisal of the therapeutic effectiveness of accurate empathy, nonpossessive warmth, and genuineness. In A. S. Gurman & A. M. Razin (Eds.), *Effective psychotherapy: A handbook of research* (pp. 482-502). Oxford, England: Pergamon Press.

Nowicki, S. (2008). Obituary: Donald J. Kiesler (1933-2007). *American Psychologist, 63*(4), 272a.

Orwell, G. (1946/1996). *Animal farm.* New York: New American Library.

Parloff, M. B., Waskow, I. E., & Wolfe, B. F. (1978). Research on therapist variables in relation to process and outcome. In S. L. Garfield & A. E. Bergin (Eds.), *Handbook of psychotherapy and behavior change: An empirical analysis* (2nd ed.) (pp. 233-282). New York, NY: Wiley.

Parloff, M. B., London, P., & Wolfe, B. (1986). Individual psychotherapy and behavior change. *Annual review of psychology,*

37(1), 321-349.

Patterson, C. H. (1966). Counseling. *Annual Review of Psychology*, *17*(1), 79-110.

Patterson, C. H. (1984). Empathy, warmth, and genuineness in psychotherapy: A review of reviews. *Psychotherapy: Theory, Research, Practice, Training, 21*(4), 431-438.

Patterson, C. H. (2000). *Understanding Psychotherapy. Fifty Years of Client-Centered Theory and Practice*. Llangarron, Ross-on-Wye, UK: PCCS Books.

Paul, G. L. (1967). Strategy of outcome research in psychotherapy. *Journal of Consulting Psychology, 31*(2), 109-118.

Phillips, J. S., & Bierman, K. L. (1981). Clinical psychology: Individual methods. *Annual review of psychology, 32*(1), 405-438.

Quinn, A. (2008). A person-centered approach to the treatment of combat veterans with posttraumatic stress disorder. *Journal of Humanistic Psychology, 48*(4), 458-476.

Quinn, A. (2011). A person-centered approach to the treatment of borderline personality disorder. *Journal of Humanistic Psychology, 51*(4), 465-491.

Quinn, A. (2013). A person-centered approach to multicultural counseling competence. *Journal of Humanistic Psychology, 53*(2), 202-251.

Rappaport, J. & Chinsky, J. M. (1972). Accurate empathy: Confusion of a construct. *Psychological Bulletin, 77*(6), 400-404.

Redfering, D. L. (1975). Differential effects of group counseling with Black and White female delinquents: One year later. *Journal of Negro Education, 44*(4), 530-537.

Rennie, D. L. (2007). Reflexivity and its radical form: Implications for the practice of humanistic psychotherapies. *Journal of Contemporary Psychotherapy, 37*(1), 53-58.

Rice, L. N. (1965). Therapist's style of participation and case outcome. *Journal of Consulting Psychology, 29*(2), 155-160.

Rice, L. (1974). The evocative function of the therapist. In D. Wexler & L. Rice (Eds.), *Innovations in client-centered therapy* (pp. 289–311). New York: John Wiley.

Rogers, C. R. (1942). *Counseling and psychotherapy: Newer concepts in practice*. Boston: Houghton Mifflin.

Rogers, C. R. (1951). *Client-centered therapy: Its current practice, implications and theory*. Boston: Houghton Mifflin.

Rogers, C. R. (1957). The necessary and sufficient conditions of therapeutic personality change. *Journal of Consulting Psychology, 21*(2), 95-103.

Rogers, C. R. (1958). A process conception of psychotherapy. *American Psychologist, 13*(4), 142-149.

Rogers, C. R. (1959a). A tentative scale for the measurement of process in psychotherapy. In E. A. Rubinstein & M. B. Parloff (Eds.), *Research in psychotherapy* (pp. 96-107). American Psychological Association.

Rogers, C. R. (1959b). A theory of therapy, personality, and interpersonal relationships, as developed in the client-centered framework. In S. Koch (Ed.), *Psychology: A Study of a Science: Vol. 3* (pp. 184-256). New York, NY: McGraw-Hill.

Rogers, C. R. (1961). On becoming a person. Boston: Houghton Mifflin.

Rogers, C. R. (1974). In retrospect: Forty-six years. *American Psychologist, 29*(2), 115-123.

Rogers, C. R. (1975). Empathic: An unappreciated way of being. *Counseling Psychologist, 5*(2), 2-10.

Rogers, C.R. (1980). *A Way of Being*. Boston: Houghton Mifflin.

Rogers, C. R. (1989). *The Carl Rogers Reader*. NewYork, NY Houghton Mifflin.

Rogers, C. R. & Dymond, R. F. (Eds.). (1954). *Psychotherapy and personality change*. Chicago, IL: University of Chicago Press.

Rogers, C. R., & Russell, D. E. (2002). *Carl Rogers: The quiet revolutionary: An oral history*. Roseville, CA: Penmarin Books.

Rogers, C. R., Gendlin, E. T., Kiesler, D. J., & Truax, C. B. (Eds.) (1967). *The therapeutic relationship and its impact: A study of psychotherapy with schizophrenics*. Madison, WI: University of Wisconsin Press.

Rogers, C., Marquis, D. G., & Hilgard, E. R. (1950). ABEPP policies and procedures. *American Psychologist, 5*(8), 407-408.

Schneider, K. J. (1999). The revival of the romantic means a revival of psychology. *Journal of Humanistic Psychology, 39*(3), 13-29.

Shadish, W. R., & Sweeney, R. B. (1991). Mediators and moderators in meta-analysis: There's a reason we don't let dodo birds tell us which psychotherapies should have prizes. *Journal of Consulting and Clinical Psychology, 59*(6), 883-893.

Shlien, J. M. (1966). Cross-theoretical criteria for the evaluation of psychotherapy. *American Journal of Psychotherapy, 20*(1), 125-134.

Shlien, J. M. (1984). A counter-theory of transference. In R. F. Levant, & J. M. Shlien (Eds), *Client-centered therapy and the person-centered approach: New directions in theory, research, and practice* (pp. 153-181). New York: Praeger.

Shlien, J. M. (1992). Theory as autobiography: The man and the movement. [Review of the book *The Carl Rogers Reader*, by Howard Kirschenbaum and Valerie Henderson (Eds.)] *PsycCRITIQUES, 37*(10), 1082-1084. doi:10.1037/031513

Shlien, J. (1997). Empathy in psychotherapy: A vital mechanism? Yes. Therapist's conceit? All too often. In A. C. Bohart & L. S. Greenberg (Eds.), *Empathy reconsidered: New directions in psychotherapy* (pp. 63– 80). Washington, DC: American Psychological Association.

Shlien, J. M. (2003). *To lead an honorable life: Invitations to think about client-centered therapy and the person-centered approach: A collection of the work of John M. Shlien.* P. Sanders (Ed.). Ross-onWye: PCCS Books.

Sloane, R. B., Staples, F. R., Cristol, A. H., Yorkston, N. J., & Whipple, K. (1975). Psychotherapy versus behavior therapy. Cambridge, MA: Harvard University Press.

Sommerbeck, L. (2002). Person-centered or eclectic? A response to Kahn. *Journal of Humanistic Psychology, 42*(2), 84-87.

Sommerbeck, L. (2012). Being nondirective in directive settings. *Person-Centered & Experiential Psychotherapies, 11*(3), 173-189.

Stiles, W. B. (2009). Responsiveness as an obstacle for psychotherapy outcome research: It's worse than you think. *Clinical Psychology: Science and Practice, 16*(1), 86-91.

Strupp, H. H. (1955). An objective comparison of Rogerian and psychoanalytic techniques. *Journal of Consulting Psychology, 19*(1), 1-7.

Strupp, H. H. (1956). Comments on Rogers' "Persons or science". *American Psychologist, 11*(3), 153-154.

Strupp, H. H., & Bergin, A. E. (1969). Some empirical and conceptual bases for coordinated research in psychotherapy: a critical review of issues, trends, and evidence. *International Journal of Psychiatry, 7*(2), 18-90.

Strupp, H. H. (1977). A reformulation of the dynamics of the therapist's contribution. In A. S. Gurman & A. M. Razin (Eds.), *Effective psychotherapy: A handbook of Research* (pp. 1-22). Oxford, England: Pergamon Press.

Strupp, H. H. (1978a). Psychotherapy research and practice: An overview. In S. L. Garfield & A. E. Bergin (Eds.), *Handbook of psychotherapy and behavior change: An empirical analysis* (2nd ed.) (pp. 3-22). New York, NY: Wiley.

Strupp, H. H. (1978b). The therapist's theoretical orientation: An overrated variable. *Psychotherapy: Theory, Research & Practice,* *15*(4), 314.

Szapocznik, J. & Prado, G. (2007). Negative effects on family functioning from psychosocial treatments: A recommendation for expanded safety monitoring. *Journal of Family Psychology,* *21*(3), 468-478.

Szapocznik, J., Feaster, D. J., Mitrani, V. B., Prado, G., Smith, L., Robinson-Batista, C., …Robbins, M. S. (2004). Structural ecosystems therapy for HIV-seropositive African American women: Effects on psychological distress, family hassles, and family support. *Journal of Consulting and Clinical Psychology,* *72*(2), 288-303.

Tinsley, H. E. & Weiss, D. J. (1975). Interrater reliability and agreement of subjective judgments. *Journal of Counseling Psychology, 22*(4), 358-376.

Tinsley, H. E. & Weiss, D. J. (2000). Interrater reliability and agreement. In H. E. Tinsley & S. D. Brown (Eds.), *Handbook of applied multivariate statistics and mathematical modeling* (pp. 95-124). San Diego, CA: Academic Press.

Truax, C.B. (1960). The process of group psychotherapy:

Relationships between hypothesized therapeutic conditions and intrapersonal exploration (Unpublished doctoral dissertation). University of Wisconsin, Madison, WI.

Truax, C. B. (1963). Effective ingredients in psychotherapy: An approach to unraveling the patient-therapist interaction. *Journal of Counseling Psychology, 10*(3), 256-263..

Truax, C. B. (1966). Therapist empathy, warmth, and genuineness and patient personality change in group psychotherapy: A comparison between interaction unit measures, time sample measures, patient perception measures. *Journal of Clinical Psychology, 22*(2), 225-229.

Truax, C. B. (1967a). A scale for the rating of accurate empathy. In C.R. Rogers, E.T. Gendlin, D.J. Kiesler, & C.B. Truax (Eds.) *The therapeutic relationship and its impact: A study of psychotherapy with schizophrenics* (pp. 555-568). Madison, WI: University of Wisconsin Press.

Truax, C. B. (1967b). Research findings: translations and premature translations into practice. *International journal of psychiatry, 3*(3), 158.

Truax, C. B. (1971). Perceived therapeutic conditions and client outcome. *Comparative Group Studies, 2*(3), 301-310.

Truax, C. B. (1972). The meaning and reliability of accurate empathy ratings: A rejoinder. *Psychological Bulletin, 77*(6), 397-399.

Truax, C. B., & Carkhuff, R. R. (1965). Experimental manipulation of therapeutic conditions. *Journal of Consulting Psychology, 29*(2), 119-124.

Truax, C. B., & Carkhuff, R. R. (1967). *Toward effective counseling and psychotherapy: Training and practice.* Chicago, IL: Aldine.

Truax, C. B., & Mitchell, K. M. (1971). Research on certain therapist interpersonal skills in relation to process and outcome. In A. E. Bergin & S. L. Garfield (Eds.), *Handbook of psychotherapy and behavior change: An empirical analysis* (1st ed.) (pp. 299-344). New York, NY: John Wiley.

Truax, C. B., Wargo, D. G., Frank, J. D., Imber, S. D., Battle, C. C., Hoehn-Saric, R., ... & Stone, A. R. (1966). Therapist empathy, genuineness, and warmth and patient therapeutic outcome. *Journal of Consulting Psychology, 30*(5), 395-401.

van der Veen, F. (1965). Effects of the therapist and the patient on each other's therapeutic behavior. *Journal of Consulting Psychology, 29*(1), 19-26.

Wampold, B. E., Mondin, G. W., Moody, M., Stich, F., Benson, K., & Ahn, H. N. (1997). A meta-analysis of outcome studies comparing bona fide psychotherapies: Empiricially, "All Must Have Prizes". *Psychological bulletin, 122*(3), 203-215.

Wampold, B. E., Imel, Z. E., Laska, K. M., Benish, S., Miller, S. D., Flückiger, C., ... & Budge, S. (2010). Determining what works in the treatment of PTSD. *Clinical Psychology Review, 30*(8), 923-933.

Warner, M. (2000). Person-centered psychotherapy: One nation, many tribes. *The Person-Centered Journal, 7*(1), 28-39.

Watson, J. C., & Wiseman, H. (2010). Laura Rice: Natural observer of psychotherapy process. In L. G. Castonguay, J. C. Muran, L. Angus, J. A. Hayes, N. Ladany, & T. Anderson (Eds.), *Bringing psychotherapy research to life: Understanding change through the work of leading clinical researchers* (pp. 175-183). Washington, DC, US: American Psychological Association.

Watson, J. C., Goldman, R. N., & Greenberg, L. S. (2011). Contrasting two clients in Emotion-Focused Therapy for Depression 1: The case of "Tom, 'Trapped in the Tunnel'". *Pragmatic Case Studies in Psychotherapy, 7*(2), 268-304.

Webb, C. A., DeRubeis, R. J., & Barber, J. P. (2010). Therapist adherence/competence and treatment outcome: A meta-analytic review. *Journal of Consulting and Clinical Psychology, 78*(2), 200-211.

Wenegrat, A. (1974). A factor analytic study of the Truax Accurate Empathy Scale. *Psychotherapy: Theory, Research & Practice, 11*(1), 48-51.

Wexler, D. & Rice, L. (Eds.). (1974). *Innovations in client-centered therapy*. New York: John Wiley.

Wiser, S. & Goldfried, M. R. (1998). Therapist interventions and client emotional experiencing in expert psychodynamic–interpersonal and cognitive–behavioral therapies. *Journal of Consulting and*

Clinical Psychology, 66(4), 634-640.

Witty, M. C. (2004). The difference directiveness makes: The ethics and consequences of guidance in psychotherapy. *The Person-Centered Journal*, *11*, 22–32.

2

A PERSON-CENTERED APPROACH TO MULTICULTURAL COUNSELING COMPETENCE [1]

During the final decades of the 20th century, the multicultural (MC) counseling competence movement emerged as a primary topic of concern in the helping professions, acquiring the status of a "fourth force" in

---

[1] The final, definitive version of this paper has been published in the *Journal of Humanistic Psychology*, 53/2, April/2013 by SAGE Publications Ltd, All rights reserved.

counseling and psychology (P. B. Pedersen, 1991). In particular, Derald Sue and colleagues' work (e.g., D. W. Sue, Arredondo, & McDavis, 1992; D. W. Sue et al., 1982; S. Sue, 1977; S. Sue & Zane, 1987) toward developing a cross-cultural counseling competencies framework had a substantial impact on theory, research, and policy at the turn of the century. As a result, a wealth of contributions toward the training and practice of the culturally competent counselor have proliferated the field, possibly comparable to the effect that Rogers (1957) and Bordin (1979) had on research and practice in the helping professions.

During the same time period, the stewards of counseling and psychotherapy research evidence (e.g., the American Psychiatric/Psychological Associations) put forth rigorous practice guidelines and validation criteria against which psychotherapy efficacy could be measured (e.g., Chambless et al., 1998). However, the U.S. Department of Health and Human Services (HHS) Surgeon General's report (HHS, 2001) later issued a stark analysis of the research studies cited by these mental health organizations. The report concluded that definitive MC research evidence demonstrating psychotherapy's relevance for minority populations was nonexistent. Since then, however, MC counseling research has emerged suggesting that culturally adapted psychotherapy may be effective compared to both unadapted forms and to no treatment. Therefore, the first section of this article will review Sue and colleagues' MC competencies, as well as historic and modern MC research trends in general.

During the formative years of Carl Rogers's person-centered therapy (PCT; ca. 1954-1974), evidence that PCT was an effective treatment for racial/ethnic minority clients was absent from the empirical literature. However, in the early 1970s a modest body of research emerged from this tradition, answering certain clinically meaningful questions regarding the effects of psychotherapy with minority clients in community settings. For reasons presented in this article, neither MC nor general PCT research would proceed further. Instead, the Rogerian research tradition receded into the annals of psychotherapy history in the United States. Remarkably, since the 1990s PCT has reemerged demonstrating equivalence to other psychotherapies across a range of Axis I and, potentially, Axis II disorders (e.g., Elliott, Greenberg, & Lietaer, 2004; Quinn, 2011).

Moreover, recent MC research studies in both the United States and countries worldwide suggest that PCT is an effective and acceptable treatment for clients from collectivist-oriented cultures-of-origin. Therefore, the latter half of this article provides (a) a brief historical review of the factors contributing to the delay of a person-centered MC research tradition; (b) evidence of this reemergence, despite considerable researcher allegiance bias, marking PCT's return to the status of an effective treatment approach across client populations; and (c) cultural adaptations to previously hypothesized PCT mechanisms of change, thus providing a competent and effective treatment system for racial/ethnic minority clients and families.

As of 2010, according to the Office of Minority Health (HHS, 2012b), African Americans composed approximately 14% of the U.S. population; Latinos(as), 16%; Asian Americans, 6% (including Pacific Islanders); Native Americans, 2%; and White Americans of European descent, 62% of the population (U.S. Census Bureau, 2011). Moreover, the Office of Minority Health (HHS, 2012a) also estimated that 7% of African Americans in the United States received mental health treatment in 2006: 7% of Latinos(as); 6% of Asian Americans; and 11% of Native Americans—compared to nearly 15% of the White population. In addition, during the same period, these four minority groups had a higher incidence of psychological distress and suicide than their White counterparts, and as expected, income level appeared to be a substantial protective factor. Specifically, distress decreased as an average minority person's income rose above two times the poverty level, which was approximately $10,500 for an individual and $21,000 for a household of four (HHS, 2012a; U.S. Census Bureau, 2010).

In comparison to their clients, when mental health counselor demographic data are examined (Manderscheid & Berry, 2006), of 361,525 therapists surveyed, an estimated 87% of clinically trained psychiatrists, psychologists, social workers, mental health counselors, and marriage and family therapists in the United States report being White; 3% report being African American; 3% Latino(a); 2% Asian American; 0.5% Native American; and approximately 5% did not specify.

Intuition suggests that knowledge of historical trends make possible a better approximation of the emerging future. In this respect, the unique potential of a MC person-centered approach in the 21st century will not likely be understood without locating in history the context in which this quiet, humanistic revolution emerged, receded, and is now entering a period of resurgence as suggested by Kirk Schneider's (2011a) recent forecast of psychology's imminent return to its existential/humanistic roots. Furthermore, evidence of this resurgence can be found in the work of humanistic psychologists Rubin (2011), Bargdill (2011), Hoffman (2009), Robbins (Olfman & Robbins, 2012), and others (see Hoffman, 2011; Schneider, 2011b). These leaders are in the process of forging the way toward the next great period in the helping professions - reminding a new generation of professionals that their full potential resides in their way of being as helping practitioners.

Consequently, this article attempts to provide both a window to the past and a vista of one possible future by contributing relevant clinical information for the case worker, counselor, and therapist working in the field. Whether the helping professional provides office and outreach therapy at a MC community mental health agency, works in a culturally diverse hospital setting, or is a private practice therapist who sees minority clients across a range of income levels, a specific, therapeutic way of being is suggested to bridge these different situations. In all, the effectiveness of a culturally adapted person-centered approach is dependent on the therapist and his or her willingness to be a person, flawed yet genuine, in the presence of the client.

The Multicultural Counseling Competencies

Multicultural counseling competence, in a broad sense, suggests a type of therapist skillfulness when helping a person, family, group, or community that struggles as a result of discriminatory and oppressive practices of the dominant group of a given culture. To clarify, culture has been defined as "the belief systems and value orientations that influence customs, norms, practices, and social institutions, including psychological processes and organizations" (American Psychological Association [APA], 2002, p. 8) and referred to as "the totality of ways being passed on from generation to generation" (National Association of Social Workers, 2007, p. 10). Specifically in the United States, along a cultural/political spectrum, a person possessing, for example, membership in all the domains of the dominant group is thought to be of White, European American descent, middle-class, male, heterosexual, Christian, young, able-bodied (mentally, physically, and emotionally), and English-speaking (Robinson, 1999). And as a result, by virtue of this dominant group membership, an individual, family, or group inherently has a higher probability, as it were, of experiencing life, liberty, and the potential pursuit of happiness across the lifespan.

According to the updated MC counseling model developed by D. W. Sue et al. (1992), a therapist's MC competence is dependent on the degree to which he or she can learn, develop, and demonstrate specific MC competencies. These MC competencies are thought to extend beyond a therapist's general counseling competence (i.e., counseling microskills; see Ridley, Mollen,& Kelly, 2011) when contributing to client outcome (Constantine, 2002). In addition, the MC competence model suggests certain competencies that extend beyond "micro-level" work, focusing on advocacy and change practices at the organizational and institutional levels (National Association of Social Workers, 2007; D. W. Sue et al., 1992). Therefore, the MC competence model centers on a therapist's ability to recognize his or her membership in one or more dominant cultural groups and to acknowledge the subsequent effects of this membership on the intra- and extratherapy relationship with a MC client, family, or community. In other words,

> a major obstacle in getting our profession to understand the negative implications of monoculturalism is that White culture is such a dominant norm that it acts as an invisible veil that prevents people from seeing counseling as a potentially biased system . . . what is needed is for counselors to become culturally aware, to act on the basis of a critical analysis and understanding on their own conditioning, the conditioning of their clients, and the sociopolitical system of which they are both a part. (D. W. Sue et al., 1992, p. 480).

Therapist knowledge, awareness, and skills

In brief, the MC counseling competencies, as put forth by D. W.

Sue et al. (1992), include three characteristics that apply to the development of the competent therapist. The therapist must develop (a) an understanding or knowledge of the client's experience as a culturally different person, (b) an awareness of his or her own assumptions about culturally diverse people, and (c) culturally appropriate therapeutic interventions and skills.

Knowledge of the client's worldview. As the therapist develops an understanding of the client's worldview, potentially rigid beliefs and attitudes toward the client's culture are unearthed. The therapist facilitates this exploration by obtaining knowledge about the client's cultural group, including the culture-specific attitudes toward mental health issues, help-seeking behavior, and appropriateness of counseling approaches. The therapist supplements this knowledge through experiential immersion in culturally different settings so that his or her "perspective of minorities is more than an academic or helping exercise" (D. W. Sue et al., 1992, p. 482).

Awareness of own assumptions. As the therapist develops cultural knowledge he or she becomes more aware of the relativity of cultural assumptions. The therapist's attitudes about his or her own culture, as well as beliefs about other cultures, move from a state of rigidity toward a more dynamic viewpoint. In tandem, the therapist develops a deeper, more accurate understanding and subsequent ownership of ways in which dominant group membership has benefited and affected him or her personally. The therapist also becomes aware of the effects that these socially constructed power differentials have on the relationship with culturally different clients - at times communicated through interpersonal style, office décor, therapy orientation, and so on. Moreover, the therapist realizes his or her own limitations and seeks out further training and education to develop culturally competent clinical skills and to understand him or herself as a racial and cultural being.

Culturally-adapted interventions. The therapist's attitudes toward helping and healing practices are extended beyond a mainstream, Westernized counseling approach. He or she moves toward respect and understanding of religious/spiritual values relating to mental and physical functioning, as well as indigenous, culturally specific healing practices, including the importance of family and community resources. As the therapist delves further into culturally different perspectives, he or she acknowledges the cultural bias affecting mainstream therapy practice, including monocultural diagnostic assessment procedures that may perpetuate barriers to mental health services.

A race/ethnicity focus

D. W. Sue et al. (1992) address an ongoing difficulty with which MC theorists struggle: the rank order of oppressions. Although D. W. Sue et al. (1992) suggest the above MC counseling competencies could likely be relevant to counseling other oppressed groups (e.g., GLBTQ [gay/lesbian/bi/transsexual/queer] groups, physically disabled people, etc.), they state that these competencies, as they are hypothesized, focus on the four "visible racial ethnic minority groups" in society: African Americans, Latinos(as), Asian Americans, and Native Americans. Moreover, Arredondo et al. (1996) include a Caucasian/European group in their operational definition of the MC competencies.

Similarly, a number of social justice and critical race theorists caution against creating an "equality of oppressions" paradigm that may dilute the legacy and ongoing effects of racial oppression persistent in racial/ethnic minorities' lives (Abrams & Moio, 2009). That is, to suggest equivalency may perpetuate a color-blind mentality that threatens to perpetuate the idea of a "universal human experience" and, as a result, would enable the continuation of oppression in the helping professions in particular. In contrast, however, some have argued that to deny a universal helping system creates a stereotype-based counseling system (Patterson, 2004) in which the counselor acts less like a genuine helper and more like a "chameleon . . . to meet the presumed characteristics of clients from varying cultures" (Patterson, 1996, p. 230). As a result, therapists may rely on theory and techniques that are generally unproven (Weinrach & Thomas, 2002). In response, others have stated that to disregard the MC competencies is equivalent to an unethical psychotherapy practice (Arredondo & Toporek, 2004).

Moving forward, Arredondo et al. (1996) observe that "an assumption is often made, although not verbalized, that MC counseling is for poor persons of color who use public services. Not only is this erroneous but it does lump all persons of color into one economic class" (p. 7). However, Bonilla-Silva and Ray (2009) balance this view

> as the research traditions of laissez-faire racism . . . symbolic racism. . . and . . . colorblind racism shows, whites have learned how to talk the talk, without walking that walk. Ignoring all evidence of the profoundly racialized system affecting most areas of social life and the fact that most blacks are still at the bottom of the well, whites have pointed to several token black figures as evidence that the long arc of white racism is indeed tilting towards justice. (p. 177)

Historical Multicultural Counseling Research Traditions

The evolution of a culturally sensitive approach to working with clients of diverse backgrounds has at minimum a 60-year history (Heine, 1950); though the late 1960s and early 1970s marked a significant movement forward in theory and initial research (Lorion, 1978), with person-centered researchers visible at the forefront (e.g., G. Banks, Berenson, & Carkhuff, 1967; Carkhuff & Banks, 1970; Lerner, 1972). However, with the Rogerian research tradition in the beginning stages of decline (at the time, arguably the oldest evidence-based research tradition in the profession), an empirical vacuum emerged into which experimental MC therapy research would not enter for two decades.

On building a multicultural research foundation

The year 1954 marked the beginning of the Rogerian research tradition, with the publication of Rogers and Dymond's (1954) experimental volume, *Psychotherapy and Personality Change.* Subsequently, during the next 20 years psychotherapy research became increasingly concerned with studies not only relating PCT but also the facilitative conditions (Rogers, 1957) of empathy, warmth, and genuineness, to outcome (e.g., Beutler, Johnson, Neville, Workman, & Elkins, 1973; Garfield & Bergin, 1971; Halkides, 1958; Truax, 1963; Truax & Carkhuff, 1967) - continuing in part the research tradition begun by Rogers and colleagues at the University of Chicago (see D. S. Cartwright, 1957). Moreover, approximately 20 years after the Rogers and Dymond volume, experimental research measuring therapeutic change with culturally diverse populations emerged from the Rogerian tradition (e.g., Lerner, 1972; Redfering, 1975). However, the apparent ascent of this PCT multicultural research paradigm - which appeared to be building on inquiries begun by Rogers and colleagues in Chicago and Wisconsin - would be short-lived. That is, the research methodologies generally employed in the numerous studies demonstrating the effectiveness of the facilitative conditions had come under sharp criticism (e.g., Chinsky & Rappaport, 1970), and by the mid-1970s, the Rogerian research tradition had receded from the literature.

During the same period, psychoanalytic and behavior therapy research was in its infancy (Luborsky & Spence, 1978; Marks, 1978), with virtually no empirical evidence contributed by the analytic tradition, and mostly applied learning studies contributed by the behaviorists (Bergin, 1966; Bergin & Strupp, 1970). Sloane, Staples, Cristol, Yorkston, and Whipple's (1975) book *Psychotherapy versus Behavior Therapy* represents one of the first controlled, well-designed psychotherapy outcome studies using actual clients to be completed outside the influence of the Rogerian research tradition: the authors found the effects of behavior therapy versus psychoanalytic psychotherapy to be comparable. Going forward 2 years, Beck's cognitive therapy entered the evidence-based domain with an initial study comparing cognitive therapy with an antidepressant (Rush, Beck, Kovacs, & Hollon, 1977). By the early 1980s, a research tradition, combining the randomized clinical trial design with advanced statistical procedures using computer software, held the promise of a coming age in which social science research would no longer be subjected to bias from the effects of unique, nonspecific personal qualities inherently introduced by the client and the therapist (Krause & Lutz, 2009; Stiles, 2009) - qualities that had previously "invalidated" Rogerian research findings (Bergin & Suinn, 1975).

By the early 1990s, interest in culturally diverse psychotherapy outcome research was again reaching prominence in therapy journals and handbooks (D'Andrea & Heckman, 2008). Accordingly, if the growth of the Rogerian research tradition were used as a timeline, hypothetically one could predict that the newer psychoanalytic and behavior therapy research traditions would begin publishing experimental MC research following a similar 20-year foundation-building time period. Therefore, using Sloan, Staples, Cristol, Yorkston, and Whipple's (1975) book as the initial marker, a post-Rogerian MC research tradition could be predicted to begin in 1995. Remarkably, a review of the literature supports this hypothesis.

In Bergin and Garfield's 1994 edition of Psychotherapy and Behavior Change, Stanley Sue and colleagues' chapter on the state of psychotherapy research with culturally diverse populations concluded that "there are virtually no studies comparing the outcomes of treated and untreated groups of ethnic minority clients" (S. Sue, Zane, & Young, 1994, p. 785); that is, no studies using actual clients in which the findings can be generalized to larger populations. However, in 1995, Muñoz et al. (1995) reported findings from a major randomized, controlled comparison study examining the effects of a culturally adapted, cognitive-behavioral depression prevention treatment with low-income, racial/ethnic minority clients (notably, Miranda et al.'s [2005] comprehensive literature review corroborates a general date of 1995 as marking the inception of modern experimental MC research as well).

Modern Multicultural Research

By the beginning of the 21st century, all forms of psychotherapy and psychosocial interventions had come under attack for assuming equal therapeutic effectiveness across racial/ethnic groups despite a lack of appropriate research evidence (Miranda et al., 2005). The 2001 Surgeon General's report (HHS, 2001) demonstrated this bleak situation in the mental health field. Miranda et al. (2005) further reviewed the data and found that of 9,266 participants in mental health care efficacy studies, only 561 (6%) African American, 99 (1%) Latino, 11 (0.1%) Asian American/Pacific Islanders, and zero Native Americans were included, severely limiting the clinical significance of any conclusive findings. Specifically, the research that was examined in the report of the Surgeon General (HHS, 2001) were those studies cited in the American Psychiatric Association's "Practice Guidelines" for bipolar disorder, major depression, and schizophrenia, and in the Agency for Healthcare Research and Quality's "Evidence Report/Technology Assessment" for attention-deficit/hyperactivity disorder in children. Also included in the report's analysis was the APA's "empirically-validated therapies" research evidence. After reviewing the literature cited by these three organizations, the Surgeon General's report concluded that "specific information about the efficacy of these interventions for racial and ethnic minority populations is unavailable" (HHS, 2001, p. 172).

Notably, following a decade of negative reactions (see Freire, 2006), the APA (2006) broadened the definition of an empirically validated treatment. At the request of 2005 APA president, and person-centered veteran, Ronald Levant (Levant, 1978), a new task force was formed to reevaluate the APA's treatment efficacy standards. As a result, the APA (2006) developed a new evaluative framework called "evidence-based practice in psychology," validating the importance of clinical observation and naturalistic and qualitative research designs in psychotherapy research.

Modern culturally adapted psychotherapy research

Since Muñoz et al.'s (1995) early study and the Surgeon General's report (HHS, 2001), reviews by Miranda et al. (2005) and Cardemil, Moreno, and Sanchez (2011) of racial/ethnic minority psychosocial intervention research report that culturally-adapted mainstream treatments can improve outcome. In particular, two therapy orientations have shown success with predominantly Latino(a) and African American clients and to a lesser extent Asian Americans: (a) culturally adapted cognitive behavior therapy (e.g., Hinton, Hofmann, Rivera, Otto, & Pollack, 2011; Miranda, Chung, et al., 2003; Muñoz et al.,1995; Tandon, Perry, Mendelson, Kemp, & Leis, 2011; Wells et al., 2004) and (b) culturally adapted interpersonal psychotherapy (e.g., Grote et al.,2009; Krupnick et al., 2008). In contrast, both approaches, and variants of them, have reported less favorable outcomes as well (culturally adapted cognitive behavior therapy: Foster, 2007; Le, Perry, & Stuart, 2011; culturally adapted interpersonal psychotherapy: Crockett, Zlotnick, Davis, Payne, & Washington, 2008). Moreover, unadapted motivational interviewing (Miller & Rose, 2009) has shown favorable results with Native American clients.

On closer inspection of these studies, though, treatment effects tend to diminish as the research migrates from the highly controlled efficacy settings to the naturalistic community settings that treat the "hardest-to-serve" clients who face multiple treatment barriers (e.g., Miranda, Chung, et al., 2003). Furthermore, naturalistic research suggests that additional case management services may be required in conjunction with culturally adapted treatment to mitigate substantial engagement and attrition problems (e.g., Miranda, Azocar, Organista, Dwyer, & Areane, 2003). Likewise, Beck and colleagues have reported similar problems in studying CBT effects in naturalistic settings (Gibbons et al., 2010; 83% White client sample reported).

Modern multicultural competence research

As interest in MC counseling research reemerged in the 1990s, multiple instruments were developed to measure therapist, client, and observer ratings of Sue's (D. W. Sue et al., 1992) therapist MC competencies (Constantine, Juby, & Liang, 2001; Worthington, Mobley, Franks, & Tan, 2000). Furthermore, process-outcome studies using primarily survey, analog, and retrospective designs have been carried out to assess relationships between training, MC competence, client satisfaction, and symptom-reduction using mostly White therapists and mixed samples of racial/ethnic college student clients (i.e., predominantly African American, Latino(a), and Asian American).

Therapist self-ratings. In studies assessing therapists' own ratings, the therapist tends to rate his or her MC skill level as higher

than, and subsequently unrelated to, the client's and judge's ratings (Constantine, 2001b; Fuertes et al., 2006; Worthington et al., 2000). Adding to this dilemma, therapist self-report MCC ratings tend to be positively related to socially desirable responding (Constantine et al., 2001; Constantine & Ladany, 2000; Worthington et al., 2000).

In terms of training and education, however, a therapist self-reported MC *knowledge* component, though not the *awareness* component, has been repeatedly found to correlate with the therapist's previous MC education (Constantine, 2001a; Constantine et al., 2001; Constantine & Ladany, 2000). One study has found both self-reported knowledge and awareness components to be positively associated with previous MC education (Chao, Wei, Good, & Flores, 2011). In contrast, therapist MC competence has consistently been found unrelated to his or her cross-cultural case conceptualization skill set (Constantine, 2001a; i.e., competence was unrelated to therapist ability to formulate a treatment plan).

Previous MC education, then, may predictably influence a White therapist's MC knowledge but may be less predictable in affecting his or her awareness and choice to take ownership of racial disparities that may affect the MC counseling situation. Interestingly, verbally demonstrating knowledge/awareness to the client as "proof" that the therapist owns his or her "Whiteness" may not be necessary or helpful in therapy (Thompson & Alexander, 2006). Troubling, though, is the finding that less therapist MC awareness is related to both increased color-blindness (i.e., lack of awareness, or denial of the existence of racism; Gushue & Constantine, 2007) and more rigid White racial identities (Constantine et al., 2001). Moreover, Chao et al. (2011) found that more trained, less color-blind White therapists had significantly higher MC knowledge scores than their more color-blind, but equivalently trained, counterparts.

Taken together, these findings tentatively demonstrate that White therapist knowledge of an MC world is easier or more readily attained than awareness of that world, but color-blind pretenses and rigid racial attitudes can obscure that knowledge. Nonetheless, despite this latter qualification a therapist will likely struggle less with MC knowledge assessment statements, such as "I am knowledgeable of acculturation models for various ethnic minority groups," versus an MC awareness statement, such as "I am aware that being born a minority in this society brings with it certain challenges that White people do not have to face" (Chao et al., 2011, p. 75). Furthermore, this discrepancy may be related to differences between cognitive (e.g., perspective-taking) and affective (e.g., concern or sympathy) components of a culturally empathic understanding system (Constantine, 2001a). For instance, once social desirability effects were controlled, Constantine (2000) found higher levels of therapist affective empathy alone to be significantly related to higher MC knowledge and awareness self-reports, whereas cognitive empathy alone was unrelated. Despite these findings, however, therapist self-reported MC competence is not specifically related to outcome, such as client satisfaction with therapy (Fuertes et al., 2006).

Client ratings. In comparison, racial/ethnic minority clients' ratings of their predominantly White therapists' MC competencies have correlated significantly with client satisfaction and symptom reduction but are possibly confounded with client ratings of general competence/credibility ratings of the therapist (i.e., expertness, attractiveness, trustworthiness). Further support for this latter finding comes from studies by Owen, Leach, Wampold, and Rodolfa (2011) and Constantine (2007) suggesting that client-rated MC competence ratings and satisfaction may be influenced by the therapist's personal qualities, such as likeability. However, client MC competence ratings have been found to account for an additional amount of client satisfaction, beyond therapist general competence and likeability (Constantine, 2002; Fuertes & Brobst, 2002). Interestingly, client ratings of therapist general and MC competence have consistently been found interrelated with client perception of the working alliance (Constantine, 2007; Fuertes et al., 2006; Owen, Tao, Leach, and Rodolfa, 2011; Wang & Kim, 2010) demonstrating that a client's perceptions of the therapist's general as well as MC competence may be substantially dependent on the particular client–therapist relationship that is formed.

In addition, client–therapist racial/ethnic match has been found unrelated to both client perception of therapist MC competence (Owen,

Leach, et al., 2011) and satisfaction with therapy (Fuertes et al., 2006). Looking beyond racial/ethnic match, Stanley Sue and colleagues (Zane et al., 2005) investigated client–therapist "cognitive match" (i.e., congruence between client/therapist perceptions of how a person relates to others, copes with problems, and the purpose of therapy). The authors found these factors to play a significant role in session impact and symptom outcome. Previously, the authors (S. Sue & Zane, 1987) had suggested that therapist credibility and a giving nature may be important components in minority clients' (a) attitudes toward therapy, (b) their inspiration for attending therapy, and (c) the overall perceived benefit from therapy.

On the whole, a minority client's satisfaction with therapy may substantially depend on a general positive regard toward and trust in the therapist, and is also modestly related to the therapist's particular MC competence. Corroborating recent research reviews (Zane et al., 2005), client-therapist racial/ethnic match similarity appears to be less important for some types of outcome criteria than previously thought.

Observer ratings. Fewer studies have reported observer-rated therapist MC competence. Among these, Constantine (2001b), using audio-taped recordings, found that observers rated the MC competence of African American and Latino counselors higher compared to White counselors. These observer ratings were neither influenced by the client's race/ethnicity nor by client/therapist racial/ethnic similarities.

In addition, observers' ratings of therapist MC competence have been found to significantly correlate with both MC-oriented verbal content and therapist attribution of client problem causation. In other words, the therapists who were rated more competent also tended to use more MC-oriented speech content and demonstrated increasingly sympathetic attitudes toward the client's problem (Worthington et al., 2000). Paralleling these findings, observer-rated empathy has also been found related to verbal content frequency (Wenegrat, 1974). For empathy, a substantial factor was found to explain this relationship: a therapist's assertiveness in approaching the client's emotions. Drawing a parallel, Worthington et al.'s (2000) finding could be interpreted as a therapist's assertiveness in approaching the client's multiculturalism. Mentioned earlier, however, Thompson and Alexander's (2006) study moderates this finding: White therapists that were instructed to initiate a discussion of race were rated no more effective by their African American clients than were White therapists instructed not to initiate a discussion. Therefore, the extent to which a therapist should intentionally demonstrate MC competence by initiating a "race discussion" is questionable.

Multicultural empathy. A number of theorists and researchers have found empathy to be a necessary therapist attribute in general (Elliott, Bohart, Watson, & Greenberg, 2011) and potentially important in MC counseling as well. P. Pedersen (2009) reviews empathy within an MC framework and suggests an "inclusive cultural empathy" paradigm through which the therapist reframes the therapy relationship into MC categories in order to "accept the counseling relationship as it is - ambiguous and complex" (p. 147). Furthermore, the author recommends developing a balance of meaningful knowledge and accurate assumptions as a means to develop appropriate social action skills (i.e., interventions).

Regarding research evidence, MC competence studies have found therapist self-reported empathy to positively affect MC case-conceptualization skills (Constantine, 2001a), and client-perceived empathy is positively related to client satisfaction (Fuertes & Brobst, 2002). In addition, Miville, Carlozzi, Gushue, Schara, and Ueda (2006) found empathic therapists more likely to embrace cultural diversity and to score high on emotional intelligence tests. Conversely, therapists with high color-blind scores were found to be less empathic when compared to low color-blind therapists (Burkard & Knox, 2004). Furthermore, client-perceived therapist MC competence was positively associated with client-perceived therapist empathy across both racially matched and racially unmatched therapy dyads (Fuertes et al., 2006). Taken together, these findings suggest that therapist empathy may be a primary ingredient in MC counseling competence.

Meta-analytic research. Bruce Wampold and colleagues

(Benish, Quintana, & Wampold, 2011) performed a meta-analysis of select comparison studies that compared "bona fide" culturally adapted therapies to comparable but unadapted therapies (bona fide therapies are considered to be treatments that possess specific, hypothesized mechanisms of change). The findings are provocative: The effectiveness of the culturally adapted therapies (beyond that of the unadapted general effects) was moderated solely by the degree to which the therapies possessed an accurate "illness myth" or culturally congruent explanation and perception of the clients' problems or illnesses. Therefore, as the types of studies analyzed are distilled to the most competitive comparisons, culturally-adapted therapies remain moderately more effective because of the presence of an accurate illness myth, a concept similar to Stanley Sue's (Zane et al., 2005) cognitive match and Derald Sue's (D. W. Sue et al., 1992) skills competencies.

With the MC research in mind, the following section will examine PCT's current and historical contributions and then suggest hypothesized cultural adaptations to a person-centered approach.

A Person-Centered Approach to the Treatment of Multicultural Clients

As is generally known, Carl Rogers is the figurehead of the person-centered movement, which, from the 1940s to 1970s, explored the effects of certain facilitative therapist conditions on personality and behavior change with individuals, families, groups, students, schools, in corporate culture, and in large groups as well. These facilitative, or core, conditions were originally defined as congruence, unconditional positive regard, and empathic understanding (Rogers, 1957). Moreover, from the early 1970s until his death in 1987, Rogers and colleagues devoted substantial time and resources toward clarifying a cross-cultural definition of the person-centered approach, providing a future foundation for therapeutic work in culturally diverse settings (e.g., Rogers, 1977; Rogers, Farson, & McGaw, 1968; Rogers & Sanford, 1987).

Remarkably, in the first decade of the 21st century, results of a survey of practicing helping professionals found Rogers to be the most influential figure of the previous quarter-century, replicating findings from two decades prior (Cook, Biyanova, & Coyne, 2009; D. Smith, 1982). Furthermore, in 2007 a prominent psychotherapy journal devoted a special section of the Fall volume to the 50-year publication anniversary of Rogers's (1957) renowned necessary and sufficient facilitative conditions article (Gelso, 2007). Paradoxically, though, across the 11 articles published in this bicentennial, celebratory volume the verdict was: probably facilitative but not sufficient - save for one-half of one article. Most support for the necessity of Rogers's theory seemed to be provided only within the context of correcting it; by adding novel components primarily related to the therapeutic orientation held by the author of each article (e.g., psychodynamic, behavioral, process-experiential, feminist, etc.).

Despite the ambivalence of professional opinion toward Rogers's contributions, the facilitative conditions tend to be regarded as the necessary preconditions for therapy to occur - that is, necessary to build a therapeutic relationship. Once this is accomplished, the helping professions have then historically focused on specific therapist techniques and interventions thought to ultimately result in client symptom reduction, or as Gordon Paul (1967) asked in his well-known question, "what treatment, by whom, is most effective for this individual with that specific problem, and under which set of circumstances?" (Paul, 1967, p. 111).

Person-centered research in the 1970s

Arguably, the Rogerian traditions of research and evidence-based practice concurrently ended in the United States in 1974. A number of methodological issues had been raised about the final 10 years of facilitative conditions research (ca. 1964-1974), spearheaded, for better or worse, by Charles Truax (Truax & Mitchell, 1971). Not by chance, this hypothesized end date corresponds with Truax's death (December 1973; Bergin & Suinn, 1975; Kirschenbaum, 1979), John M. Butler's death in 1975 (Wexler & Butler, 1976), and, in a broader sense, the deaths of Maslow in 1970 and Buhler and Jourard in 1974 (Greening, 2007). Consequently, by the time Rogers (1975) published his well-known article entitled "Empathic: An Unappreciated Way of Being," Bergin and Suinn (1975) had performed a quick and cursory review of the arguments on both sides of the ongoing methodological dispute (e.g.,

Bozarth & Krauft, 1972; Chinsky & Rappaport, 1970; Gurman, 1973b; Mintz & Luborsky, 1971; Rappaport & Chinsky, 1972; Truax, 1972) and had concluded, "these findings may invalidate much of this program of research [including the Wisconsin schizophrenia project (Rogers, Gendlin, Kiesler, & Truax, 1967)]" (p. 515). However, Bergin and Suinn (1975) had overlooked evidence contradicting much of the criticism leveled at Truax and colleagues' use of observer-rated research measures (Beutler, Johnson, Neville, & Workman, 1973; Gurman, 1973a; Wenegrat, 1974). Later, additional clarification and evidence supporting Truax emerged as well (Beutler, 1976; Friedlander et al., 1988).

Despite evidence to the contrary, literature published in the late-1970s continued to rely on the negative reviews and research findings published earlier that decade (e.g., Parloff, Waskow, & Wolfe, 1978). Finally, the proverbial nail-in-the-coffin came from the PCT camp. Mitchell, Bozarth, and Krauft (1977) found no correlation between the conditions and measurable change in clients, though the finding emerged from a therapist sample possessing minimal abilities to provide sufficient facilitative conditions, as rated by trained observers. Surprising, though understated, were findings that client-perceived facilitative condition measures were consistently related to positive outcome (Barrett-Lennard, 1981; Bergin & Suinn, 1975; Gurman, 1977).

Though debatable, the Rogerian practice tradition was discredited along with research on the facilitative conditions. Looking back, interpersonal conflict stemming from events that took place during the "Wisconsin years" may have largely contributed to PCT's decline rather than overwhelming evidence disproving Rogers's theory and the effectiveness of PCT (Kirschenbaum, 1979). To be clear, despite unfavorable reviews (e.g., Parloff et al., 1978), the evidence did not conclusively demonstrate the alleged inadequacies of either the research or the practice - though an exhaustive review of the numerous articles supporting this point is beyond the scope of this article. However, after reviewing Parloff et al.'s (1978) influential chapter, C. H. Patterson (1984) exemplifies the general trend: "they recognize that there are positive findings, but emphasize the negative, failing to note that there are more positive than negative studies, or to note that the negative studies are not without serious problems or flaws" (p. 433). Furthermore, when the studies cited by Parloff et al. (1978), in particular, are examined in detail, a researcher allegiance bias comparable to "necessary, not sufficient" becomes apparent (e.g., Bergin & Jasper, 1969; Garfield & Bergin, 1971; Mintz, Luborsky, & Auerbach, 1971; Sloane et al., 1975). As a result - and given recent concessions that allegiance does affect outcome (McLeod, 2009) - this bias may have seriously affected the intentions of both the researchers and the non-PCT therapists in these studies, resulting in their unequivocal conclusions of "no relationship" between the conditions and outcome. In retrospect, why substantial time, book, and journal space were devoted to dismantling 20 years of empirical support for Rogers's facilitative conditions - and the subsequent affect on the helping professions and on society in general - is grounds for consideration.

Historical multicultural research

Noted in the previous section of this article, although the Rogerian tradition was ending, research influenced by the PCT tradition was accumulating that examined the effects, for example, of person-centered and egalitarian therapist attitudes on racial/ethnic minority clients from a variety of backgrounds (including college students and clients living in impoverished communities). Moreover, these initial studies contributed meaningful empirical findings, such as "both race and social class of both patient and counselor appear to be significant sources of effect upon the depth of self-exploration of patients in initial clinical interviews" (Carkhuff & Pierce, 1967, p. 634), "the evidence thus suggests that counselor experience per se may be independent of counseling effectiveness with [African American] counselees . . . race and type of orientation and training appear more relevant variables" (G. Banks et al., 1967, p. 71), and furthermore, "systematic training in interpersonal skills, then, was effective in 'shaping' higher and more effective levels of communication . . . between races" (Carkhuff & Banks, 1970, p. 417).

Furthermore, in addition to the work of Banks, Carkhuff, and colleagues (e.g., Redfering, 1975), Barbara Lerner published the well-known book Therapy in the Ghetto, as well as follow-up studies, on differential therapist attitudes in relation to outcome with low-income, African American clients (Lerner, 1972, 1973; Lerner & Fiske, 1973). A few years later, in a major review of psychotherapy with disadvantaged populations (a previous version of Stanley Sue's pivotal chapter cited earlier [S. Sue et al., 1994]), Lorion (1978) referred to Lerner's work as "a single systematic evaluation of insight-oriented psychotherapies for ghetto residents" (p. 920). Lerner, who began her work in the person-centered research tradition (R. Cartwright & Lerner, 1963), received further praise and criticism from Stanley Sue (1973). In particular, echoing the critique he would make 20 years later of psychoanalytic and behavior therapy research (S. Sue et al., 1994), Sue pointed out that Lerner's naturalistic research design lacked a comparable control group against which the positive outcomes could be further substantiated. Sue's criticisms were answered by Lerner (1974) in which she referred to her companion study (Lerner, 1973) that supported her original findings of a positive relationship between White therapists' nonauthoritarian, "democratic" values and improved outcomes with African American clients. Despite these early empirical precedents being set, little culturally diverse experimental therapy research was carried out in subsequent years, though Stanley Sue (along with Derald Sue, as already cited) would continue to demonstrate evidence of severe disparities in racial/ethnic minority mental health treatment over the years (e.g., S. Sue, 1977; S. Sue et al., 1994; S. Sue & Zane, 1987; Zane et al., 2005). Similarly, the humanistic/person-centered movement would also become dormant in the United States for the next few decades. In writing about the revival of meaning in psychology, Kirk Schneider (1999) substantiates this view: "since about 1975 [. . .] the humanistic psychology movement [. . .] has been relegated to a quaint afterthought in the curriculum of most APA-accredited doctoral programs in psychology" (p. 14).

The person-centered movement never fully achieved Sue's (S. Sue, 1973; S. Sue et al., 1994) recommendations regarding the use of research methods that would allow for further generalization of results with racial/ethnic minority clients. However, the likelihood of the Rogerian tradition executing additional MC research using control/comparison groups was substantially stronger than that of other research traditions still in the beginning phases of building a research base (e.g., Di Loreto, 1971; Kernberg, 1973; Mintz et al., 1971). That is, from its inception, Rogerian research had been engaged in scientific inquiry and the use of rigorous and meaningful control conditions (i.e., the two Rogerian research volumes were practically graduate-level methodology courses unto themselves; see Rogers & Dymond, 1954; Rogers, Gendlin, Kiesler, & Truax, 1967). Therefore, the Rogerian group would have had a 20-year foundation of experience, training, and know-how to contribute toward the implementation of further randomized, controlled MC research projects. However, the published literature in the 1970s suggests that PCT researchers, rather than pursuing novel avenues of empirical inquiry, devoted substantial time in defending PCT against - what now appear to be - unfounded claims made by a group of social scientists who held significant professional interest in seeing through the dismantling of the person-centered approach.

The status of modern person-centered research

According to the original APA standards for empirically validated therapies (Chambless et al., 1998), PCT meets criteria as a well-established treatment intervention for depression (Goldman, Greenberg, & Angus, 2006; Greenberg & Watson, 1998; Teusch, Bohme, Finke, Gastpar, & Skerra, 2003; Teusch, Bohme, & Gastpar, 1997; Ward et al., 2000) and meets criteria as a potentially efficacious treatment for panic and anxiety disorders (Cottraux et al., 2008; Teusch et al., 1997) and for personality disorders (Cottraux et al., 2009; Teusch, Bohme, Finke, & Gastpar, 2001; Turner, 2000). Furthermore, Elliott et al.'s (2004) meta-analysis found that PCT - once researcher allegiance was controlled - was equivalent in effect size to both process-experiential therapies (i.e., PCT plus process-direction) and cognitive, behavioral, and psychodynamic approaches across a range of Axis I disorders. Unfortunately, PCT is also comparable to modern established treatments by merit of an insubstantial MC research base (HHS, 2001).

Multicultural person-centered studies

However, a number of 21st-century research studies have

provided strong support for the person-centered approach as an effective and equivalent treatment for culturally diverse populations, despite probable researcher allegiance bias in some. The following studies report findings from Brazil, Malaysia, Iran, and the United States.

Brazil. Freire, Koller, Piason, and da Silva (2005) reported on a program in Southern Brazil that provided PCT to impoverished children and adolescents living at either a residential shelter or attending day treatment. The authors observed that a nondirective, person-centered therapist intention toward promoting client autonomy and self-determination resulted in notable symptom and behavior change. After six months, the children and adolescents who received or were receiving counseling had demonstrated observable improvements in their relationships with the shelter staff, their peers, and their families (with whom many of the children were able to visit on the weekends). Surprisingly, this pattern of change was reportedly independent of the children's particular use of time in therapy: positive outcomes were observed in those children who chose only to play cards and games with their therapists, those children who openly discussed their feelings and experiences, and those who talked only about sports and movies.

Confirming these clinical observations, Teusch and Bohme (1999) provide quantitative evidence of client change in PCT, despite an absence of a specific symptom-reduction treatment plan: "our findings underline the hypothesis that client-centered treatment influences the reduction of anxiety symptoms using other mechanisms than would behavioral exposure treatment" (p. 119).

Malaysia. Mohamad, Mokhtar, and Samah (2011) provide findings from a qualitative study of four PCT clients' perceptions of their inner experiences and personal growth. After 12 sessions, the clients reported constructive change as assessed by interpersonal process recall methods; in particular, increased openness to exploring spiritual, cultural, and moral issues in their lives.

For example, one young woman reported improved personal understanding of the teachings of the Qur'an, which paralleled a closer connection to and understanding of her mother's life experiences. Another client, dissatisfied with her religion, had lost her faith in prayer prior to starting therapy. However, shortly after therapy began, she renewed her morning prayer routine:

> that day after the counseling session. . . . I went home . . . then I thought and thought about all those things. . . . I still did not pray. . . . I came back here . . . suddenly it was like . . . I don't know, it came naturally . . . that morning when I woke up at 5.30, I performed my prayers again. (Mohamad et al., 2011, p. 2121)

In addition, Din, Noor, and Kahn's (2008) quantitative study provides further support for PCT's effectiveness in Southeast Asia.

Moderately educated, predominantly married, and depressed Malay women reported symptom improvement after receiving four sessions of PCT during an 8-week period. Clients receiving PCT reported a large decrease in depression (assessed by the Malay version of the Beck Depression Inventory [BDI]) at post-treatment (BDI = 13.93) and follow-up (BDI = 9.80), and compared to a waitlist control. Moreover, the clients' clinical improvement is substantial, particularly when compared to nondepressed Malay samples (BDI = 12.4; Muhktar & Oei, 2010). The authors concluded,

> the three necessary therapeutic conditions, namely, congruence, unconditional positive regards [sic] and empathy provided without any directed intervention during the therapy resulted in significant positive outcome. Beck's hypothetical statement that the therapist's qualities as 'necessary but not sufficient' . . . to produce positive outcome was not observed in most of the participants in this experimental study. (Din et al., 2008, p. 12)

Iran. Yoosefi (2011) compared change in client self-differentiation scores among a sample of divorced Muslim men and women in Iran, randomly assigned to PCT, rational-emotive behavior therapy (REBT), or a control group condition. The women, whose sample size was twice the men's, tended to be predominantly unemployed and living with their parents, whereas the men tended to be employed, living alone. Furthermore, compared to the men, the women were less educated, earning one-sixth the income.

Briefly, self-differentiation has been defined as "the capacity of a family system and its members to manage emotional reactivity, remain thoughtful in the midst of strong emotion, and experience both intimacy and autonomy in relationships" (Skowron, Stanley, & Shapiro, 2009, p. 4). Specifically, higher scores on Skowron and Friedlander's (1998) Differentiation of Self Inventory (DSI) relate to higher client self-differentiation, and vice versa. Skowron et al. (2009) have found that greater self-differentiation was positively related to interpersonal and psychological well-being in White samples. Furthermore, the DSI has shown relevance in cross-cultural and marital relationship studies as a measure of emotional reactivity, ability to take the "I" position, and degree of emotional cut-off/fusion with others (Yoosefi, 2011). Select normative comparison scores have been reported for the following: (a) White, married men and women in the United States (M = 3.9 and M = 3.6, respectively; Skowron & Friedlander, 1998), (b) married Iranian men and women (M = 3.5 and M = 3.3, respectively; Yousefi [sic] et al., 2009), and (c) college students in Tehran (M = 3.4, men and women combined; Gharehbaghy, 2011). Moreover, in Gharehbaghy's (2011) latter study, higher self-differentiation scores were positively associated with greater family harmony.

Going forward, Yoosefi (2011) found no significant differences between PCT and REBT treatment effects on client self-differentiation scores. Surprisingly, self-differentiation scores for both therapies had decreased about three points from pretreatment (PCT: M = 5.0; REBT: M = 4.7) to post-treatment (PCT: M = 2.0; REBT: M = 1.9) remaining stable at follow-up, while control group scores held at pretreatment levels across time.

Examined through a Western cultural lens, Yoosefi's (2011) findings are startling. First, the divorced clients on average were found to possess a higher individuated self-concept at pretreatment compared to both the demographically-similar sample of married Iranians and the sample of Iranian college students (Gharehbaghy, 2011; Yousefi [sic] et al., 2009). Furthermore, the cognitive-behavior therapy variation (i.e., REBT) and the PCT were found to equally change client self-differentiation scores, though in an unexpected direction when viewed from an individualistic, Western perspective.

Drawing from a MC perspective, however, these findings may be easier explained. It is reasonable to assume that, within a more collectivist-oriented culture, holding status as a divorcee might result in a defensive reaction within the individual - particularly the women - that would presumably be related to an unusually strong individualistic client stance (i.e., higher than "culturally normal" self-differentiation scores). As a result of therapy, the person becomes less defensive over time, returning to a more balanced self-concept that would include both individual and collectivist attributes (i.e., a lower self-differentiation score). Partially explaining this phenomenon, early psychotherapy research (Butler & Haigh, 1954) provided evidence of a convergent relationship between clients' actual-self and ideal-self scores after receiving PCT. Across a predominantly White client sample, Butler and Haigh (1954) found that PCT facilitated equilibrium between the client's self-concept and the client's ideal of who he or she should or could be, assumed to be partly influenced by the client's culture. Depending on the point of view, this correlation was referred to as "congruence" or "discrepancy," but the degree of self-ideal match was suggested to measure a client's self-esteem (Shlien, 1962).

Likewise, Yoosefi's (2011) research may demonstrate convergence between a client's personal view of self and a collective-influenced ideal. Specifically, in a person-centered therapeutic climate, where the therapist's intent is toward a nonjudgmental attitude, the client will likely be encouraged to explore individually chosen aspects of his or her worldview. Within a MC context, the tendency toward self-actualization - hypothesized to be the meta-mechanism of change within a person-centered relationship (Quinn, 2011) - may operate within a client by moving him or her toward individual-collective equilibrium. In the process, the client accommodates and embraces various aspects of his or her culture-of-origin, while also retaining unique personal qualities as well. In this way, the client can remain a unique person, but within the context of relationship with and responsibility to/for others. Thus, increased self-esteem will not always predict increased individuation.

Rather, self-esteem will be the outcome of an increased sense of personal choice.

United States. Szapocznik et al. (2004; Feaster, Brincks, et al., 2010; Feaster, Burns, et al., 2010) reported a study assessing change among a sample of low-income, HIV-positive, African American mothers randomly assigned to one of three conditions: (a) structural ecosystems therapy (SET; an adaptation of a brief family therapy), (b) a PCT attention-control condition, and (c) a community referral control. Specifically, PCT "was incorporated in the study to control for common factors . . . in therapy such as attention, supportiveness, and empathy" (Szapocznik et al., 2004, p. 291).

Previously, I reported on the tendency of research studies to provide PCT in a diluted format as a TAU or minimal treatment control condition. Despite these handicaps, PCT demonstrated results comparable to the experimental treatment conditions (Quinn, 2011). In contrast, the current study provides a less-diluted version of the PCT condition. Specifically, PCT training and adherence measures were instituted, including an initial PCT workshop and monthly adherence check-ins provided by the late Barbara Brodley, a well-known person-centered therapist (e.g., Brodley, 2006b). However, a substantial bias likely remained because of constraints placed on the PCT therapists' choice of responses and the subsequent outcome criteria against which PCT was measured. The PCT condition "was included to compare the family and systems-oriented SET to a person-oriented therapeutic modality that did not address the family or other systems in which the women are embedded" (Feaster, Burns, et al., 2010, p. 206). Presumably, the researchers wished to assess additional effects of their approach (i.e., SET), beyond the effects of an individualized, non-technique-oriented treatment. However, when the researchers formulated their subsequent conclusions, they failed to account for the substantial advantage given to the SET treatment on family assessment measures, in particular due to the PCT constraints, which may have produced spuriously inflated differences between treatments. However, despite this apparent researcher partisanship, PCT demonstrated comparable results on most measures.

The initial study published by Szapocznik et al. (2004) found that clients receiving SET demonstrated significantly better retention rates on average (M = 12.45, SD = 12.85) compared to PCT clients (M = 5.74, SD = 5.23), though initial engagement rates were the same (i.e., at least two sessions attended). Related to these retention rates, the authors state: "assessors and therapists contacted each woman to set and confirm appointments for each assessment or therapy session," however, "for women in the SET condition, therapists also contacted family members to remind them to be available for therapy sessions" (Szapocznik et al., 2004, p. 292). In comparison, "[PCT] methods were limited to contact with the woman only and nondirected attempts to build empathy, unconditional positive regard, and congruence" (Feaster, Burns, et al.,

2010, p. 208).

Statistical analysis indicated that all three conditions were found to significantly decrease psychological distress over time, though overall decrease in the clients' distress was small for each of the three conditions. Moreover, the PCT condition was more effective with the most severely distressed clients, whereas SET was more effective with the least distressed. Specifically, no difference in distress was found between the active treatment conditions at the 3-month and 6-month post-baseline assessments. However, SET clients compared to their PCT counterparts reported a significant improvement in distress at the 9-month assessment, whereas PCT client distress rose slightly. Unexpectedly, SET and PCT clients reported no difference in overall distress improvement at the final 18-month assessment, as PCT clients' distress subsequently decreased over the final period. Of interest, the above findings parallel reports by Greenberg and Watson (1998), Teusch and Bohme (1999), and Cottraux et al. (2008). In these studies, the more directive therapy condition demonstrated stronger mid-treatment and/or post-treatment effects but at follow-up assessments these differences between treatments had disappeared.

Differences between treatment conditions were also reported for client-perceived family hassles scores. In brief, an adapted version of the Hassles Scale (L. Smith et al., 2001) was used by Szapocznik et al. (2004) to assess the extent to which clients reported family hassles occurring daily, for example, in relation to their children, parents, ex-spouse, neighbors, money for health care, another's smoking or drinking, their children's future, social/support services, and transportation (L. Smith et al., 2001). A hassles score "was obtained by counting the number of family-related hassles items that the woman had endorsed" (Szapocznik et al., 2004, p. 292). No difference between conditions was reported at the 3- and 6-month assessments. However, clients who had received PCT reported an increase in family hassles at both 9 months (compared to both SET and the control) and 18 months (compared to SET only).

Lastly, Szapocznik et al. (2004) assessed changes in client-perceived family support across time. The family support measure sums the number of reported family relationships on whom the client feels she can depend. No differences were found across conditions: all three conditions demonstrated declines in reported family support over time, stabilizing between 9- and 18-month assessments.

Six years later, a subsequent study analyzing the same data (Feaster, Brincks, et al., 2010) reported a significant difference between the SET and PCT conditions relating to HIV medication adherence. Though client-reported "percentage of pills taken" in the PCT condition was significantly greater compared to SET at first (i.e., at 3- and 6-month assessments), and comparable after 9 months, clients in the PCT condition had a significantly lower medication adherence at 18 months compared to the SET and the control groups, which had similar adherence rates.

A third analysis of a subset of the data was undertaken by Feaster, Burns, et al. (2010), examining differences in substance use relapse. PCT clients demonstrated a significantly greater relapse rate compared to the SET and control groups - which is surprising given the impact of therapist empathy on substance users treated with motivational interviewing (Miller & Rose, 2009). A mediation analysis was performed to assess the impact that psychological distress scores, family hassles, and extra-therapy service usage had on the differences between treatments. Overall, none of these variables were found to mediate relapse, though conspicuously, change in client-reported family hassles were reported to have partially explained the SET/ PCT relapse difference. In addition, Feaster, Burns, et al. (2010) found that therapy attendance significantly accounted for the differences in relapse between SET and PCT. Like medication adherence, the SET relapse rates were not significantly better than the control group.

A "constraint effect" in psychotherapy research.

The final cluster of studies by Szapocznik (2004); Feaster, Brincks, et al. (2010); and Feaster, Burns, et al. (2010) adds to a group of psychotherapy studies (Quinn, 2011) demonstrating comparable results between a "showcased" treatment and PCT, despite consistent and overwhelming advantage given to the former. In this case (Szapocznik et al., 2004), researcher allegiance bias was introduced, not by providing a PCT condition with minimally trained therapists, but by constraining the PCT therapists' range of responses (e.g., instructions to focus solely on individual client characteristics). Statistically speaking, this bias or "constraint effect" would then theoretically lead to nonrandom or systematic error being introduced into the data. For example, the effect of systematically constraining PCT therapist response would likely lead to a significant correlation between the PCT treatment condition and a unidirectional outcome measure that is sensitive only to an increase of client problems (i.e., family hassles scale). The inflated client-perceived family hassles scores found for the PCT condition substantiates this hypothesis. To be clear, the above bias is analogous to asking a 7-foot tall athlete to crouch, then measuring the athlete's height under these conditions, and subsequently cutting him or her from the basketball team for being too short. In a similar way, after instructing the PCT therapists to avoid family issues (i.e., rendering the therapists less effective with their clients) the researchers proceeded to evaluate PCT using a family assessment measure that would predictably favor the family therapy (SET). Therefore, drawing conclusions from this data set regarding differences in treatment effects is ill-conceived at best. Remarkably, however, the authors would conclude that PCT was a harmful treatment approach (Szapocznik & Prado, 2007).

In a separate article regarding harmful effects in family therapy, Szapocznik and Prado (2007) employ broad strokes in presenting their conclusions: that PCT, in particular, is an iatrogenic psychosocial treatment. To build their case, the authors first cite a number of research studies, primarily depending on Allen Bergin's research from the 1960s, which suggested that psychotherapy could produce a "deterioration effect" (Barlow, 2010; Bergin, 1966, 1971). In brief, Bergin had originally developed his conception of a deterioration effect by attending a meeting of Rogers's schizophrenia research project at the University of Wisconsin in the early 1960s. Moreover, Truax - who, at the time, was the administrative coordinator for this research project - is reported to have presented evidence during this meeting suggesting that some clients might get worse from psychotherapy (see Lambert, Bergin, & Collins, 1977; notably, Truax's conclusions supported tentative evidence found a decade prior [see Rogers & Dymond, 1954]). In short, Truax would go on to provide substantial evidence (e.g., Truax, 1963) that psychotherapy could be "for better or for worse" - and the primary protective factors against deterioration, bridging treatment approaches, were found to be high levels of Rogers's facilitative conditions (Truax & Carkhuff, 1965, 1967; Truax & Mitchell, 1971). Later, Bergin (1966, 1971) would cite Truax's research in support of his similar and historically more popular concept (see Barlow, 2010).

Next, Szapocznik and Prado (2007) state,

> there was a transitory iatrogenic effect [. . .] with the person-centered approach having significantly more family stressors than

either the experimental family condition or the community control. However, the significance of these differences was not sustained at the 18-month follow-up [to be accurate, the SET advantage remained significant at 18-months, as reported by Szapocznik et al. (2004)]. (p. 474)

Similarly, others have found their voices as well. Berk and Parker (2009) interpret these findings as follows: "Szapocznik and Prado detailed how interventions may have adverse effects on families and friends [. . .] particularly if the individual undergoing therapy becomes more self-absorbed or self-centered" (p. 789). Likewise, Moos (2005) states "person-centered treatment also may engender an individualistic and self-centered world-view, which may be associated with deterioration in social and family functioning" (p. 600).

Redfering (1975). Consequently, the potential inaccuracies and broad generalizations contained in the above conclusions are particularly troubling given that previous PCT research has demonstrated positive effects on African American women's attitudes toward their families. Briefly, Redfering (1975) conducted a 1-year follow-up study of the differential effects of person-centered group therapy (using White therapists) on personal meanings that young African American and White institutionalized, juvenile-delinquent females placed on their concepts of "father," "mother," "myself," and "peers." Remarkably, following PCT treatment the African American women placed significantly greater positive meanings on these family concepts, at posttreatment, at a 1-year follow-up, and compared to their White counterparts after 1 year. Moreover, significantly more of the African American clients had been released from incarceration within the year, living with their parents and gainfully employed. Surprisingly, Redfering (1975) found that "with the exception of 'myself,' the black group's mean scores on the experimental concepts improved" (p. 534). In other words, according to the criteria of improvement suggested by Szapocznik and Prado (2007), Berk and Parker (2009), and Moos (2005), these African American women were significantly freed from their "self-absorbed" and "self-centered" attitudes as a result of a PCT treatment.

Hypothesized Mechanisms of Change in the Treatment of Multicultural Clients

Like all psychotherapies and psychosocial interventions (Kazdin, 2009), a causal relationship between Rogers's hypothesized mechanisms of change (Rogers, 1957, 1959) and outcome criteria have yet to be definitively proven. Similarly, as the field of psychotherapy currently begins the process of demonstrating that orientation-specific mechanisms of change are causally linked to temporary or lasting symptom reduction, the results become ambiguous. For example, the effectiveness of adherence to techniques, such as therapist prescription of homework, is questioned (Strunk, Brotman, & DeRubeis, 2010), and more difficult patients have been found to be less treatable, regardless of therapist competence in providing specific techniques (Strunk, Brotman, DeRubeis, & Hollon, 2010). Furthermore, a meta-analysis of mechanisms of change research found therapist adherence and therapist competence unrelated to outcome, concluding that "it may be that a more important set of factors are those that are common to most or all forms of psychotherapy, such as the quality of the therapeutic alliance" (Webb, DeRubeis, & Barber, 2010, p. 207).

Previously, hypothesized mechanisms of change in PCT (Quinn, 2011) were described in the context of treating a client population that possessed two primary characteristics: (a) the likelihood of experiencing trauma and (b) low trust of the therapist (i.e., put coarsely, possessing a "sensitive bullshit meter"; Quinn, 2008, p. 464). Furthermore, a plausible predictive relationship has been suggested to exist between a client's experience of trauma and a subsequent decrease in trust toward the therapist (Quinn, 2008). Given that many racial/ethnic minority clients will also possess these characteristics, as a result of racism and oppression in particular (Pole, Gone, & Kulkarni, 2008), the remainder of this article will use MC research evidence to develop a set of MC mechanisms of change.

The facilitative mechanisms

Rogers (1957, 1959) suggested that when a client and therapist are in psychological contact, and the client is incongruent (e.g., the client's illness myth is incongruent with societies' illness myth), then the therapist facilitative mechanisms of congruence, unconditional positive regard, and empathic understanding will likely result in a process of positive client change. However, these mechanisms must be both communicated by the therapist and perceived by the client. As stated earlier, research has consistently found Rogers's facilitative mechanisms to be predictive of client outcome when provided by PCT therapists (Barrett-Lennard, 1981; Truax & Mitchell, 1971) and nonpredictive when provided by non-PCT therapists (Parloff et al., 1978).

The MC research reviewed in this article supports Rogers's hypothesis. The evidence suggests that two necessary facilitative mechanisms of change are needed for the therapist to provide a culturally competent therapy experience: (a) therapist self-congruence (e.g., emotional intelligence) and (b) an accurate empathic understanding of the client's internal frame of reference (i.e., empathy was earlier found related to client satisfaction, therapist case conceptualization, and a pro-diversity therapist stance). However, if mechanisms (a) and (b) describe the competent PCT therapist, then a final mechanism must be included for the therapist to be effective, which is hypothesized to be (c) a therapist's tendency for unconditional positive regard toward the client, also referred to as radical acceptance (Linehan, 1993). Therefore, assuming the conditions of psychological contact, client incongruence, and minimal communication and perception are met, then, if the PCT therapist can provide these three facilitative mechanisms within a culturally adapted framework (described shortly), these mechanisms are hypothesized to be sufficient to facilitate a process of positive change for MC clients and families.

Accordingly, these hypothesized mechanisms of change are integrative with D. W. Sue et al. (1992) MC competencies. That is, the effective person-centered therapist must possess MC knowledge (cognitive empathy) and awareness (affective empathy plus self-congruence) to sufficiently provide the skills (communication of unconditional positive regard) necessary for a process of change to occur with racial/ethnic minority clients. However, these competencies are not suggested to be mandates within the PCT framework: much of the MC knowledge and awareness that a PCT therapist acquires is invariably from a personal/professional motivation toward further self-congruence and unconditional positive self-regard. In support, MC research suggests that an empathic therapist (presumably, a more integrated, self-accepting, and emotionally intelligent person) is less color-blind and has a more fluid racial identity.

However, these facilitative mechanisms are hypothesized to be effective only if the therapist provides them with a genuine, unconditional intention (Quinn, 2011). Others (Brodley, 2006b; Merry & Brodley, 2002) have referred to this intention as "nondirective," which is equivalent, though typically misconceived by the field at large as "indirectness" or "indifference" on the part of the therapist. Nonetheless, if the therapist does not possess this type of intention in providing these mechanisms, then these mechanisms will fail to be sufficient. Moreover, this "genuinely unconditional" therapist intention likely differentiates the PCT therapist from other therapists who may view or use the facilitative mechanisms for contingent purposes, such as a means by which the client will more readily engage in a therapist-prescribed course of treatment, or to more willingly accept the therapist's transference interpretations (e.g., J. S. Beck, 1995; Gabbard, 2004; Linehan, 1993). Thus, for PCT to be effective,

> it is hypothesized that the therapist wants to understand for no other reason but to understand. If the therapist is motivated to understand solely to be a change agent for the client [e.g., by using a reflective listening technique], then the facilitative mechanisms may not be sufficient because a tendency toward unconditional acceptance will not effectively emerge. (Quinn, 2011, p. 482)

Of note, this last point may explain why the motivational interviewing research group includes a "spirit of MI" component in their mechanisms theory and in their therapist competence measure (Miller & Rose, 2009).

The process mechanisms

Rogers (1959) outlines a comprehensive process theory of change hypothesized to occur within the client as a result of experiencing the facilitative mechanisms. This process has been distilled into six mechanisms: (a) an increase of an accurate awareness of experience, both internal and external; (b) an increase of an internal locus of control and decrease of an external locus of control; (c) an ability to assimilate previously threatening experience into the self-concept; (d) decreased defensiveness and reactivity, increased self-acceptance; (e) increased acceptance of others; and (f) an increased reliance on an internal locus of evaluation of experience (Quinn, 2011). Briefly, research has consistently found a positive relationship between higher levels of the therapist facilitative mechanisms, higher levels of the client process mechanisms, and improved client outcome (Kiesler, 1971; van der Veen, 1967). However, the findings from studies investigating the relationship between change in process levels during therapy and subsequent outcome have been equivocal, due in part to nonlinear trends found during the process of therapy (D. S. Cartwright, 1955). In other words, assumptions of a linear, or straight-line, model of client process change related to outcome have led to ambiguous and inconclusive findings, due to client change measures tending to be curvilinear over time, for instance, U-shaped in form (Kiesler, 1971; see Pachankis & Goldfried, 2007, for a critique of historical linear assumptions related to process research).

Of importance, MC research has found a relationship between higher levels of therapist empathy and increased process depth with African American clients, but only when provided by racially-matched therapists in the study (W. M. Banks, 1972). In contrast, Redfering (1975) demonstrated cross-racial PCT effectiveness, but did not provide data regarding specific characteristics of the person-centered therapists or measures of the mechanisms of change. Therefore, the question remains: how can PCT be adapted to achieve effectiveness when provided to culturally diverse client populations by nonracially matched therapists, in particular?

Culturally competent adaptations to person-centered therapy

Two cultural adaptations to the facilitative mechanisms of change are hypothesized: (a) therapist congruence with the client's (or family's) illness myth (Benish et al., 2011) and (b) therapist empathic understanding of the client's emerging perceptions of, and attitudes toward, the therapist. In other words, the former adaptation focuses on entering the client's world, whereas the latter adaptation focuses on understanding the client's perception of the therapist. These adaptations, when met, are hypothesized to account for the suggested MC deficiencies in PCT (MacDougall, 2002; Usher, 1989) and are also hypothesized to result in a sufficient MC PCT treatment approach. Although specific in-session therapy phenomena (e.g., anger, "projective identification," self-harming, homework, etc.) are not addressed at length because of space considerations, therapist response patterns have previously been discussed (see Bozarth, 1984; Brodley, 2006a; Merry & Brodley, 2002; Quinn, 2011).

Adaptation (a). The therapist must accurately understand the client's illness myth, that is, his or her perception of and solution to

205

the particular reason for treatment (i.e., by modern Western standards, the dominant culture's illness myth is called a disorder, such as depression or anxiety, and can be treated, for example, by controlling one's automatic thoughts [J. S. Beck, 1995] as well as taking psychotropic medications). Furthermore, the therapist develops this understanding through the use of Sue's (D. W. Sue et al., 1992) MC knowledge and awareness guidelines and, in tandem, by developing an individualized understanding of the client by accurately listening to and communicating with the client. Specifically, in order for therapist listening and communicating to result in accurate understanding, a therapist's internal frame of reference, or awareness, must become increasingly congruent with the events taking place in the external environment (e.g., client verbal and nonverbal communication), resulting in accurate knowledge of the client's moment-to-moment experience (Quinn, 2008). By frequently checking or testing his or her perceived and subceived understanding of the client's experience, the therapist's knowledge of the client will accumulate, resulting in a steady increase of accurate conceptualizations of the client's cultural worldview. This recursive process of understanding, in the context of Sue's recommendations, will become the medium through which the therapist perceives the client's illness myth and, gradually, as a result of this nonjudgmental intention to create a client-therapist cognitive match (Zane et al., 2005) the therapist will communicate unconditional positive regard to the client. As a result, it is hypothesized that this genuine positive regard and unconditional communication of acceptance and understanding of the client, or family, will become increasingly integrated into the client's self-concept, or each family member's "self-in-group" concept, resulting in a tendency toward unconditional positive self-regard: "it is the therapist's genuine congruence in the relationship that authenticates this positive regard as real and something the client is able to own and believe in" (Quinn, 2011, p. 485).

Adaptation (b). The focus of Adaptation (b) rests within Rogers's sixth condition, which states that both therapist communication of (Rogers, 1957) and client perception of (Rogers, 1959) the facilitative mechanisms must be minimally achieved - hypothesized here to be the "bridge" between the facilitative and process mechanisms of successful culturally adapted PCT. The therapist's consistent intention to accurately understand the client's perceptions of the therapist, with increasing precision, is this adaptation's purpose; though taking care to realize that the therapist, whether he or she be Carl Rogers, Barbara Brodley, or a graduate student, may initially appear quite fake and incongruent through the eyes of the client or family. Adaption (b), then, could be thought of as the "here-and-now" aspect of the therapeutic encounter that addresses and resolves barriers between the therapist and client as the therapist continues to develop further precision in understanding the client's worldview informed by Adaptation (a).

Hypothetically, a racial/ethnic minority client may experience difficulties in trusting that a PCT therapist's genuine and prizing way of being is real and not a façade through which the therapist will attempt to gain leverage or control of the client's behaviors. Moreover, research suggests that some clients who are less acculturated to Western living may perceive the therapeutic relationship differently than their more acculturated counterparts (Wang & Kim, 2010). Therefore, when therapy begins, a minority client may not believe or trust that a White therapist, in particular, genuinely holds the client's best interests in mind. That is, the client's perception of the therapist may not match the therapist's more benign self-perception, as MC competence research has shown. When possessing a genuine intention, if the PCT therapist recognizes client distrust or suspicion, he or she does not switch to a more analyzing, advice-giving, or coaching therapeutic stance which, at minimum, may result in avoidance of important issues in the client's life (e.g., developing hope, reuniting with family, building community supports by attending church or other social functions, setting limits with others, pursuing higher education, etc.) and, at worse, promote racial microaggressions to emerge (Constantine, 2007). Rather, the therapist is asked to accept the ambivalence and "stay in the muck" by remaining within the client's frame of reference, tentatively addressing the therapist's feeling with the client, and allowing the client to move the moment forward.

To reiterate, as MC research suggests the therapist's self-perception means little in terms of the client's perceptions of the therapist. Thus, for the facilitative mechanisms to be sufficient, the therapist must engage in a reciprocal return to the core question regarding how the client is perceiving the therapist at all emerging points in time. Constantine's (2007) findings clearly support this position. The author found that client perceptions of therapist general and MC competence, as well as the working alliance, failed to mediate the negative relationship between perceived therapist racial microaggressions and satisfaction with therapy. Furthermore, since an intention to provide sufficiently high levels of the facilitative mechanisms are hypothesized to facilitate a change process in PCT, and if, according to Truax (Truax & Carkhuff, 1965; Truax & Mitchell, 1971), high levels of the facilitative mechanisms likely mediate therapist-induced client deterioration (presumably, therapist racial microaggressions as well), a therapist's primary intention must be to provide these facilitative mechanisms continually, thereby providing maximal levels of these attitudes, in the client's presence across the course of treatment. In other words, a consistent and genuine intention to provide these mechanisms will likely preclude actions such as agenda setting, Socratic questioning, or homework assigning (see Brodley, 2006a, on PCT homework). If these directive actions are taken, the PCT therapist will likely fail to monitor his or her emerging behaviors, as well as the client's reactions to the therapist's behaviors, which will likely increase the prevalence of client-perceived racial microaggressions. Therefore, to be therapeutically effective, a PCT therapist must consistently adhere to the facilitative mechanisms, as opposed to a therapist using a different treatment approach, such as cognitive therapy, which may require more directive therapist responses:

> let me interrupt you for a moment. It's important to me to understand the big picture of your week and to get the details later in the session. For right now, could you just tell me about your week in two or three or four sentences? . . . It sounds to me like you're saying, "I had a pretty hard week. I had a fight with a friend, and I was really anxious about going out, and I had trouble concentrating on my work." That's the big picture I was talking about that helps me get a sense of what's really important to put on the agenda and find out more about later. (J. S. Beck, 1995, pp. 64-65)

Furthermore, Adaptation (b) does not suggest that the therapist should somehow convince the client to trust him. Rather, the focus for the therapist to be continually open to the potential for client feelings of distrust, whether or not verbalized, may be illustrated by the following:

> well, I guess I'd like to say that, "I'm here to be of help" . . . I'd like to hear about your life, but I also suspect that it would be hard to say things to me . . . because, who am I to act like I know who you are and what you've been through . . . I guess I usually think I'm pretty trustworthy, but it's up for you to decide, really . . . but I'd like to hear about what's on your mind . . . Or, if you'd

like we could go for a walk for our time together, and see how that is - if you'd like to, I'd like to do that too.

To briefly clarify: this is not to say that, when meeting with a family, a therapist will take a walk with a whole family, though possibly this could occur; or, similar to other approaches, the therapist might meet the client or family at home occasionally; or the individual client will wish to walk and talk sometimes, and talk in the office at other times. This is to illustrate the intention of the therapist to accept that the client may not like or trust the therapist (particularly during initial sessions), but will not usually verbalize this. Thus, the therapist must continue to provide high levels of the facilitative mechanisms, "roll with resistance," and wait for the client to gradually perceive the mechanisms as being real and not a facade.

In providing this hypothesized facilitative climate that allows the client to gradually feel trusting toward the therapist, the therapist may feel as though little if any "progress" is happening. Again, the PCT therapist does not switch therapy orientations. Rather, he or she trusts in the process that results from providing these facilitative mechanisms consistently, genuinely, and with an unconditional intention. Furthermore, given higher attrition rates found in MC treatment settings (Cardemil et al., 2011), if the client continues to return to therapy each week therapy is likely progressing in a positive direction, though it may not always seem so to the therapist.

Consequently, the therapist will know that a minimally sufficient client trust has been reached when a new and meaningful "familiarity" in his or her relationship with the client emerges; sometimes merely from the client consistently attending therapy over time, or sometimes from a specific event or experience while together. For example, Dave Mearns's concept of "meeting at relational depth," which also happens gradually, may be equivalent (Mearns & Cooper, 2005). Similarly, MC consultants frequently refer to this familiarity as "breaking bread" with the client or family; though this concept arguably leads to a technique and, consequently, an item on a therapist's checklist: "ok . . . breaking bread, check . . . now let us proceed with the therapy." In contrast to the latter concept, a culturally adapted PCT approach anticipates that the process of facilitating this familiarity or trust happens gradually, in a variety of ways which, research suggests, is due to the unique characteristics inherent in each client-therapist dyad (Moos & MacIntosh, 1970, Owen, Leach, et al., 2011; Truax et al., 1966).

Once this familiarity is achieved, the process mechanisms of change are hypothesized to proceed, though the therapist does not go on autopilot. The therapist's manner or way of being with the client - which resulted in their relationship reaching this point of familiarity - is assumed to continue because, according to research evidence, therapist-provided facilitative mechanisms tend to be predictably stable across time, after a slight instability during the early sessions (Gurman, 1973a; Rogers et al., 1967; Truax et al., 1966). However, the client or family may ebb and flow in their levels of trust toward and familiarity with the therapist, which substantiates the ongoing need for the therapist to adhere to the facilitative mechanisms, thereby consistently attending to the client's emerging perceptions as therapy progresses.

A concluding transcript (Rogers, 1977) demonstrates this nonjudgmental adherence to the client's perspective. Rogers exemplifies the use of Adaptation (b) in reciprocally facilitating a climate of unconditional acceptance of the client's anger, which, arguably, resulted from incongruence between the client's illness myth and that of society's:

> Client: You know, [. . .] what has happened to me didn't just start when I found out that I, you know, was going to die.

> (T: Mmm.) Kind of thing.

> Therapist: Let me see if I understand that. That you feel as though, um, what the culture and people and so on have . . . have done to you . . . that's really caused you more suffering than the leukemia. Is that what you're saying?

> Client: I think so [. . .] I don't know what would have happened if I had died or if I will or whatever, but I certainly know what's happening now and what happened [. . .]

> Client: And to some extent that . . . that kind of leukemia, that kind of deterioration of the body is the same kind of thing that happened to my mind [. . .]

213

Therapist: So really, what the culture did to you was give you a cancer of the mind.

Client: Yeah [. . .] I really . . . I think, I really want to say that my culture [. . .] is saying that it's not all that good to be angry, you know, because [. . .] traditionally, you know, when blacks become angry they're, they're not angry . . . they're militant. (T: Mmm.) You know what I mean (slight laughter)?

Therapist: I know. Another label [. . .] I get what you're saying and I also feel quite strongly that I want to say, "it's OK with me if you're angry here" . . .

Client: (Pause) . . . But I don't, you know . . . it's hard to know how to be angry, you know . . . hard to . . .

Therapist: Sure, sure, I'm not saying you have to be. (C: Sure). I'm just saying it's OK with me. [. . .] If you feel like being angry, you can be angry.

Client: You really believe that?

Therapist: Damn right.

Client: (12 second pause.) Well. (15 second pause.) (Sigh.) I'm not sure how to respond to that at all, you know, because a part of that anger is, you know, the . . . the hurt, and maybe if I'm . . . maybe what's happening is that if I'm . . . if I become angry and

I really let it hang out, that I really will see how hurt I am [. . .]

Therapist: Perhaps at a deeper level you're afraid of the hurt that you may experience if you let yourself experience the anger.[. . .]

Client: [agreeing] (Small laugh. Pause.) Um, whew . . . (Pause.) I keep getting these blocks, you know . . . these, you know . . . when I come to something like that, you know, because, you know, to me that's a revelation and I'm not really sure that, uh, risking being angry I guess . . . (T: Mmm.) or something like that, you know

[. . .]

Therapist: I really do get that . . . that this . . . this realization that, "Maybe what I'm most afraid of is the hurt that I might experience," um, makes you more cautious about whether you should, whether you should or could really let go of the . . . of the anger (Rogers, 1977, pp. 86-89).

Conclusion

If a therapist can be a person that possesses a genuine and accepting way of being, then he or she will likely move toward providing these person-centered, culturally adapted facilitative mechanisms of change for the client or family. If the MC client or family perceives these mechanisms to be a genuine aspect of the therapist's way of being, then trust and familiarity will likely occur, resulting in a process of change to occur, which is hypothesized to resemble the process mechanisms. Though these mechanisms are not a magic bullet, they are sufficient for this process of change to occur both during and beyond therapy. The client or family may return to therapy someday, or these therapy experiences may have been sufficient to continue a process of "becoming" for the rest of their lives. Ultimately, in the process of becoming one's own person, or in becoming "their own family," so to speak, the client may choose the family, and the family may choose its members, but this valuing process lies beyond the scope of the therapist's personal and clinical judgments. Rather, this process emerges from within the client.

References

Abrams, L. S., & Moio, J. A. (2009). Critical race theory and the cultural competence dilemma in social work education. *Journal of Social Work Education, 45*, 245-261.

American Psychological Association. (2002). *Guidelines on multicultural education, training, research, practice, and organizational change for psychologists.* Retrieved from http://www.apa.org/pi/oema/resources/policy/multicultural-guideline.pdf

American Psychological Association. (2006). Evidence-based practice in psychology. *American Psychologist, 61*, 271-285.

Arredondo, P., & Toporek, R. (2004). Multicultural counseling competencies equals ethical practice. *Journal of Mental Health Counseling, 26*(1), 44-55.

Arredondo, P., Toporek, R., Brown, S. P., Jones, J., Locke, D. C., Sanchez, J., & Stadler, H. (1996). Operationalization of the multicultural counseling competencies. *Journal of Multicultural Counseling and Development, 24*(1), 42-78.

Banks, G., Berenson, B. G., & Carkhuff, R. R. (1967). The effects of counselor race and training upon counseling process with Negro clients in initial interviews. *Journal of Clinical Psychology, 23*, 70-72.

Banks, W. M. (1972). The differential effects of race and social class in helping. *Journal of Clinical Psychology, 28*, 90-92.

Bargdill, R. (2011). The youth movement in humanistic psychology. *Humanistic Psychologist, 39*, 283-287.

Barlow, D. H. (2010). Negative effects from psychological treatments: A perspective. *American Psychologist, 65*, 13-20.

Barrett-Lennard, G. T. (1981). The empathy cycle: Refinement of a nuclear concept. *Journal of Counseling Psychology, 28*, 91-100.

Beck, J. S. (1995). *Cognitive therapy: Basics and beyond.* New York, NY: Guilford Press.

Benish, S. G., Quintana, S., & Wampold, B. E. (2011). Culturally adapted psychotherapy and the legitimacy of myth: A direct-comparison meta-analysis. *Journal of Counseling Psychology, 58*, 279-289.

Bergin, A. E. (1966). Some implications of psychotherapy research for therapeutic practice. *Journal of Abnormal Psychology, 71*, 235-246.

Bergin, A. E. (1971). The evaluation of therapeutic outcomes. In A. E. Bergin & S. L. Garfield (Eds.), *Handbook of psychotherapy and behavior change: An empirical analysis* (pp. 217-270). New York, NY: Wiley.

Bergin, A. E., & Jasper, L. G. (1969). Correlates of empathy in psychotherapy: A replication. *Journal of Abnormal Psychology, 74,* 477-481.

Bergin, A. E., & Garfield, S. L. (Eds.). (1994). *Handbook of psychotherapy and behavior change: An empirical analysis.* New York, NY: Wiley.

Bergin, A. E., & Strupp, H. H. (1970). The directions in psychotherapy research. *Journal of Abnormal Psychology, 76,* 13-26.

Bergin, A. E., & Suinn, R. M. (1975). Individual psychotherapy and behavior therapy. *Annual Review of Psychology, 26,* 509-556.

Berk, M., & Parker, G. (2009). The elephant on the couch: Side-effects of psychotherapy. *Australian and New Zealand Journal of Psychiatry, 43,* 787-794.

Beutler, L. E. (1976). More sources of variance in accurate empathy ratings: A response. *Journal of Consulting and Clinical Psychology, 44,* 860-861.

Beutler, L. E., Johnson, D. T., Neville, C. W., & Workman, S. N. (1973). Some sources of variance in "accurate empathy" ratings. *Journal of Consulting and Clinical Psychology, 40,* 167-169.

Beutler, L. E., Johnson, D. T., Neville, C. W., Workman, S. N., &

Elkins, D. (1973). The A-B therapy-type distinction, accurate empathy, nonpossessive warmth, and therapist genuineness in psychotherapy. *Journal of Abnormal Psychology, 82*, 273-277.

Bonilla-Silva, E., & Ray, V. (2009). When Whites love a Black leader: Race matters in Obamerica. *Journal of African American Studies, 13*, 176-183.

Bordin, E. S. (1979). The generalizability of the psychoanalytic concept of the working alliance. *Psychotherapy: Theory, Research & Practice, 16*, 252-260.

Bozarth, J. D. (1984). Beyond reflection: Emergent modes of empathy. In R. F. Levant & J. M. Shlien (Eds.), *Client-centered therapy and the person-centered approach: New directions in theory, research and practice* (pp. 59-75). Boston, MA: Praeger.

Bozarth J. D., & Krauft C. C. (1972). Accurate empathy ratings: Some methodological considerations. *Journal of Clinical Psychology, 28*, 408-210.

Brodley, B. T. (2006a). Client-initiated homework in client-centered therapy. *Journal of Psychotherapy Integration, 16*, 140-161.

Brodley, B. T. (2006b). Non-directivity in client-centered therapy. *Person-Centered & Experiential Psychotherapies, 5*(1), 36-52.

Burkard, A. W., & Knox, S. (2004). Effect of therapist color-blindness on empathy and attributions in cross-cultural counseling. *Journal of Counseling Psychology,51*, 387-397.

Butler, J. M., & Haigh, G. V. (1954). Changes in the relation between self-concepts and ideal concepts consequent upon client-centered counseling. In C. R. Rogers & R. F. Dymond (Eds.), *Psychotherapy and personality change: Coordinated research studies in the client-centered approach* (pp. 55-75). Chicago, IL: University of Chicago Press.

Cardemil, E. V., Moreno, O., & Sanchez, M. (2011). One size does not fit all: Cultural considerations in evidence-based practice for depression. In D. W. Springer, A. Rubin, & C. G. Beevers (Eds.), *Treatment of depression in adolescents and adults* (pp. 221-243). Hoboken, NJ: John Wiley.

Carkhuff, R. R., & Banks, G. (1970). Training as a preferred mode of facilitating relations between races and generations. *Journal of Counseling Psychology, 17*, 413-418.

Carkhuff, R. R., & Pierce, R. (1967). Differential effects of therapist race and social class upon patient depth of self-exploration in the initial clinical interview. *Journal of Consulting Psychology, 31*, 632-634.

Cartwright, D. S. (1955). Success in psychotherapy as a function of certain actuarial variables. *Journal of Consulting Psychology, 19*, 357-363.

Cartwright, D. S. (1957). Annotated bibliography of research and theory construction in client-centered therapy. *Journal of Counseling Psychology, 4*, 82-100.

Cartwright, R. D., & Lerner, B. (1963). Empathy, need to change and improvement with psychotherapy. *Journal of Consulting Psychology, 27*, 138-144.

Chambless, D. L., Baker, M., Baucom, D. H., Beutler, L., Calhoun, P., Crits-Christoph, P., . . . Woody, S. R. (1998). Update on empirically validated therapies II. *Clinical Psychologist, 51*, 3-16.

Chao, R. C. L., Wei, M., Good, G. E., & Flores, L. Y. (2011). Race/ethnicity, color-blind racial attitudes, and multicultural counseling competence: The moderating effects of multicultural counseling training. *Journal of Counseling Psychology, 58*, 72-82.

Chinsky, J. M., & Rappaport, J. (1970). Brief critique of the meaning and reliability of "accurate empathy" ratings. *Psychological Bulletin, 73*, 379-382.

Constantine, M. G. (2000). Social desirability attitudes, sex, and affective and cognitive empathy as predictors of self-reported multicultural counseling competence. *Counseling Psychologist, 28*, 857-872.

Constantine, M. G. (2001a). Multicultural training, theoretical orientation, empathy, and multicultural case conceptualization ability in counselors. *Journal of Mental Health Counseling, 23*, 357-372.

Constantine, M. G. (2001b). Predictors of observer ratings of multicultural counseling competence in Black, Latino, and White American trainees. *Journal of Counseling Psychology, 48*, 456-462.

Constantine, M. G. (2002). Predictors of satisfaction with counseling: Racial and ethnic minority clients' attitudes toward counseling and ratings of their counselors' general and multicultural counseling competence. *Journal of Counseling Psychology, 49*, 255-263.

Constantine, M. G. (2007). Racial microaggressions against African American clients in cross-racial counseling relationships. *Journal of Counseling Psychology, 54*, 1-16.

Constantine, M. G., & Ladany, N. (2000). Self-report multicultural counseling competence scales: Their relation to social desirability attitudes and multicultural case conceptualization ability. *Journal of Counseling Psychology, 47*, 155-164.

Constantine, M. G., Juby, H. L., & Liang, J. J. C. (2001). Examining multicultural counseling competence and race-related attitudes among White marital and family therapists. *Journal of Marital and Family Therapy, 27*, 353-362.

Cook, J. M., Biyanova, T., & Coyne, J. C. (2009). Influential psychotherapy figures, authors, and books: An Internet survey of over 2,000 psychotherapists. *Psychotherapy: Theory, Research, Practice, Training, 46*(1), 42-51.

Cottraux, J., Note, I. D., Boutitie, F., Milliery, M., Genouihlac, V., Yao, S. N., . . .Gueyffier, F. (2009). Cognitive therapy versus Rogerian supportive therapy in borderline personality disorder: Two-year follow-up of a controlled pilot study. *Psychotherapy and*

Psychosomatics, 78, 307-316.

Cottraux, J., Note, I., Yao, S. N., de Mey-Guillard, C., Bonasse, F., Djamoussian, D., . . . Chen, Y. (2008). Randomized controlled comparison of cognitive behavior therapy with Rogerian supportive therapy in chronic post-traumatic stress disorder: A 2-year follow-up. *Psychotherapy and Psychosomatics, 77*, 101-110.

Crockett, K., Zlotnick, C., Davis, M., Payne, N., & Washington, R. (2008). A depression preventive intervention for rural low-income African-American pregnant women at risk for postpartum depression. *Archives of Women's Mental Health, 11*, 319-325.

D'Andrea, M., & Heckman, E. F. (2008). A 40-year review of multicultural counseling outcome research: Outlining a future research agenda for the multicultural counseling movement. *Journal of Counseling & Development, 86*, 356-363.

Di Loreto, A. O. (1971). *Comparative psychotherapy*. Chicago, IL: Aldine-Atherton.

Din, M. O., Noor, N. M., & Kahn, R. K. A. W. (2008). An experimental study on psychotherapy for women with major depression. *International Journal of Behavioral Science, 3*(1), 1-15. Retrieved from http://bsris.swu.ac.th/journal/i3/inter31.pdf

Elliott, R., Bohart, A. C., Watson, J. C., & Greenberg, L. S. (2011). Empathy. *Psychotherapy, 48*(1), 43-49.

Elliott, R. K., Greenberg, L. S., & Lietaer, G. (2004). Research on experiential psychotherapies. In M. J. Lambert (Ed.), *Bergin and Garfield's handbook of psychotherapy and behavior change* (pp. 493-539). New York: Wiley.

Feaster, D. J., Brincks, A. M., Mitrani, V. B., Prado, G., Schwartz, S. J., & Szapocznik, J. (2010). The efficacy of structural ecosystems therapy for HIV medication adherence with African American women. *Journal of Family Psychology, 24*(1), 51-59.

Feaster, D. J., Burns, M. J., Brincks, A. M., Prado, G., Mitrani, V. B., Mauer, M. H., & Szapocznik, J. (2010). Structural ecosystems therapy for HIV+ African-American women and drug abuse relapse. *Family Process, 49*, 204-219.

Foster, R. M. P. (2007). Treating depression in vulnerable urban women: A feasibility study of clinical outcomes in community service settings. *American Journal of Orthopsychiatry, 77*, 443-453.

Freire, E. S. (2006). Randomized controlled clinical trial in psychotherapy research: An epistemological controversy. *Journal of Humanistic Psychology, 46*, 323-335.

Freire, E. S., Koller, S. H., Piason, A., & da Silva, R. B. (2005). Person-centered therapy with impoverished, maltreated, and neglected children and adolescents in Brazil. *Journal of Mental Health Counseling, 27*, 225-237.

Friedlander, M. L., Ellis, M. V., Siegel, S. M., Raymond, L., Haase, R. F., & Highlen, P. S. (1988). Generalizing from segments to sessions: Should it be done? *Journal of Counseling Psychology, 35*,

243-250.

Fuertes, J. N., & Brobst, K. (2002). Clients' ratings of counselor multicultural competency. *Cultural Diversity and Ethnic Minority Psychology, 8*, 214-223.

Fuertes, J. N., Stracuzzi, T. I., Bennett, J., Scheinholtz, J., Mislowack, A., Hersh, M., & Cheng, D. (2006). Therapist multicultural competency: A study of therapy dyads. *Psychotherapy: Theory, Research, Practice, Training, 43*, 480-490.

Gabbard, G. O. (2004). *Long-term psychodynamic psychotherapy: A basic text.* Arlington, VA: American Psychiatric Publishing.

Garfield, S. L., & Bergin, A. E. (1971). Therapeutic conditions and outcome. *Journal of Abnormal Psychology, 77*, 108-114.

Gelso, C. J. (2007). Editorial. *Psychotherapy: Theory, Research, Practice, Training, 44*, 239.

Gharehbaghy, F. (2011). An investigation into Bowen family systems theory in an Iranian sample. *Iranian Journal of Psychiatry and Behavioral Sciences, 5*(1) 56-63. Retrieved from http://www.mazums.ac.ir/dorsapax/Data/Sub_15/File/etoolsfile1gharehbaghi_2.pdf

Gibbons, C. J., Fournier, J. C., Stirman, S. W., DeRubeis, R. J., Crits-Christoph, P., & Beck, A. T. (2010). The clinical effectiveness of cognitive therapy for depression in an outpatient clinic. *Journal of Affective Disorders, 125*, 169-176.

Goldman, R. N., Greenberg, L. S., & Angus, L. (2006). The effects of adding emotion-focused interventions to the client-centered relationship conditions in the treatment of depression. *Psychotherapy Research, 16*, 536-546.

Greenberg, L. S., & Watson, J. (1998). Experiential therapy of depression: Differential effects of client-centered relationship conditions and process experiential interventions. *Psychotherapy Research, 8*, 210-224.

Greening, T. (2007). Five basic postulates of humanistic psychology. *Journal of Humanistic Psychology, 47*(1).

Grote, N. K., Swartz, H. A., Geibel, S. L., Zuckoff, A., Houck, P. R., & Frank, E. (2009). A randomized controlled trial of culturally relevant, brief interpersonal psychotherapy for perinatal depression. *Psychiatric Services, 60*, 313-321.

Gurman, A. S. (1973a). Effects of therapist and patient mood on the therapeutic functioning of high- and low-facilitative therapists. *Journal of Consulting and Clinical Psychology, 40*, 48-58.

Gurman, A. S. (1973b). Instability of therapeutic conditions in psychotherapy. *Journal of Counseling Psychology, 20*, 16-24.

Gurman, A. S. (1977). The patient's perception of the therapeutic relationship. In A. S. Gurman & A. M. Razin (Eds.), *Effective psychotherapy: A handbook of research.* (pp. 503-543). Oxford, England: Pergamon Press.

Gushue, G. V., & Constantine, M. G. (2007). Color-blind racial attitudes and white racial identity attitudes in psychology trainees. *Professional Psychology: Research and Practice, 38*, 321-328.

Halkides, G. (1958). *An experimental study of four conditions necessary for therapeutic change* (Unpublished doctoral dissertation). University of Chicago, Chicago, IL.

Heine, R. W. (1950). The Negro patient in psychotherapy. *Journal of Clinical Psychology, 6*, 373-376.

Hinton, D. E., Hofmann, S. G., Rivera, E., Otto, M. W., & Pollack, M. H. (2011). Culturally adapted CBT (CA-CBT) for Latino women with treatment-resistant PTSD: A pilot study comparing CA-CBT to applied muscle relaxation. *Behaviour Research and Therapy, 49*, 275-280.

Hoffman, L. (2009). Introduction to existential psychotherapy in a cross-cultural context: An East-West dialogue. In L. Hoffman, M. Yang, F. J. Kaklauskas, & A. Chan (Eds.), *Existential psychology East-West* (pp. 1-67). Colorado Springs, CO: University of the Rockies Press.

Hoffman, L. (Ed.). (2011). First international conference on existential psychology [Special issue]. *Humanistic Psychologist, 39*(3).

Kazdin, A. E. (2009). Understanding how and why psychotherapy leads to change. *Psychotherapy Research, 19*, 418-428.

Kernberg, O. F. (1973). Summary and conclusions of "Psychotherapy and psychoanalysis: Final report of the Menninger Foundation's psychotherapy research project." *International Journal of Psychiatry, 11*(1), 62-77.

Kiesler, D. J. (1971). Patient experiencing and successful outcome in individual psychotherapy of schizophrenics and psychoneurotics. *Journal of Consulting and Clinical Psychology, 37*, 370-385.

Kirschenbaum, H. (1979). *On becoming Carl Rogers*. New York, NY: Delacorte Press.

Krause, M. S., & Lutz, W. (2009). Process transforms inputs to determine outcomes: Therapists are responsible for managing process. *Clinical Psychology: Science and Practice, 16*(1), 73-81.

Krupnick, J. L., Green, B. L., Stockton, P., Miranda, J., Krause, E., & Mete, M. (2008). Group interpersonal psychotherapy for low-income women with posttraumatic stress disorder. *Psychotherapy Research, 18*, 497-507.

Lambert, M. J., Bergin, A. E., & Collins, J. L. (1977). Therapist-induced deterioration in psychotherapy. In A. S. Gurman & A. M. Razin (Eds.), *Effective psychotherapy: A handbook of research* (pp. 452-481). New York, NY: Pergamon Press.

Le, H. N., Perry, D. F., & Stuart, E. A. (2011). Randomized controlled trial of a preventive intervention for perinatal depression in high-risk Latinas. *Journal of Consulting and Clinical Psychology, 79*, 135-141.

Lerner, B. (1972). *Therapy in the Ghetto*. Baltimore, MD: Johns

Hopkins University Press.

Lerner, B. (1973). Democratic values and therapeutic efficacy: A construct validity study. *Journal of Abnormal Psychology, 82*, 491-498.

Lerner, B. (1974). Liked review. *PsycCRITIQUES, 19*, 248-249. doi:10.1037/0012578

Lerner, B., & Fiske, D. W. (1973). Client attributes and the eye of the beholder. *Journal of Consulting and Clinical Psychology, 40*, 272-277.

Levant, R. F. (1978). Family therapy: A client-centered perspective. *Journal of Marriage and Family Counseling, 4*(2), 35-42.

Linehan, M. M. (1993). *Cognitive-behavioral treatment of borderline personality disorder*. New York, NY: Guilford Press.

Lorion, R. P. (1978). Research on psychotherapy and behavior change with the disadvantaged: Past, present, and future directions. In S. L. Garfield & A. E. Bergin (Eds.), *Handbook of psychotherapy and behavior change: An empirical analysis* (pp. 903-938). New York, NY: Wiley.

Luborsky, L., & Spence, D. P. (1978). Quantitative research on psychoanalytic therapy. In S. L. Garfield & A. E. Bergin (Eds.), *Handbook of psychotherapy and behavior change: An empirical analysis* (pp. 331-368). New York, NY: Wiley.

MacDougall, C. (2002). Rogers's person-centered approach: Consideration for use in multicultural counseling. *Journal of*

Humanistic Psychology, 42, 48-65.

Manderscheid, R. W., & Berry, J. T. (Eds.). (2006). *Mental health, United States, 2004* (DHHS Publ. No. 06-4195). Rockville, MD: Substance Abuse and Mental Health Services Administration, Center for Mental Health Services. Retrieved from http://store.samhsa.gov/shin/content/SMA06-4195/SMA06-4195.pdf

Marks, I. M. (1978). Behavioural psychotherapy of adult neurosis. In S. L. Garfield & A. E. Bergin (Eds.), *Handbook of psychotherapy and behavior change: An empirical analysis* (pp. 493-589). New York, NY: Wiley.

McLeod, B. D. (2009). Understanding why therapy allegiance is linked to clinical outcomes. *Clinical Psychology: Science and Practice, 16*(1), 69-72.

Mearns, D., & Cooper, M. (2005). *Working at relational depth in counselling and psychotherapy.* London, England: Sage.

Merry, T., & Brodley, B. T. (2002). The nondirective attitude in client-centered therapy: A response to Kahn. *Journal of Humanistic Psychology, 42,* 66-77.

Miller, W. R., & Rose, G. S. (2009). Toward a theory of motivational interviewing. *American Psychologist, 64,* 527-537.

Mintz, J., & Luborsky, L. (1971). Segments versus whole sessions: Which is the better unit for psychotherapy process research? *Journal of Abnormal Psychology, 78,* 180-191.

Mintz, J., Luborsky, L., & Auerbach, A. H. (1971). Dimensions of psychotherapy: A factor-analytic study of ratings of psychotherapy sessions. *Journal of Consulting and Clinical Psychology, 36,* 106-120.

Miranda, J., Azocar, F., Organista, K. C., Dwyer, E., & Areane, P. (2003). Treatment of depression among impoverished primary care patients from ethnic minority groups. *Psychiatric Services, 54,* 219-225.

Miranda, J., Bernal, G., Lau, A., Kohn, L., Hwang, W. C., & LaFromboise, T. (2005). State of the science on psychosocial interventions for ethnic minorities. *Annual Review of Clinical Psychology, 1*(1), 113-142.

Miranda, J., Chung, J. Y., Green, B. L., Krupnick, J., Siddique, J., Revicki, D. A., & Belin, T. (2003). Treating depression in predominantly low-income young minority women: A randomized controlled trial. *Journal of the American Medical Association, 290,* 57-65.

Mitchell, K., Bozarth, J., & Krauft, C. (1977). Reappraisal of the therapeutic effectiveness of accurate empathy, nonpossessive warmth, and genuineness. In A. S. Gurman & A. M. Razin (Eds.), *Effective psychotherapy: A handbook of research* (pp. 482-502). Oxford, England: Pergamon Press.

Miville, M. L., Carlozzi, A. F., Gushue, G. V., Schara, S. L., & Ueda, M. (2006). Mental health counselor qualities for a diverse clientele: Linking empathy, universal-diverse orientation, and emotional intelligence. *Journal of Mental Health Counseling, 28,* 151-165.

Mohamad, M., Mokhtar, H. H., & Samah, A. A. (2011). Person-centered counseling with Malay clients: Spirituality as an indicator of personal growth. *Procedia - Social and Behavioral Sciences, 30,* 2117-2123.

Moos, R. H. (2005). Iatrogenic effects of psychosocial interventions for substance use disorders: Prevalence, predictors, prevention. *Addiction, 100,* 595-604.

Moos, R. H., & MacIntosh, S. (1970). Multivariate study of the patient-therapist system: A replication and extension. *Journal of Consulting and Clinical Psychology, 35,* 298-307.

Muhktar, F., & Oei, T. (2010). Exploratory and confirmatory factor validation and psychometric properties of the Beck Depression Inventory for Malays (BDI-Malay) in Malaysia. *Malaysian Journal of Psychiatry.* Advance online publication. Retrieved from http://mjpsychiatry.com/index.php/mjp/article/view/27 /27.

Muñoz, R. F., Ying, Y. W., Bernal, G., Pérez-Stable, E. J., Sorensen, J. L., Hargreaves, W. A., . . . Miller, L. S. (1995). Prevention of depression with primary care patients: A randomized controlled trial. *American Journal of Community Psychology, 23,* 199-222.

National Association of Social Workers. (2007). *Indicators for the achievement of the NASW standards for cultural competence in social work practice.* Retrieved from http://www.socialworkers.org/practice/standards/naswculturalstandardsindicators2006.pdf

Olfman, S., & Robbins, B. D. (Eds.). (2012). *Drugging our children.* Santa Barbara, CA: Praeger.

Owen, J., Leach, M. M., Wampold, B., & Rodolfa, E. (2011). Client and therapist variability in clients' perceptions of their therapists' multicultural competencies. *Journal of Counseling Psychology, 58,* 1-9.

Owen, J. J., Tao, K., Leach, M. M., & Rodolfa, E. (2011). Clients' perceptions of their psychotherapists' multicultural orientation. *Psychotherapy, 48,* 274-282.

Pachankis, J. E., & Goldfried, M. R. (2007). On the next generation of process research. *Clinical Psychology Review, 27,* 760-768.

Parloff, M. B., Waskow, I. E., & Wolfe, B. F. (1978). Research on therapist variables in relation to process and outcome. In S. L. Garfield & A. E. Bergin (Eds.), *Handbook of psychotherapy and behavior change: An empirical analysis* (pp. 233-282). New York, NY: Wiley.

Patterson, C. H. (1984). Empathy, warmth, and genuineness in psychotherapy: A review of reviews. *Psychotherapy: Theory, Research, Practice, Training, 21,* 431-438.

Patterson, C. H. (1996). Multicultural counseling: From diversity to universality. *Journal of Counseling & Development, 74*, 227-231.

Patterson, C. H. (2004). Do we need multicultural counseling competencies? *Journal of Mental Health Counseling, 26*(1), 67-73.

Paul, G. L. (1967). Strategy of outcome research in psychotherapy. *Journal of Consulting Psychology, 31*, 109-118.

Pedersen, P. (2009). Inclusive cultural empathy: A relationship-centred alternative to individualism. *South African Journal of Psychology, 39*, 143-156.

Pedersen, P. B. (1991). Multiculturalism as a generic approach to counseling. *Journal of Counseling & Development, 70*, 6-12.

Pole, N., Gone, J. P., & Kulkarni, M. (2008). Posttraumatic stress disorder among ethnoracial minorities in the United States. *Clinical Psychology: Science and Practice, 15*(1), 35-61.

Quinn, A. (2008). A person-centered approach to the treatment of combat veterans with posttraumatic stress disorder. *Journal of Humanistic Psychology, 48*, 458-476.

Quinn, A. (2011). A person-centered approach to the treatment of borderline personality disorder. *Journal of Humanistic Psychology, 51*, 465-491.

Rappaport, J., & Chinsky, J. M. (1972). Accurate empathy: Confusion of a construct. *Psychological Bulletin, 77*, 400-404.

Redfering, D. L. (1975). Differential effects of group counseling with Black and White female delinquents: One year later. *Journal of Negro Education, 44*, 530-537.

Ridley, C. R., Mollen, D., & Kelly, S. M. (2011). Beyond microskills: Toward a model of counseling competence. *Counseling Psychologist*, 39, 825-864.

Robinson, T. L. (1999). The intersections of dominant discourses across race, gender, and other identities. *Journal of Counseling & Development, 77*, 73-79.

Rogers, C. R. (1957). The necessary and sufficient conditions of therapeutic personality change. *Journal of Consulting Psychology*, 21, 95-103.

Rogers, C. R. (1959). A theory of therapy, personality, and interpersonal relationships, as developed in the client-centered framework. In S. Koch (Ed.), *Psychology: A study of a science* (pp. 184-256). New York, NY: McGraw-Hill.

Rogers, C. R. (1975). Empathic: An unappreciated way of being. *Counseling Psychologist, 5*(2), 2-10.

Rogers, C. R. (1977). Carl Rogers counsels an individual on anger and hurt [Film Transcript]. In B.T. Brodley & G. Lietaer (Eds.). (2006), *Transcripts of Carl Rogers' Therapy Sessions, Volume 12, Dione* (pp. 68-109). Retrieved from http://pcayorks.blogspot.com

Rogers, C. R., & Dymond, R. F. (Eds.). (1954). *Psychotherapy and personality change*. Chicago, IL: University of Chicago Press.

Rogers, C. R., & Sanford, R. (1987). Reflections on our South African Experience (January-February 1986). *Counseling and Values,*

32(1), 17-20.

Rogers, C. R. (Therapist), Farson, R. E. (Therapist), & McGaw, W. (Producer). (1968). *Journey into self [Documentary]*. USA: Western Behavioral Sciences Institute. Retrieved from www.youtube.com

Rogers, C. R., Gendlin, E. T., Kiesler, D. J., & Truax, C. B. (Eds.). (1967). *The therapeutic relationship and its impact: A study of psychotherapy with schizophrenics*. Madison: University of Wisconsin Press.

Rubin, S. (2011). The future is now: Report from the HECTOR project and the fourth annual society for humanistic psychology conference. *Journal of Humanistic Psychology, 51*, 432-435.

Rush, A. J., Beck, A. T., Kovacs, M., & Hollon, S. (1977). Comparative efficacy of cognitive therapy and pharmacotherapy in the treatment of depressed outpatients. *Cognitive Therapy and Research, 1*(1), 17-37.

Schneider, K. J. (1999). The revival of the romantic means a revival of psychology. *Journal of Humanistic Psychology, 39*, 13-29.

Schneider, K. J. (2011a). Humanistic psychology's chief task: To reset psychology on its rightful existential–humanistic base. *Journal of Humanistic Psychology, 51*, 436-438.

Schneider, K. J. (2011b). The 50th anniversary of JHP: Reflections on the state of the field [Special Issue]. *Journal of Humanistic of Psychology, 51*(4).

Shlien, J. M. (1962). Toward what level of abstraction in criteria? In H. H. Strupp & L. Luborsky (Eds.), *Research in psychotherapy* (pp. 142-154). Washington, DC: American Psychological Association.

Skowron, E. A., & Friedlander, M. L. (1998). The Differentiation of Self Inventory: Development and initial validation. *Journal of Counseling Psychology, 45*, 235-246.

Skowron, E. A., Stanley, K. L., & Shapiro, M. D. (2009). A longitudinal perspective on differentiation of self, interpersonal and psychological well-being in young adulthood. *Contemporary Family Therapy: An International Journal, 31*(1), 3-18.

Sloane, R. B., Staples, F. R., Cristol, A. H., Yorkston, N. J., & Whipple, K. (1975). *Psychotherapy versus behavior therapy*. Cambridge, MA: Harvard University Press.

Smith, D. (1982). Trends in counseling and psychotherapy. *American Psychologist, 37*, 802-809.

Smith, L., Feaster, D. J., Prado, G., Kamin, M., Blaney, N., & Szapocznik, J. (2001). The psychosocial functioning of HIV+ and HIV-African American recent mothers. *AIDS and Behavior, 5*, 219-231.

Stiles, W. B. (2009). Responsiveness as an obstacle for psychotherapy outcome research: It's worse than you think. *Clinical Psychology:*

Science and Practice, 16(1), 86-91.

Strunk, D. R., Brotman, M. A., & DeRubeis, R. J. (2010). The process of change in cognitive therapy for depression: Predictors of early inter-session symptom gains. *Behaviour Research and Therapy, 48,* 599-606.

Strunk, D. R., Brotman, M. A., DeRubeis, R. J., & Hollon, S. D. (2010). Therapist competence in cognitive therapy for depression: Predicting subsequent symptom change. *Journal of Consulting and Clinical Psychology, 78,* 429-437.

Sue, D. W., Arredondo, P., & McDavis, R. J. (1992). Multicultural counseling competencies and standards: A call to the profession. *Journal of Counseling & Development, 70,* 477-486.

Sue, D. W., Bernier, J. E., Durran, A., Feinberg, L., Pedersen, P., Smith, E. J., & Vasquez-Nuttall, E. (1982). Position paper: Cross-cultural counseling competencies. *Counseling Psychologist, 10,* 45-52.

Sue, S. (1973). Therapy with Blacks and the poor: A bold attempt. [Review of the book Therapy in the Ghetto: Political impotence and personal disintegration by B. Lerner]. *PsycCRITIQUES, 18,* 529-530. doi:10.1037/0011725

Sue, S. (1977). Community mental health services to minority groups: Some optimism, some pessimism. *American Psychologist, 32,* 616-624.

Sue, S., & Zane, N. (1987). The role of culture and cultural techniques in psychotherapy: A critique and reformulation. *American Psychologist, 42*, 37-45.

Sue, S., Zane, N., & Young, K. (1994). Research on psychotherapy with culturally diverse populations. In A. E. Bergin & S. L. Garfield (Eds.), *Handbook of psychotherapy and behavior change* (pp. 783-820). New York, NY: Wiley.

Szapocznik, J., Feaster, D. J., Mitrani, V. B., Prado, G., Smith, L., Robinson-Batista, C., . . . Robbins, M. S. (2004). Structural ecosystems therapy for HIV-seropositive African American women: Effects on psychological distress, family hassles, and family support. *Journal of Consulting and Clinical Psychology, 72*, 288-303.

Szapocznik, J., & Prado, G. (2007). Negative effects on family functioning from psychosocial treatments: A recommendation for expanded safety monitoring. *Journal of Family Psychology, 21*, 468-478.

Tandon, S. D., Perry, D. F., Mendelson, T., Kemp, K., & Leis, J. A. (2011). Preventing perinatal depression in low-income home visiting clients: A randomized controlled trial. *Journal of Consulting and Clinical Psychology, 79*, 707-712.

Teusch, L., & Bohme, H. (1999). Is the exposure principle really crucial in agoraphobia? The influence of client-centered "nonprescriptive" treatment on exposure. *Psychotherapy Research, 9*, 115-123.

Teusch, L., Bohme, H., Finke, J., & Gastpar, M. (2001). Effects of client-centered psychotherapy for personality disorders alone and in combination with psychopharmacological treatment. *Psychotherapy and Psychosomatics, 70*, 328-336.

Teusch, L., Bohme, H., Finke, J., Gastpar, M., & Skerra, B. (2003). Antidepressant medication and the assimilation of problematic experiences in psychotherapy. *Psychotherapy Research, 13*, 307-322.

Teusch, L., Bohme, H., & Gastpar, M. (1997). The benefit of an insight-oriented and experiential approach on panic and agoraphobia symptoms. *Psychotherapy and psychosomatics, 66*, 293-301.

Thompson, V. L. S., & Alexander, H. (2006). Therapists' race and African American clients' reactions to therapy. *Psychotherapy: Theory, Research, Practice, Training, 43*(1), 99-110.

Truax, C. B. (1963). The empirical emphasis in psychotherapy: A symposium. Effective ingredients in psychotherapy: An approach to unraveling the patient-therapist interaction. *Journal of Counseling Psychology, 10*, 256-263.

Truax, C. B. (1972). The meaning and reliability of accurate empathy ratings: A rejoinder. *Psychological Bulletin, 77*, 397-399.

Truax, C. B., & Carkhuff, R. R. (1965). Experimental manipulation of therapeutic conditions. *Journal of Consulting Psychology, 29*, 119-124.

Truax, C. B., & Carkhuff, R. R. (1967). *Toward effective counseling and psychotherapy: Training and practice.* Chicago, IL: Aldine.

Truax, C. B., & Mitchell, K. M. (1971). Research on certain therapist interpersonal skills in relation to process and outcome. In A. E. Bergin & S. L. Garfield (Eds.), *Handbook of psychotherapy and behavior change: An empirical analysis* (pp. 299-344). New York, NY: John Wiley.

Truax, C. B., Wargo, D. G., Frank, J. D., Imber, S. D., Battle, C. C., Hoehn-Saric, R., . . . Stone, A. R. (1966). The therapist's contribution to accurate empathy, non-possessive warmth, and genuineness in psychotherapy. *Journal of Clinical Psychology, 22,* 331-334.

Turner, R. M. (2000). Naturalistic evaluation of dialectical behavior therapy-oriented treatment for borderline personality disorder. *Cognitive and Behavioral Practice, 7,* 413-419.

U.S. Census Bureau. (2010). *Poverty thresholds 2006.* Retrieved from http://www.census.gov/hhes/www/poverty/data/threshld/thresh 06.html

U.S. Census Bureau. (2011). *The White population: 2010.* Retrieved from http://www.census.gov/prod/cen2010/briefs/c2010br-05.pdf

U.S. Department of Health and Human Services. (2001). *Mental health: Culture, race, and ethnicity: A supplement to mental health: A report of the Surgeon General* (DHHS Pub No. 01-3613).

Retrieved from http://www.surgeongeneral.gov/ library/mentalhealth/cre/sma-01-3613.pdf

U.S. Department of Health and Human Services, Office of Minority Health. (2012a). *Data/statistics.* Retrieved from http://minorityhealth.hhs.gov/templates/browse.aspx?lvl=1&lvlI D=2

U.S. Department of Health and Human Services, Office of Minority Health. (2012b). *Mental health data/statistics.* Retrieved from http://minorityhealth.hhs.gov/templates/ browse.aspx?lvl=3&lvlid=9

Usher, C. H. (1989). Recognizing cultural bias in counseling theory and practice: The case of Rogers. *Journal of Multicultural Counseling and Development, 17*(2), 62-71.

van der Veen, F. (1967). Basic elements in the process of psychotherapy: A research study. *Journal of Consulting Psychology, 31*, 295-303.

Wang, S., & Kim, B. S. K. (2010). Therapist multicultural competence, Asian American participants' cultural values, and counseling process. *Journal of Counseling Psychology, 57*, 394-401.

Ward, E., King, M., Lloyd, M., Bower, P., Sibbald, B., Farrelly, S., . . . Addington-Hall, J. (2000). Randomised controlled trial of non-directive counselling, cognitive-behaviour therapy, and usual general practitioner care for patients with depression I: Clinical effectiveness. *British Medical Journal, 321*, 1383-1388.

Webb, C. A., DeRubeis, R. J., & Barber, J. P. (2010). Therapist adherence/competence and treatment outcome: A meta-analytic review. *Journal of Consulting and Clinical Psychology, 78*, 200-211.

Weinrach, S. G., & Thomas, K. R. (2002). A critical analysis of the multicultural counseling competencies: Implications for the practice of mental health counseling. *Journal of Mental Health Counseling, 24*(1), 20-35.

Wells, K., Sherbourne, C., Schoenbaum, M., Ettner, S., Duan, N., Miranda, J., . . . Rubenstein, L. (2004). Five-year impact of quality improvement for depression: Results of a group-level randomized controlled trial. *Archives of General Psychiatry, 61*, 378-386.

Wenegrat, A. (1974). A factor analytic study of the Truax Accurate Empathy Scale. *Psychotherapy: Theory, Research & Practice, 11*(1), 48-51.

Wexler, D. A., & Butler, J. M. (1976). Therapist modification of client expressiveness in client-centered therapy. *Journal of Consulting and Clinical Psychology, 44*, 261-265.

Worthington, R. L., Mobley, M., Franks, R. P., & Tan, J. A. (2000). Multicultural counseling competencies: Verbal content, counselor attributions, and social desirability. *Journal of Counseling Psychology, 47*, 460-468.

Yoosefi, N. (2011). Comparison of the effectiveness of family therapy based on rational emotive behavioral therapy (REBT) and person centered therapy (PCT) on self-differentiation among divorce applicant clients. *International Journal of Psychology and Counselling, 3*, 176-185. Retrieved from http://www.academicjournals.org/ JPC/PDF/Pdf2011/Dec/Yoosefi.pdf

Yousefi [sic], N., Etemadi, O., Bahrami, F., Fatehzadeh, M., Ahmadi, S. A., & Beshlideh, K. (2009). Structural relationships between self-differentiation and subjective wellbeing, mental health and marital quality: "Fitting Bowen's theory." *Iranian Journal of Psychiatry and Behavioral Sciences, 3*(2), 4-14. Retrieved from http://www.sid.ir/en/VEWSSID/J_pdf/118620100202.pdf

Zane, N., Sue, S., Chang, J., Huang, L., Huang, J., Lowe, S., . . . Lee, E. (2005). Beyond ethnic match: Effects of client-therapist cognitive match in problem perception, coping orientation, and therapy goals on treatment outcomes. *Journal of Community Psychology, 33*, 569-585.

3

A PERSON-CENTERED APPROACH TO THE TREATMENT OF BORDERLINE PERSONALITY DISORDER [2]

꿒

Since the beginning of the 21st century, an increase of research has resulted in accumulated evidence demonstrating the effectiveness of a number of treatment approaches for borderline personality disorder (BPD). Four mainstream modalities examined in this article have

---

[2] The final, definitive version of this paper has been published in the *Journal of Humanistic Psychology*, 51/4, October/2011 by SAGE Publications Ltd, All rights reserved.

emerged as viable and competing methods of reducing observable symptoms and improving psychopathologic characteristics of BPD. These treatment approaches are transference-focused psychotherapy (TFP), mentalization-based therapy (MBT), schema-focused therapy (SFT), and dialectical behavior therapy (DBT).

These four approaches hold a number of similarities. All suggest a developmental view of BPD etiology that accounts for biological and environmental precipitants. All approaches primarily view "borderline" maladaptive functioning from a lens of developmental trauma during which the client's ability to observe, describe, and reflect on experience was significantly frustrated. Furthermore, these four approaches address a common treatment approach that consists of building a therapeutic relationship high in trust and rapport, then facilitating change through the use of approach-specific strategies. In particular, TFP and MBT, with psychodynamic leanings, depict similar meta-strategies of change through the creation of a transference relationship; the former approach relying heavily on interpretation, and the latter emphasizing a combination of empathy and here-and-now interpretations. Likewise, SFT and DBT both suggest meta-strategies that combine cognitive and behavioral theory within a larger framework that suggests aspects of humanistic therapies. All therapies emphasize a combination of acceptance and change strategies.

In contrast to these mainstream approaches, person-centered

therapy (PCT) has received scant consideration as a viable treatment for BPD likely, in part, as a result of its overall decline in the United States in the past 40 to 50 years. Current research trends tend to employ PCT in a diluted version as a supportive therapy or treatment-as-usual (TAU) control in studies that are primarily interested in the performance of a cognitive–behavioral or psychodynamic treatment condition. Despite the "watered-down" format, PCT has demonstrated comparable effectiveness as a treatment approach for Axis I disorders (Elliott, Greenberg, & Lietaer, 2004). In this article, I examine research evidence that supports PCT as a viable approach for Axis II disorders as well, particularly for BPD.

Since the 1970s, common factors research indicates that up to 85% of therapy outcome is due to variables other than orientation-specific interventions, such as the quality of the therapeutic relationship and client hope and resilience. These common factors and the extent that each factor may account for therapy outcome are suggested as follows: (a) client and extratherapeutic factors - 40%, (b) therapist-client relationship factors - 30%, (c) placebo and expectancy effects - 15%, and (d) specific techniques and therapy model factors - 15% (Asay & Lambert, 1999).

Likewise, the mainstream BPD treatments examined in this article possess both common and specific factors. Although it is debatable, one could argue that at least 85% of the emphasis within mainstream BPD approaches focuses on specific techniques unique to a singular approach. However, research suggests that the success of BPD approaches is not dependent on the type or dose of intervention. That is, the BPD research evidence presented in this article indicates that psychodynamic, behavioral, and humanistic treatments may be comparable. Furthermore, the common factors hypothesis does not preclude the use of specific techniques but highlights the likelihood that interpersonal aspects of therapy significantly outweigh intervention and treatment planning in positive outcome. In other words, behind every good plan is a good relationship.

What follows is an account of current and possibly future trends in the treatment of BPD. The intent of this review and selection of these particular therapies is twofold. The first aim is to offer the frontline clinician a condensed and accessible snapshot of current trends in thinking from influential figures in the field of BPD, namely, Kernberg, Fonagy, Young, and Linehan (for expanded explanations of each approach see the April 2006 issue of the Journal of Clinical Psychology, Thorn [2006]). Subsequently, with these current trends in mind, the second aim is to outline a person-centered approach to the treatment of BPD and, in doing so, attempt to describe the highly personal interactions that a clinician may encounter anywhere that psychological contact is made with this very difficult-to-treat population.

Finally, a personal encounter is the foundation from which a clinician's treatment of choice will arise, whether the therapy occurs on an inpatient unit, at a partial hospitalization or day treatment setting, within an assertive community treatment outpatient framework, and/or in biweekly or weekly outpatient therapy. Included in this choice of treatment is a way of being a therapist, characteristically an imprecise concept. Regardless of the clinician's choice of treatment approach, this article attempts to clarify this way of being.

Current Views of Borderline Personality Disorder

BPD, prevalent in approximately 1% of the general population, 10% of psychiatric outpatient, and possibly 20% of psychiatric inpatient settings (Levy et al., 2006; Paris, 2003), might be described as a consistently empty state of internal experiencing that results in a polarized, subjective perception of self and the world, oscillating between extremes of good and bad. According to the Diagnostic and Statistical Manual of Mental Disorders, fourth edition, text revision (DSM-IV-TR; American Psychiatric Association, 2000), BPD is described as "a pervasive pattern of instability of interpersonal relationships, self-image, and affects, and marked impulsivity beginning by early adulthood and present in a variety of contexts" characterized by the following nine indicators: (a) frantic efforts to avoid real or imagined abandonment, (b) a pattern of unstable and intense interpersonal relationships characterized by alternating between extremes of idealization and devaluation, (c) identity disturbance: markedly and persistently unstable self-image or sense of self, (d) impulsivity in at least two areas that are potentially self-damaging (e.g., spending, sex, substance abuse, reckless driving, binge eating), (e) recurrent suicidal behavior, gestures, or threats, or self-mutilating behavior, (f) affective instability because of a marked reactivity of mood (e.g., intense episodic dysphoria, irritability, or anxiety usually lasting a few hours and only rarely more than a few days), (g) chronic feelings of emptiness, (h) inappropriate, intense anger, or difficulty controlling anger (e.g., frequent displays of temper, constant anger, recurrent physical fights), (i) transient, stress-related paranoid ideation or severe dissociative symptoms.

Transference-focused therapy

Kernberg, Clarkin, and Levy developed TFP based on an object relations view of development. TFP focuses primarily on reactivating the primitive object relations of a borderline client in a controlled setting. The mechanisms of change in TFP are suggested to be an integration of the polarized concepts of self and others stemming from an increased capacity to reflectively think about thoughts, feelings, and experiences. Moreover, Levy et al. (2006) outline the facilitative mechanisms provided by a TFP therapist through which client change occurs: (a) the structured treatment approach that includes a treatment manual, a treatment contract, a hierarchy of problems addressed, and group supervision for therapists; (b) clarification as a technique of evoking the client's internal states and to encourage reflective thinking; (c) confrontation as a means to inquire about contradictions and highlight obstacles toward goals; and (d) tranference interpretations that increase the client's ability to differentiate between self and other (i.e., self-representation and object representation). From a stance of objectivity and a nonjudgmental attitude, the TFP therapist "suspends the ordinary reaction of the social environment . . . [and] lets the patient live out his or her internal representations in the treatment setting" (p. 489) with the goal of client understanding, modifying, and integrating his or her split-off internal representations. Furthermore, Clarkin, Yeomans, and Kernberg (2006) argue that during a borderline client's development, internal representations of self and other are restricted: "These individuals retain the primitive, and not necessarily accurate, internal representations of self and other from early life, resulting, first, in a view of the world where nurturing objects and punitive depriving objects alternate with no realistic middle ground" (pp. 19-20).

Preliminary evidence has been found to support TFP's efficacy. Clarkin et al. (2001) found that TFP was a potential viable treatment for reducing completed suicides, reducing acute hospitalizations, and number of days in an inpatient psychiatric hospital setting. Further evidence supports the viability of TFP. Clarkin, Levy, Lenzenweger, and Kernberg (2007) reported on a study comparing TFP, DBT, and a supportive therapy in the treatment of BPD. Although all three therapies demonstrated positive outcome on depression, anxiety, global functioning, and social adjustment measures, only TFP and DBT significantly reduced suicidality.

Mentalization-based therapy

In contrast to mainstream psychodynamic thinking regarding the primacy of the therapeutic frame in BPD treatment (McWilliams, 1994), Bateman and Fonagy (2004) argue that "the potential effectiveness of all treatments depends not so much on their frame but on their ability to increase a patient's capacity to mentalize" (p. 46). MBT, according to Fonagy and Bateman (2006a), considers the borderline client's psychopathology as resulting from a deficit in this capacity to mentalize. The authors propose that this deficit results in three modes of representations of experiencing, referred to as psychic equivalence, pretend mode, and teleological mode. Respectively, these modes either provide the borderline client with an experience of concrete equivalence between thought and reality, a capacity to pretend or dissociate from experience, or a capacity to only accept subjective experience through confirmation from an external source (i.e., external locus of control). The authors describe a therapist "holding in mind" of the borderline client that results reciprocally in the client learning to hold mental states in mind as well.

Fonagy and Bateman (2006a) view mechanisms of change in MBT as occurring through a combination of enhancing the client's ability to mentalize in the context of an attachment relationship. To activate this attachment relationship, the authors propose four "largely unconscious" therapist guidelines that focus on arousing the client's attachment system: (a) discussing current attachment relationships; (b) discussing past attachment relationships; (c) in creating an environment promoting affect regulation, the therapist is able to encourage and regulate the client's attachment bond to him or her; and (d) in a group setting, the therapist attempts to encourage attachment bonds between members. The therapist also encourages the borderline client to experience a titration of negative emotions through confronting aversive/traumatic memories.

The authors outline certain therapist techniques to encourage reflective thought: (a) the therapist focuses exclusively on current client mental states to "build up" representations of internal states, (b) the therapist avoids situations in which the client discusses mental states that cannot be linked to subjectively felt reality, (c) the therapy creates a transitional area of relatedness in which thoughts and emotions can be "played with," and (d) client interpersonal in-session behaviors are interpreted or understood in terms of the immediate client experience, while interpretations of unconscious meanings are avoided.

Mentalization-base therapy has also demonstrated empirical success. In a study comparing a mentalization-based psychoanalytic approach to TAU, 19 borderline clients were found to significantly reduce self-harm behaviors, depression, anxiety, length of hospitalization, improve social adjustment, and maintain this improvement 18 months, 36 months, and 8 years after treatment (Bateman & Fonagy, 1999, 2001, 2008).

253

Schema-focused therapy

Possessing similarities to Beck's cognitive therapy for personality disorders (Pretzer & Beck, 2005), Jeffrey Young developed SFT that integrates cognitive, behavioral, and experiential techniques focused around the concept of schemas and their influence on a borderline client's functioning and experience. In addition, the therapeutic relationship is used in a greater capacity as a vehicle of change, early life experiences take a more central role of discussion, and affective experience is encouraged and directed in-session (Giesen-Bloo et al., 2006).

Schema-focused therapy is guided by four main constructs: early maladaptive schemas, schema domains, schema processes, and schema modes. Respectively, these four constructs provide a framework that examines (a) dysfunctional relationship themes with primary caregivers, (b) the categories into which maladaptive schemas fall (e.g., disconnection and rejection, impaired autonomy, etc.), (c) the processes through which a borderline client maintains these intact maladaptive schemas (avoidance, compensation, etc.), and (d) the schema mode that is "currently active," functioning as the primary means through which a borderline client views the world (McGinn & Young, 1996). In particular, the five categories of schema modes consist of the abandoned/abused child, the angry/impulsive child, the detached protector, the punitive parent, and the healthy adult, the goal mode of therapy (Kellogg & Young, 2006). Notably, these modes seem to be reminiscent of the ego states of Berne's transactional analysis (Steiner, 1974) such as the "little professor" or "pig parent."

Four mechanisms of change are suggested to facilitate successful outcome in SFT: limited reparenting, experiential techniques, cognitive techniques, and behavioral pattern breaking. The therapist provides limited reparenting by facilitating a safe, stable, and accepting therapy climate as the precursor to experiential/gestalt techniques such as guided imagery work, empty chair and two chair techniques, and letter writing in an effort to externalize the punitive parent mode or critical inner voice. Cognitive techniques provide education and cognitive restructuring to address the angry/impulsive child and detached protector modes, exhibited by behaviors of interpersonal anger and emotional numbing. Finally, behavioral pattern breaking applies in-therapy learning to the external world. Included are behavioral techniques of relaxation training, anger management, and exposure to feared situations in an effort to move the client toward autonomy and to becoming his or her own healthy adult. Through the interaction and facilitation of these mechanisms of change emerge three stages of treatment: bonding and emotional regulation, schema mode change, and development of autonomy.

A 3-year study (Giesen-Bloo et al., 2006) comparing SFT with TFP found that both treatments at 12 months had successfully reduced BPD symptoms, such as parasuicidality, impulsivity, general psychopathologic symptoms, and had significantly improved quality-of-life measures. Change was maintained at 3 years. SFT was found to possess significantly less attrition rates than TFP and demonstrated stronger effect sizes in the reduction of maladaptive personality traits.

Dialectical behavior therapy

Linehan's DBT approach is a prominent and highly regarded treatment for parasuicidal borderline clients. DBT has found success in significantly reducing suicides, suicide attempts, parasuicidality, and frequency of hospitalization while having inconsistent effect on client hope, depression, and reasons for living measures (Linehan et al., 2006; Lynch, Chapman, Rosenthal, Kuo, & Linehan, 2006). Across studies, DBT tends to have lower attrition rates than the treatment comparison (Linehan et al., 1999; Linehan et al., 2006; Verheul et al., 2003) save for a particular comparison study (Linehan et al., 2002) in which a validation therapy had both a lower attrition rate and was comparable to DBT on outcome measures of self-harm, hospital utilization, and social adjustment. In most studies, the DBT condition has also tended to possess a higher number of quality sessions with trained clinicians than did the treatment comparisons (Koons et al., 2001; Linehan et al., 1999; Linehan et al., 2006). In addition, there is some evidence that DBT loses efficacy on parasuicidality measures with more severe cases or cases that are comorbid with substance abuse (Koons et al., 2001; Linehan et al., 1999; Linehan et al., 2002; Linehan et al., 2006; Verheul et al., 2003).

Dialectical behavior therapy combines Buddhist perspectives of mindfulness, acceptance, and dialectics with cognitive and behavioral change strategies. This acceptance/change dialectic is mirrored in both the therapist's interventions (e.g., validation/behavioral techniques) as well as the client's therapy process (radical acceptance/skills training). Linehan and colleagues (Lynch et al., 2006) outline four treatment strategies that facilitate the summarized goal of therapy as the "reduction of ineffective action tendencies linked with dysregulated emotions" (p. 475): (a) mindfulness, (b) opposite action, (c) behavioral targeting and chain analysis, and (d) dialectics. Furthermore, the mechanisms of change that arise from these strategies are hypothesized as (a) exposure, response prevention (E/RP), and extinction, (b) learning of novel, skillful responses to evocative stimuli (emotion regulation skills training, problem solving), (c) enhancing attentional control and stimulus discrimination (refocusing, distracting, and recognizing), and (d) balancing and sustaining effective treatment (radical acceptance through therapist validation). Lynch et al. (2006) further suggest that a process occurs as a result of these mechanisms of change that creates in the client self-acceptance leading to a nonjudgmental attitude. From this, the client becomes less reactive, providing opportunity to develop new associations with internal/external events that result in an increase of adaptive behaviors.

In addition, therapist validation, a primary component in DBT treatment, is operationalized into six behaviors or levels: (a) active listening, (b) accurate reflection of feeling, (c) articulating unverbalized thoughts or feelings, (d) expressing to the client that the dysfunctional behavior is logical in view of past experience, (e) normalizing dysfunctional behavior in the current context, and (f) acting in a manner that is genuine (Lynch et al., 2006).

Some similarities and differences between DBT and the person-centered approach

Similar in spirit to Rogers's (1980) person-centered approach, Linehan has recognized the theoretical parallels between DBT and PCT: "I discovered recently that I must have stolen this, unconsciously so to speak, from Rogers whom I had read in the original many years ago. In re-reading him recently, I was stunned at how radical Rogers is" (Hellinga, van Luyn, & Dalewijk, 2000, as cited in van Blarikom, 2008, p. 28). Furthermore, Linehan's focus on mindfulness seems to parallel Rogers's focus on the importance of congruence between a person's awareness and his or her subjective experience. However, in contrast to Rogers, Linehan explicitly states that much of the relationship or rapport building in which a DBT therapist engages is a facade, used later to leverage a client to decrease parasuicidal behaviors such as cutting and to assist in amplifying teaching methods that focus on increasing emotion regulation and decreasing maladaptive interpersonal relationships. Linehan (1993) states, "DBT has been called 'blackmail therapy' by some, since the therapist is willing to put the quality of the relationship on the line in a trade for improved behavior on the part of the patient" (p. 98). Therefore, the DBT therapist's genuineness and prizing seems to take a backseat to measurable outcomes. As Linehan and colleagues (Lynch et al., 2006) state, "The therapist might increase his or her level of validation and genuineness when the patient exhibits particularly skillful behavior in session [. . .] and withdraw or decrease validation when the patient's behavior in session is dysfunctional" (p. 468). One conclusion could be drawn that the therapist not only wishes to change the borderline client's maladaptive behaviors, but by using the relationship as a lever, the therapist may be in danger of also rejecting the person as well.

As a result, some questions are raised regarding principles and values in psychotherapy: (a) does external, observable symptom reduction take precedence over a genuine interpersonal relationship and the promotion of self-acceptance; does one lead to the other and, if so, which comes first?, (b) by using the relationship as a "bargaining chip" toward behavior change, does the therapist encourage client hope and self-acceptance or simply stifle and reject those unattractive, socially unconventional aspects of the person?, and (c) is this level of therapist manipulation necessary with such a dysfunctional and at-risk population?

Person-Centered Therapy and Research

Carl Rogers's person-centered approach has been called nondirective therapy, client-centered therapy, and, most recently, person-centered therapy (Rogers, 1980). As research investigating the viability of this therapy progressed, Rogers and colleagues (Rogers & Dymond, 1954; Rogers, Gendlin, Kiesler, & Truax, 1967) discovered that for positive client change to occur, an effective therapist tended to possess certain attitudes toward the client that, when conveyed through therapist interpersonal behaviors, created change-promoting conditions in a therapy setting. Having moved away from the idea of a nondirective technical skill, Rogers suggested that these therapist conditions of congruence, unconditional positive regard, and empathic understanding were both necessary in all helping relationships and sufficient to produce successful outcomes (Rogers, 1957). The therapist conditions were found to facilitate a client process that led to increased accurate awareness of experience, personal agency, and self-acceptance. This movement toward an internal locus of control and confidence in one's ability to accurately evaluate experience were considered the primary ingredients in behavioral change. Furthermore, research during the 1960s and 1970s confirmed these "core conditions" as primary factors associated with outcome success across therapy orientations (Patterson, 1984; Truax & Mitchell, 1971). As time went on, variations to this approach emerged, such as Gendlin's (1978) experiential therapy and focusing method and Greenberg, Rice, and Elliot's (1993) emotion-focused approach. However, these experiential therapies (i.e., PCT plus process direction) have received criticism within the person-centered community for lacking the spirit of Rogers's original thesis (Patterson, 1990; see Brodley

[1990] for a critical comparison of PCT and experiential therapy; see Elliott & Freire [2007] for a relatively recent update on "classical PCT versus experiential").

Following an extensive analysis of research findings in the treatment of anxiety and phobias, trauma, depression, anger, schizophrenia, and health-related psychological distress, Elliott et al. (2004) found experiential therapies in general and PCT in particular to demonstrate strong effect sizes (i.e., >0.8) consistently in pre–post measures, in wait-list and no-treatment controls, and when compared with CBT and psychodynamic approaches. Experiential therapy demonstrated a "trivial" but significantly stronger effect size than PCT when compared with CBT/dynamic treatments, suggesting that a process-directive component may enhance the PCT approach. However, the authors point out the possible "dilution" of PCT's effectiveness because of it being used as the TAU control/comparison condition in most studies reviewed. As a result, PCT's effectiveness would be confounded with researcher allegiance bias favoring the experimental treatment condition. Not surprisingly, when the authors controlled for allegiance effects in their analysis, PCT was found to possess equivalent effectiveness to experiential, CBT, and dynamic approaches across diagnostic populations. In addition, PCT has demonstrated initial effectiveness in the treatment of personality disorders, BPD in particular (Teusch, Bohme, Finke, & Gastpar, 2001).

Studies examining PCT effectiveness with borderline clients

Currently, PCT is in decline in the United States in the domains of research, training, and practice, whereas in Europe and Asia, PCT is quite prominent (Bozarth, Zimring, & Tausch, 2002; Cooper, O'Hara, Schmid, & Wyatt, 2007). Only three BPD treatment studies could be found that were published in English and that included a PCT treatment condition. These studies are presented in detail to highlight the strengths and weaknesses of this type of therapy in the treatment of BPD. Despite possible researcher and therapist biases as a result of the approach being couched as the TAU control/comparison condition in two of three studies, PCT demonstrates strong effect sizes overall.

Turner (2000). A study by Turner (2000) compared a DBT-oriented treatment with PCT in a community mental health clinic. Both therapy conditions were provided by the same therapists and PCT was offered as a supportive therapy control condition. That is, therapists alternated between providing the PCT condition for one group of clients and the DBT condition for the other group. The therapists possessed a background in psychodynamic, PCT, and family systems approaches and received training in DBT prior to and during the study. The DBT condition was modified by incorporating some psychodynamic components, while the skills training group found in typical DBT was condensed to in-session skills training with the therapist. In comparison, the PCT condition was based on Robert Carkhuff's (1969, as cited in

Turner, 2000) version of PCT and "provided patients with a safe therapeutic environment and accurate empathic reflection only" (p. 416). The therapists when providing the PCT condition met with clients twice a week, developed a treatment contract that stipulated elimination of suicide/self-harm during treatment, and in place of a structured agenda the therapists "instructed patients to express what was on their minds at each session" (p. 416). PCT was found to produce positive effects beyond what would occur by chance.

Specifically, the PCT condition produced significant gains at both 6 and 12 months on parasuicidal, suicidality, and self-harm measures; on emotional functioning (including impulsivity, anger, depression, and anxiety measures); and global mental health functioning. When compared with the DBT condition, PCT was equivalent on anxiety measures at both 6 and 12 months. On depression and impulsiveness measures, PCT was equivalent to DBT at 6 months only. DBT demonstrated stronger improvement in parasuicidal, suicidality, and self-harm at both 6 and 12 months. DBT also reduced number of hospitalization days significantly more at 6 and 12 months.

Turner's (2000) study also investigated movement of client symptoms below clinically significant cutoff scores. That is, did improvement extend to reducing the symptoms to a normal level of clinical functioning? DBT significantly moved more clients below the cutoff score on suicidality/self-harm measures. However, no difference in clinical reduction was found between treatment conditions for impulsivity and anger. Clinical reduction of depression measures was equivocal, as DBT demonstrated an improvement on the Beck Depression Inventory, but the Hamilton Rating Scale for Depression reported no significant difference between treatment conditions. Furthermore, comparisons on global mental health cutoff scores were equivocal as well.

Finally, the quality of the helping relationship was assessed at 6 months. No significant difference was found between treatments on this measure. Following analysis, the helping relationship ratings were found to account for as much variance in client improvement as the differences in treatment conditions. That is, the impact of the helping relationship on symptom reduction was equal to the influence of whether the client experienced the PCT or DBT condition. In a post hoc analysis of therapist differences, Turner (2000) found that one of four therapists was more effective in providing the PCT condition than in providing the DBT condition; three of four therapists were more effective in providing the DBT condition. This led the author to conclude that "the provision of PCT with the right therapist worked well for some BPD clients" and that "the provision of a strategic and integrated set of therapeutic strategies adds to the provision of supportive elements for many borderline clients" (p. 419).

Cottraux et al. (2009). In a more recent comparison study,

Cottraux et al. (2009) investigated the differential effects of cognitive therapy (CT) versus "Rogerian Supportive Therapy" (RST) at two sites in France. Similar to Turner's (2000) study, the therapists in this study provided both the CT and PCT conditions. Furthermore, the therapists in the study possessed "CBT diplomas" and had received formal training and supervision from an American CT trainer who travelled to France to perform three 2-day workshops on the cognitive treatment of BPD. In contrast to this focused preparation afforded to the CT condition, "the principles and methods of RST were taught in 10 [hours] by role-playing and had been previously used by the same two research teams." Furthermore, the PCT condition was operationalized into 10 principles that, in addition to Rogers's core conditions, included directions such as "the therapists were to have an unconditionally positive regard for the patients, whatever they said," "the patients were to be reassured when they expressed negative feelings," and "the therapists were to politely ignore or refuse requests for advice, directive behaviors, homework, behavioral experiments, cognitive schema, modification, problem solving, or exposure to feared mental images or real-life situations." Again, the PCT condition emerged quite favorably.

Cognitive therapy compared with the PCT condition showed very little significant difference throughout treatment and at follow-up. PCT was found to be equivalent to CT on depression, anxiety, and suicidality/self-harm measures across the 6-, 12-, and 24-month time line. Furthermore, no difference in dropout rates occurred across treatments. CT was significantly more effective with regard to hopelessness at 6 months, but no difference emerged at the end of treatment and follow-up. CT did demonstrate a significant change compared with the PCT condition on a 7-point global improvement scale at the 2-year follow-up. This study by Cottraux et al. (2009) demonstrated the viability of even a diluted version of PCT in the treatment of BPD. In conclusion the authors state, although "administration of CT and RST by the same CT-oriented therapists may constitute a bias in favour of CT [. . .] studies with experts in client centred therapy should be carried out to replicate or contradict our study" (pp. 313-315).

Teusch et al. (2001). In a final study at an inpatient setting in Germany conducted by Teusch et al. (2001), the effects of PCT plus medication was compared with a PCT only condition in the treatment of four subgroups of personality disorders (paranoid/schizoid, emotional instability/borderline, histrionic/narcissistic, and obsessive-compulsive/dependent). Hospital patients received a combination of individual and group PCT. In addition to using a measure similar to the Hamilton Depression Scale, this study used the Giessen Test, a measure similar to the self-concept Q-sort developed by Rogers's group (Rogers & Dymond, 1954) to assess self-perception on a number of measures including social perceptions, mood stability, and realistic perceptions of others. Overall, the PCT only condition was found to be as effective for improvement in mood, self-esteem, and social comprehension across all personality disorder subgroups. However, a significant effect occurred favoring the PCT only condition in reduction of depression in the borderline personality subgroup. This was a large effect size (>0.8). In addition, PCT alone as well as with medication was found to have a significant positive effect across the four subgroups of personality disorders on social perception and social behavior.

A final notable effect was found at follow-up. The clients who received the PCT only treatment tended to continue with psychotherapy alone following discharge, whereas the clients who received the PCT plus medication condition tended to receive follow-up services of both therapy and medication.

Hypothesized Mechanisms of Change in PCT

Person-centered therapy, in contrast to process-directive variations, provides a therapy experience such that the client perceives no specific, preplanned agenda in the beginning or during the course of therapy. If, during the therapy relationship, a client perceives a planned agenda on the part of the therapist, then we are no longer speaking of PCT in its intended form. However, a slight twist exists in the practice of PCT: the person-centered therapist may at times be quite direct, may facilitate homework, may have a client involuntarily committed for psychiatric evaluation, may provide information on behavioral exercises, and may disagree or communicate dissonance with the client. However, this directivity is of a different nature than therapy approaches founded on directive theory. Directiveness in PCT emerges as a complement or companion to the client's ongoing self-actualization process in therapy. Therefore, as Brodley (2006) discusses, homework or experimenting with cognitive and behavioral strategies may arise from an interest or need by the client, articulated by the client, and facilitated or encouraged by the therapist because this is the client's frame of reference. Therefore, the therapist continues the process of providing an environment for the client to examine feelings and attitudes, test hypotheses, attend to here-and-now emotions as they arise (e.g., transference feelings), and develop a more congruent concept of self as well as self in relation to others. However, this environment tends to arise in vivo each session (e.g., in person or by telephone), as the client-therapist interaction begins anew. The therapist has chosen to note certain thoughts or feelings about the client but looks to the client to provide the initial plan for the session. Brodley (2006) provides a transcribed example that helps clarify this seemingly contradictory stance of client autonomy versus therapist directiveness:

> Client: The meds aren't doing enough. I get into a panic and I can't even see how it is connected to anything I'm doing or thinking about. A terrible anxiety just wells up inside me. (T: Mhm, hmm) (Pause three seconds) I was wondering (Pause). [Dr. Burke] said you might have some techniques that could help me.

Therapist: Mhm, hmm. You still get terribly anxious and it completely gets its way with you. (C: Oh, Yeah. It really does.) So you wonder if I might know some things you might do to calm yourself when it happens.

Client: Yeah. Do you know what he's talking about? (T: Uhm, hmm, nodding) He said there are things anybody can learn, and I might feel better with it, along with the meds and the therapy.

Therapist: Yeah, there are some techniques one can learn that sometimes help. I'm not expert in those things, but I know some of the procedures.

Client: Can you teach them to me? (T: Sure . . .) I'll do anything not to be so anxious. It's awful (Pause). Sometimes I can't stand it!

Therapist: You feel so terrible (Pause). You're open to anything (C: I am.). Do you want to think about it more or try something right now?

Client: Let's try it now. (p. 155)

Noteworthy is the therapist's tone, which sends the subtle but essential message of client trust and prizing. Almost seeming to shy away from giving advice, the person-centered therapist "holds the line," as it were, but also goes with the client. Brodley (2006), in personal communication with another PCT therapist, Jerold Bozarth, states that,

I share Bozarth's concern [that "the concept of homework" misses the essence of CCT . . . the idea promotes the therapy as a problem oriented therapy rather than focused upon therapeutic personality change that in turn allows the client to resolve her own problems... (as cited in Brodley, 2006, p. 152)], and acknowledge that using the term "homework" in client-centered therapy can be considered a stretch [. . .] "homework" borrowing from Bozarth above, is between-sessions action that emerges from therapy and is usually further discussed during therapy. (p. 152)

As Rogers (1951) stated, if a persistent feeling is experienced by the therapist, the therapist may communicate this to the client, but from an "ownership-of-the-feeling" standpoint. This is consistent with how a therapist might address the borderline client's intense anger that may arise toward the therapist. If the therapist takes ownership of his or her feelings and communicates them in this type of genuine way, much of the further escalation of feelings may be diverted in the presence of this nondefensive stance.

Likewise, when the borderline client behaviors intensify to suicidal and self-harming levels, the therapist approaches the client from the strength of a genuine regard for the client's well-being, for example,

I'm very concerned. We cannot go on until we talk about your safety. It is important that we come up with a plan before you leave today because I'm worried that you may continue to hurt yourself or worse. I suspect you might hate me, but I'm willing to take the risk because I can tell that you're hurting and it hurts me to see you feel this way about yourself.

This is not to say that other approaches do not genuinely regard a client's well-being. This is to say that the PCT therapist attempts to preserve the client's autonomy consistently even during crisis. "Nonpossessive" describes this idea well. This stance, conveyed either implicitly or explicitly, holds the message, "it is my responsibility to make sure you and others remain safe, but that does not mean that I in some way think I am better than or judge you." Again, this is not to suggest that non-PCT therapists disregard client autonomy, but to accent the importance of remaining in the client's frame of reference as a path toward self-actualization, the primary metamechanism of change in PCT.

Self-actualization

The tendency for the self to actualize (differentiate) in a positive or negative direction is fundamental to Rogers's approach. If the self has been cultivated in a "nutrient-rich" environment (i.e., the caregiver(s) tended toward unconditional positive regard), then the self will move in a direction congruent with the overall organismic experiencing and valuing capacities. However, if the self has been cultivated in a "nutrient-deficient" environment, which possessed high levels of external conditions of worth (e.g., criticism, judgment, or trauma), then the self will move less in a direction of congruence with experience and more in a direction shaped by internalized expectations of others. Underlying self-development is the actualizing tendency. Regardless of how the self was formed, the actualizing tendency is a stable, positive movement forward. However, if the person is in a state of incongruence, the actualizing tendency may be distorted and cannot fully function in the person. It is when the person is provided a positive, correcting relationship that the distortions are removed and the self can actualize in a positive direction.

Rogers and colleagues (Rogers & Dymond, 1954; Rogers et al., 1967) provide evidence of a process or tendency toward self-actualization that occurs in PCT. In addition, Patterson and Joseph (2007), drawing from self-determination theory and positive psychology literature, present further empirical evidence. In brief, the authors found that positive self-actualization tends to occur in a prizing, understanding environment and that self-actualization is positively correlated with psychological well-being.

The remainder of this article outlines hypothesized mechanisms of change in PCT. Similar to the other approaches reviewed in this article, a person-centered approach consists of facilitative mechanisms provided by the therapist and process mechanisms that describe how the borderline client improves. The primary facilitative mechanisms consist of therapist congruence, unconditional positive regard, and empathic understanding, and at least to a minimal degree, the client must perceive these facilitative mechanisms to be present. The primary process mechanisms are hypothesized to consist of (a) an increase of accurate awareness of experience, both internal and external; (b) an increase of internal locus of control and decrease of external locus of control; (c) ability to assimilate previously threatening experience into the self-concept; (d) decreased defensiveness and reactivity, increased self-acceptance, (e) increased acceptance of others; and (f) increased reliance on internal locus of evaluation of experience. Other mechanisms exist such as client pretreatment characteristics, placebo effects, and unique therapist-client interactive relationship characteristics, but these are not unique to the specific hypothesized mechanisms of change in PCT. Incidentally, these hypothesized mechanisms may become obscured or diluted when mechanisms from other theories of BPD treatment are provided by the therapist. Said another way: "when the wrong man uses the right tools, the right tools work in the wrong way" (Watts, 1975).

The facilitative mechanisms of change

Congruence. To provide and maintain the facilitative mechanisms that create a person-centered climate, a therapist must be living as an authentic person in the therapy relationship. Furthermore, the degree to which the therapist can be authentic or congruent, will likely dictate how sensitive a listener and responder he or she will be in-session. If the therapist is integrated sufficiently in his or her own awareness of experience, such that the therapist can be accurate with his or her subceived and received reactions to the content of the perceptual field, then he or she can be authentic and congruent in receiving and responding to the client's verbal and physical communications. In this way, an authentic therapist is responsible for being a companion only. That is, the therapist's purpose is to help the client understand his or her experience more accurately, not to particularly evaluate or impose conditions on the client's experience in an expert role.

Unconditional positive regard (UCPR). Already a therapist has, to a degree, become congruent and integrated in an interpersonal, experiencing relationship with the client. As a result, the potential increases for the therapist to experience toward the client unconditional positive regard, or radical acceptance, as Linehan (1993) calls it. In contrast, without this radical acceptance from the therapist, the client will struggle to develop, as Linehan states, "acceptance of what is." If the client does not perceive sufficiently this therapist radical acceptance, then a tendency toward radical (or unconditional) self-acceptance cannot emerge.

In conveying UCPR, the PCT therapist's primary motivation is to understand the client's internal frame of reference. Hypothetically, the more authentic and congruent the therapist, the more he or she is motivated to attempt to understand the client. This motivation is a silent, but necessary, primary means of facilitating the process mechanisms of change. That is, the therapist both wishes to genuinely understand and also knows (i.e., reinforced by previous experience) that providing a climate of understanding will more than likely facilitate the process mechanisms. This is of primary importance to the sufficiency of these facilitative mechanisms to create change, and will be expanded below: The therapist wants to understand for no other reason but to understand. If the therapist is motivated to understand solely to be a change agent for the client, then the facilitative mechanisms may not be sufficient because a tendency toward unconditional acceptance will not effectively emerge. When the therapist presents an agenda (of change), already undue and ill-needed conditions have been placed on the relationship, and trust in the client's natural tendencies toward change have been discarded.

Furthermore, the more the therapist can accept what is (i.e., radical therapist self-acceptance) and, therefore, not be stifled by an agenda or treatment plan, the less is the threat that an agenda of countertransference will emerge in the therapy. Therefore, the more the therapist can mediate countertransference, including projective identification, the more he or she can differentiate between the therapist's and the client's experience in-session. By attuning in this person-centered way, the therapist can more easily tease out ownership of his or her feelings toward the client, navigate these feelings, and mitigate them. These mechanisms are therefore of a facilitative sort because countertransference and subsequent projective identification (e.g., becoming that very abuser the client expects) tend to be of greatest threat to therapeutic work with borderline clients. Therefore, these mechanisms are facilitative because they work to remove these primary barriers to BPD treatment and consequently facilitate the process mechanisms of change.

Empathy. Implied above, empathic understanding is the facilitative mechanism that provides the vehicle of UCPR (radical acceptance) for the client. However, as Linehan likewise illustrates in her six-tier definition of validation, therapist understanding does not always emerge as an encapsulated reflection-of-feeling statement. The error in mainstream thought of the person-centered approach seems to stem from this misunderstanding, particularly when considering PCT with borderline clients. A reflection of feeling statement or something similar that can be operationalized and measured implies a "moving forward" on the therapist's part; that is, an agenda or a means to an end. This type of empathic response pattern cannot be used very often with borderline clients because of the client's "fragile process" as Warner (1998) calls it. As will be seen with the hypothesized process mechanisms, reflection of feeling statements become less threatening to the client over the course of therapy but are not a primary means through which the mechanism of empathic understanding will tend to operate in facilitating the process mechanisms.

Experience has taught me that the process mechanisms emerge through a cyclical "returning to" the client's here-and-now relationship experience. In this way, understanding as opposed to interpreting, explaining, or convincing mitigates the barriers of therapist countertransference and projective identification and increases the likelihood that the therapist can experience a sufficient feeling of this radical acceptance toward the client. However, this unconditional, radical acceptance is highly threatening for the client, resulting in projective feelings toward the therapist. The therapist then attempts to understand in such a way to minimize his or her (the therapist's) problematic feelings that may unwittingly be projected back to the client as countertransference.

Mitigating countertransference. This person-centered interpersonal transaction is somewhat different from the creation of a transference neurosis for two reasons: (a) the therapist does not intentionally induce this and (b) the therapist does not explain or interpret this phenomenon to the client. Similar to other approaches, the therapist does not regard these client behaviors as barriers to the actual treatment but as the treatment in itself. However, these client behaviors, though likely to occur, are not particularly necessary for change to proceed in a PCT framework. Paradoxical, but essential to this approach, for the therapist to understand, he or she at times must express negative feelings toward the client that have persisted over sufficient time to be in need of conveyance. In other words, the therapist must take the risk of addressing with the borderline client the perceived "elephant in the room," as a way to check understanding, to test accuracy of feelings, and to convey fallibility and genuineness to the client. If this is not accomplished when needed - though it must be done with extreme sensitivity and personal ownership - it is hypothesized that these facilitative mechanisms will fail to be sufficient. The facilitative mechanisms of change therefore operate in a recursive fashion that maintains the therapist's ability to consistently provide these mechanisms, which subsequently generate the process mechanisms of change.

The spirit of PCT, a way of being. Touched on earlier, for the process mechanisms of change to emerge for the client, the facilitative mechanisms must be provided sufficiently, consistently, and without impediment. However, a paradox arises in that the therapist must want to provide a way of being for the client that is guided by these mechanisms, but the therapist does not manufacture these mechanisms as a means to purposely change the client. If these facilitative mechanisms of PCT are taken to be "mechanical," as it were, then the therapy will be more like eating the menu instead of the actual dinner (Watts, 1957); that is, more intellect and less experience. Therefore, if these facilitative mechanisms can be sufficiently provided, then the greater the likelihood the therapist will respond in a fashion that does not impose impediments or contingencies to the client's perception of a genuine way of being.

The process mechanisms of change

The process mechanisms of change begin when the client perceives at least minimal therapist levels of the facilitative mechanisms. Based on a theory of personality development outlined by Rogers (1959), "conditions of worth" of a traumatic nature were the general influence that resulted in the borderline client's personality formation. It is the reversal of these conditions of worth as unconditional positive self-regard that underlies the process of change, or the self-actualization of the person. Because of space limitations, a person-centered theory of BPD development will not be suggested (see Rogers [1959] for a PCT theory of personality).

Increased accurate awareness. Initially, the facilitative mechanisms create a safe environment for the borderline client to examine internal and external experience in less conventional, more novel ways. Furthermore, because of the nature of these facilitative mechanisms, the client engages in a tendency to choose increasingly accurate perspectives of his or her experience. This implies a movement from "unreal" interpretation of experience to significantly more reality-based, accurate understanding of experience. In this movement from interpretation to understanding, an underlying change occurs from a former stance of evaluation or judgment to a latter stance of nonjudgment or acceptance; that is, from conditional to condition-less. The nonjudgment and acceptance of the therapist provides situations in which the client can sift through and remain open to further experiential data that assists in developing a closer approximation of experience. It is not up to the therapist, in most cases, to assign values to the client's awareness or to evaluate perceptual accuracy. In this framework of therapy, feedback as a means to promote increased accurate awareness is not necessary and, if engaged in consistently, may render these PCT mechanisms insufficient. Therefore, it is hypothesized that subjective awareness of experience moves toward more accurate approximations when in a relationship that provides the facilitative mechanisms.

This increase in accurate awareness is the first hypothesized mechanism in BPD improvement and, as does all the mechanisms, operates along a continuum and is not static.

Internal locus of control. As this tendency toward accurate awareness continues, client feelings of mastery of experience begin to emerge. This mastery of experience can be described as a movement from an external to internal locus of control. The client learns that experience can be examined, understood, owned, and subsequently accepted. This internal locus of control is the second mechanism of change and emerges slowly over time.

Assimilate previously threatening experience. As the client understands and feels sufficiently in control of the internal and external world, experiences previously interpreted as threatening to his or her self-concept or personhood can be assimilated. Increasingly, because the client has become more accurate in awareness and masterful, experiences that promote the actualizing of the self will be assimilated; those that do not promote this will be examined and discarded through a nonreactive valuing process. Therefore, it is hypothesized that when this third mechanism emerges from the presence of accurate awareness and a felt internal locus of control, positive regard can be assimilated into the self (e.g., "I am a lovable person").

From defensiveness to acceptance. The client has now tentatively entered the region on the continuum of the process mechanisms in which movement from defensiveness to self-acceptance will become more the rule and less the exception. Noted earlier, typical reflective statements of empathy can be quite threatening to a borderline client. As the client more frequently assimilates therapist positive regard into his or her self-concept, the client begins to own this idea of being worthy of prizing. Notably, it is the pervasive condition-less stance - the nonpossession - of the therapist's prizing that releases this positive regard from therapist to client. Of equal importance, it is the therapist's genuine congruence in the relationship that authenticates this positive regard as real and something the client is able to own and believe in. Without the ongoing facilitative mechanisms - most important, the conveyance of a genuinely conditionless attitude - this transmission of positive regard from therapist to client is less likely to occur.

During this transition from defensiveness to self-acceptance, the therapist may experience increased client attempts to disprove and refute his or her congruent, unconditional stance. It is hypothesized that the facilitative mechanisms, provided as undiluted as possible, are exceedingly crucial for further process movement to take place. In addition, during this time period, the client may demonstrate increased suicidality and self-harm behaviors that test the therapist's clinical skills as well as his or her strengths in weathering the storm of possibly hospitalizing the client. Contrary to current zero tolerance, cost-of-care attitudes/concerns, a hospitalization can be the "grist for the mill" that propels the client further toward change. If the therapist regards a hospitalization as a personal embarrassment or a client weakness, a blemish on the therapist's skill set, or a means to leverage or manipulate the client, then these conditional attitudes will inevitably be conveyed to the client as well. However, if accepted by the therapist, if the therapist can "roll with resistance" and accept the client despite his or her "drain" on the health care system, then further therapeutic work can be had, and eventually, therapy consistency will return. Self-acceptance emerges from reoccurring experiences of absorbing external positive regard, from the therapist in particular. From this experience in therapy, the borderline client develops a capacity to experience external positive regard from others, though in practice, this may proceed slowly. It is when this fourth process mechanism of self-acceptance becomes frequently experienced that a borderline client begins to accept others.

Increased acceptance of others. Increased acceptance of others, the fifth and penultimate process mechanism, is hypothesized to significantly occur once the borderline client has internalized sufficient self-acceptance. Standing in these new feelings of accuracy, mastery, ability to receive and experience acceptance of self, the borderline client develops stronger values toward being treated with decency by others.

Hypothetically, the actualizing tendency toward congruence between self and experience will also influence the client toward validating and prizing environments more often while discarding unhealthy relationships that possess significant conditions of worth. Gradually, the client's increased ability to accurately understand, experience, and accept what is will promote a less reactive, empathic feeling toward others. The client may realize a new sense of personal power and learn that to engage in past tendencies of "fight or flight" results in a loss of personal power and self-esteem. Therefore, the client will tend toward less engagement in tumultuous transactions with others. Similar to a posttraumatic stress disorder combat veteran's emergent addiction to safety following a traumatic event (Quinn, 2008), I suggest that a borderline client develops an addiction to chaotic relationships. In other words, the client learns to self-sooth through dramatic, self-harmful gestures and interpersonal turmoil in an effort to escape from a feeling of existential emptiness. Furthermore, as the client's addiction to chaotic relationships is lessened, the client may also reduce suicidal and self-harm behaviors by way of a decreased need to build relationship through these dysfunctional means.

Reliance on self-evaluation. The sixth and final process mechanism of change is less an ultimate step as it is a summary statement of the overall process of becoming a person. That is, *the process of developing an increased reliance on an internal locus of evaluation of experience.* Once this reliance or self-confidence begins to emerge, the client will have developed the tools to proceed forth in life demonstrating adaptable decision making. Frequently, but not the rule, the more the client has been traumatized in life, the more difficult his or her process of developing an internal evaluation of experience. For some borderline clients, the process mechanisms will occur sufficiently that the self-actualizing tendency will move the client toward further becoming, and the therapist will no longer be needed in the client's life. Other clients may have their tendency toward self-actualization so disrupted that they will seek longer term work in therapy to remove the blocks of trauma and abuse. The mechanisms are not presented as a "magic bullet," but as a lifelong movement toward health; a movement that helps the client see that "happiness is choice." And so, if a therapist can facilitate for the client a reliance on an internal locus of evaluation of experience, then the client has stepped into the process of becoming one's own person.

Conclusion

A borderline client, in some ways, remains a vulnerable little boy or little girl who was thrust into an adult world of trauma and interpersonal betrayal at an early age. However, over the years this little boy or little girl has become an adult and has developed a "prickly" exterior as protection against an untrustworthy world. As this article outlines, an evidence-informed approach that emphasizes the therapy relationship and the client's resources provides a unique therapeutic way of being that allows the client to exist as this prickly person, while trusting, that through a prizing and consistent relationship, movement toward health, happiness, and stability will occur. As the process of therapy unfolds, the borderline client gradually comes down from the "borderlands" of life and, through a new found sense of confidence and positive self-esteem, begins the process of becoming one's own person.

References

American Psychiatric Association. (2000). *Diagnostic and statistical manual of mental disorders* (4th ed., Text revision). Washington, DC: Author.

Asay, T. P., & Lambert, M. J. (1999). The empirical case for the common factors in therapy: Quantitative findings. In M. A. Hubble, B. L. Duncan, & S. D. Miller (Eds.), *The heart and soul of change: What works in therapy* (pp. 23-55). Washington, DC: American Psychological Association.

Bateman, A., & Fonagy, P. (1999). Effectiveness of partial hospitalization in the treatment of borderline personality disorder: A randomized controlled trial. *American Journal of*

Psychiatry, 156, 1563-1569.

Bateman, A., & Fonagy, P. (2001). Treatment of borderline personality disorder with psychoanalytically oriented partial hospitalization: An 18-month follow-up. *American Journal of Psychiatry, 158*, 36-42.

Bateman, A. W., & Fonagy, P. (2004). Mentalization-based treatment of BPD. *Journal of Personality Disorders, 18*, 36-51.

Bateman, A., & Fonagy, P. (2008). 8-year follow-up of patients treated for borderline personality disorder: Mentalization-based treatment versus treatment as usual. *American Journal of Psychiatry, 165*, 631-638.

Bozarth, J. D., Zimring, F. M., & Tausch, R. (2002). Client-centered therapy: The evolution of a revolution. In D. J. Cain & J. Seeman (Eds.), *Humanistic psychotherapies: Handbook of research and practice* (pp. 147-188). Washington, DC: American Psychological Association.

Brodley, B. T. (1990). Client-centered and experiential: Two different therapies. In G. Lietaer, J. Rombauts, & R. Van Balen (Eds.), *Client-centered and experiential psychotherapy in the Nineties* (pp. 87-107). Leuven, Belgium: Leuven University Press.

Brodley, B. T. (2006). Client-initiated homework in client-centered therapy. *Journal of Psychotherapy Integration, 16*, 140-161.

Clarkin, J. F., Foelsch, P. A., Levy, K. N., Hull, J. W., Delaney, J. C., & Kernberg, O. F. (2001). The development of a psychodynamic treatment for patients with borderline personality disorder: A preliminary study of behavioral change. *Journal of Personality Disorders, 15*, 487-495.

Clarkin, J. F., Levy, K. N., Lenzenweger, M. F., & Kernberg, O. F. (2007). Evaluating three treatments for borderline personality disorder: A multiwave study. *American Journal of Psychiatry, 164*, 922-928.

Clarkin, J. F., Yeomans, F. E., & Kernberg, O. F. (2006). *Psychotherapy for borderline personality: Focusing on object relations*. Washington, DC: American Psychiatric Publishing.

Cooper, M., O'Hara, M., Schmid, P. F., & Wyatt, G. (Eds.). (2007). *Handbook of Person-Centred Psychotherapy*. Basingstoke, England: Palgrave Macmillan.

Cottraux, J., Note, I. D., Boutitie, F., Milliery, M., Genouihlac, V., Yao, S. N., . . . Gueyffier, F. (2009). Cognitive therapy versus Rogerian supportive therapy in borderline personality disorder: Two-year follow-up of a controlled pilot study. *Psychotherapy and Psychosomatics, 78*, 307-316.

Elliott, R., & Freire, E. (2007). Classical person-centered and experiential perspectives on Rogers (1957). *Psychotherapy: Theory, Research, Practice, Training, 44*, 285-288.

Elliott, R. K., Greenberg, L. S., & Lietaer, G. (2004). Research on experiential psychotherapies. In M. J. Lambert (Ed.), *Bergin and Garfield's handbook of psychotherapy and behavior change* (pp. 493-

539). New York: Wiley.

Fonagy, P., & Bateman, A. W. (2006a). Mechanisms of change in mentalization-based treatment of BPD. *Journal of Clinical Psychology, 62*, 411-444.

Gendlin, E. T. (1978). *Focusing*. New York, NY: Everest House.

Giesen-Bloo, J., van Dyck, R., Spinhoven, P., van Tilburg, W., Dirksen, C., van Asselt, T., . . . Arntz, A. (2006). Outpatient psychotherapy for borderline personality disorder: Randomized trial of schema-focused therapy versus transference-focused psychotherapy. *Archives of General Psychiatry, 63*, 649-658.

Greenberg, L. S., Rice, L. N., & Elliott, R. (1993). *Facilitating emotional change: The moment-by-moment process*. New York, NY: Guilford Press.

Kellogg, S. H., & Young, J. E. (2006). Schema therapy for borderline personality disorder. *Journal of Clinical Psychology, 62*, 445-458.

Koons, C. R., Robins, C. J., Tweed, J. L., Lynch, T. R., Gonzalez, A. M., Morse, J. Q., . . . Bastian, L. A. (2001). Efficacy of dialectical behavior therapy in women veterans with borderline personality disorder. *Behavior Therapy, 32*, 371-390.

Levy, K. N., Clarkin, J. F., Yeomans, F. E., Scott, L. N., Wasserman, R. H., & Kernberg, O. F. (2006). The mechanisms of change in the treatment of borderline personality disorder with transference focused psychotherapy. *Journal of Clinical Psychology, 62*, 481-501.

Linehan, M. M. (1993). *Cognitive-behavioral treatment of borderline personality disorder*. New York, NY: Guilford Press.

Linehan, M. M., Comtois, K. A., Murray, A. M., Brown, M. Z., Gallop, R. J., Heard, H. L., & Korslund, K. E. (2006). Two-year randomized controlled trial and follow-up of dialectical behavior therapy vs. therapy by experts for suicidal behaviors and borderline personality disorder. *Archives of General Psychiatry, 63*, 757-766.

Linehan, M. M., Dimeff, L. A., Reynolds, S. K., Comtois, K. A., Welch, S. S., Heagerty, P., & Kivlahan, D. R. (2002). Dialectical behavior therapy versus comprehensive validation plus 12-step for the treatment of opioid dependent women meeting criteria for borderline personality disorder. *Drug and Alcohol Dependence, 67*, 13-26.

Linehan, M. M., Schmidt, H., Dimeff, L. A., Craft, J. C., Kanter, J., & Comtois, K. A. (1999). Dialectical behavior therapy for patients with borderline personality disorder and drug-dependence. *American Journal on Addiction, 8*, 279-292.

Lynch, T. R., Chapman, A. L., Rosenthal, M. Z., Kuo, J. R., & Linehan, M. M. (2006). Mechanisms of change in dialectical behavior therapy: Theoretical and empirical observations. *Journal of Clinical Psychology, 62*, 459-480.

McGinn, L. K., & Young, J. E. (1996). Schema focused therapy. In P. M. Salkovskis (Ed.), *Frontiers in cognitive therapy* (pp. 182-207).

New York, NY: Guilford Press.

McWilliams, N. (1994). *Psychoanalytic diagnosis: Understanding personality structure in the clinical process.* New York, NY: Guildford Press.

Paris, J. (2003). *Personality disorders over time: Precursors, course, and outcome.*Arlington, VA: American Psychiatric Publishing.

Patterson, C. H. (1984). Empathy, warmth, and genuineness in psychotherapy: A review of reviews. *Psychotherapy, 21,* 431-438.

Patterson, C. H. (1990). On being client-centered. *Person-Centered Review, 5,* 425-432.

Patterson, T. G., & Joseph, S. (2007). Person-centered personality theory: Support from self-determination theory and positive psychology. *Journal of Humanistic Psychology, 47,* 117-139.

Pretzer, J. L., & Beck, A. T. (2005). A cognitive theory of personality disorders. In M. A. Hubble, B. L. Duncan, & S. D. Miller (Eds.), *Major theories of personality disorder* (pp. 43-113). New York, NY: Guilford Press.

Quinn, A. (2008). A person-centered approach to the treatment of combat veterans with posttraumatic stress disorder. *Journal of Humanistic Psychology, 48,* 458-476.

Rogers, C. R. (1951). *Client-centered therapy: Its current practice, implications and theory.* Boston: Houghton Mifflin.

Rogers, C. R. (1957). The necessary and sufficient conditions of therapeutic personality change. *Journal of Consulting Psychology,*

21, 95-103.

Rogers, C. R. (1959). A theory of therapy, personality, and interpersonal relationships, as developed in the client-centered framework. In S. Koch (Ed.), *Psychology: A study of a science.* New York, NY: McGraw-Hill.

Rogers, C. R. (1980). *A way of being.* Boston, MA: Houghton Mifflin.

Rogers, C. R., & Dymond, R. F. (1954). *Psychotherapy and personality change.*Chicago: University of Chicago Press.

Rogers, C. R., Gendlin, E. T., Kiesler, D. J., & Truax, C. B. (1967). *The therapeutic relationship and its impact: A study of psychotherapy with schizophrenics.* Madison: University of Wisconsin Press.

Steiner, C. (1974). Scripts people live: Transactional analysis of life scripts. New York, NY: Grove Press.

Teusch, L., Bohme, H., Finke, J., & Gastpar, M. (2001). Effects of client-centered psychotherapy for personality disorders alone and in combination with psychopharmacological treatment. *Psychotherapy and Psychosomatics, 70*, 328-336.

Thorn, B. E. (Ed.). (2006). Putative mechanisms of action in the psychotherapy treatment of borderline personality disorder [Special issue]. *Journal of Clinical Psychology, 62*(4).

Truax, C. B., & Mitchell, K. M. (1971). Research on certain therapist interpersonal skills in relation to process and outcome. In A. E. Bergin & S. L. Garfield (Eds.), *Handbook of psychotherapy and behavior change: An empirical analysis* (pp. 299-344). New York,

NY: John Wiley.

Turner, R. M. (2000). Naturalistic evaluation of dialectical behavior therapy-oriented treatment for borderline personality disorder. *Cognitive and Behavioral Practice, 7*, 413-419.

van Blarikom, J. (2008). A person-centered approach to borderline personality disorder. *Person-Centered and Experiential Psychotherapies, 7*, 20-36.

Verheul, R., van den Bosch, L. M. C., Koeter, M. W. J., de Ridder, M. A. J., Stijnen, T., & van den Brink, W. (2003). Dialectical behaviour therapy for women with borderline personality disorder: 12-month, randomised clinical trial in the Netherlands. *British Journal of Psychiatry, 182*, 135-140.

Warner, M. S. (1998). A client-centered approach to therapeutic work with dissociated and fragile process. In L. Greenberg, J. Watson, & G. Lietaer (Eds.), *Handbook of experiential psychology* (pp. 368-387). New York, NY: Guilford Press.

Watts, A. (1957). *The way of Zen.* New York, NY: Pantheon Books.

Watts, A. (Writer), & Jacobs, H. (Producer). (1975). *A conversation with myself* [Television broadcast]. San Francisco, CA: KQED. Retrieved from www.youtube.com

4

A PERSON-CENTERED APPROACH TO THE TREATMENT OF COMBAT VETERANS WITH POSTTRAUMATIC STRESS DISORDER [3]

The two topics discussed in this article - congruence and posttraumatic stress disorder (PTSD) following military combat trauma - are concepts rooted in the subjective, lived experience of a person. Congruence is

---

[3] The final, definitive version of this paper has been published in the *Journal of Humanistic Psychology*, 48/4, October/2008 by SAGE Publications Ltd, All rights reserved.

considered the degree to which individuals are aware of their internal, subjective experiencing and how they express this awareness to the environment. This article distinguishes diverging types of therapeutic congruence: utilitarian congruence and genuine congruence. Moreover, a military veteran's experience during and following one or more combat traumas is not only personally subjective, it also greatly affects a veteran's perceptions of and ability to communicate with the world afterward.

According to the National Center for Posttraumatic Stress Disorder (2007a, 2007b), PTSD owing to combat trauma may impact 12% to 20% of U.S. soldiers having served their country in Iraq (Operation Iraqi Freedom). Moreover, 6% to 11% of soldiers returning from Afghanistan (Operation Enduring Freedom) will experience symptoms consistent with PTSD. For perspective on these estimates, the prevalence of PTSD in Gulf War veterans was 10% and in Vietnam veterans, 30%, and in the general adult population in the United States, the prevalence of PTSD is 3% to 4%. Furthermore, if Vietnam statistics are a predictor, then Iraq and Afghanistan veterans who develop PTSD symptoms may have an increased lifetime prevalence of alcohol and drug abuse.

I argue that the person-centered approach is an underutilized and generally ignored therapeutic orientation in the treatment of combat PTSD. Furthermore, this approach, as put forth by Carl Rogers, has a unique conceptualization of what it means for therapists to experience congruence in themselves and in therapy relationships. As a result, this approach most closely captures the essence of a true subjective encounter with another in an interpersonal relationship. Therefore, therapists who choose this way of being in their professional endeavors may possess the best chance of assisting PTSD combat veterans in reintegrating their old selves with their new selves - this final statement being the pillar upon which this article rests.

A Brief Discussion of Interpersonal Communication

The degree to which a listener can understand a speaker's subjective experiencing is limited by the listener's internal frame of reference. In other words, the listener perceives the speaker's internal experiencing from a less-than-accurate external vantage point. This external vantage point (i.e., the listener) collects information based on behavioral communication, verbal and physical, of which the accuracy of the listener's understanding is in part contingent on the speaker's ability to express subjective awareness through articulation and body language.

This accuracy of the listener's understanding is dependent on the accuracy of the speaker's awareness of experience, the speaker's ability to accurately communicate this awareness to the environment and listener, and the accuracy of the listener in perceiving the speaker's communications. Furthermore, the amount of inaccuracy at any of these stages becomes roadblocks in the listener's attempts to understand the speaker's internal frame of reference - that is, the underlying emotional and cognitive content. If the listener can demonstrate, to a degree, an understanding of the speaker's internal frame of reference, then the speaker will more closely sense having been heard.

As will follow, according to Rogers, Gendlin, Kiesler, and Truax (1967) and accumulated research (e.g., Bozarth, Zimring, & Tausch, 2002; Truax & Carkhuff, 1967), a listener's ability to accurately perceive the speaker's experiencing - that is, the listener's empathic understanding - facilitates positive therapeutic reorganization of the speaker's view of self, as long as this understanding is somewhat communicated to the speaker. And the extent to which a listener can allow for congruence between external hearing and internal understanding will predict the degree of accurate listening.

In a therapeutic relationship and in accordance with the above statements, six stages of obscuring communication (roadblocks) occur between therapist and client, or three identical stages flowing in opposite directions. From the speaker's standpoint:

subjective perceiving - how accurately the speaker's experiential stimuli (e.g., thoughts, emotions, physiology, and behavior) are perceived in conscious awareness;

communication - how accurately the speaker's perceptions of awareness are then communicated verbally and physically (facial expressions, body posture, etc.) by the speaker to the environment; and *external understanding* - how accurately the listener in the environment perceives the speaker's communication.

Following this, from the listener's standpoint:

subjective perceiving - how accurately the listener experientially perceives the speaker's communications;

communication - how accurately the listener can then communicate understanding of both the spoken content and the content possibly just outside the speaker's awareness; and

external understanding - how accurately the speaker experiences the listener's understanding.

I feel it is safe to say that at each stage, an indeterminate portion of the raw experience of the speaker is lost, if you will, to the ether. Similarly, the degree of a listener's accurate understanding is dependent on his or her perceptual faculties. Thus, the degree to which a speaker has been accurately understood is directly proportional to the listener's degree of congruence, or accurate and expansive conscious awareness.

So, it would seem that with sufficient congruence in the listener, we are speaking of the prerequisites of Rogers's concept (1975) of empathic understanding of another's internal frame of reference. Not only does accurate communication of the speaker's awareness undergo obscuring before reaching the listener, the communication then undergoes additional diffusion as it is integrated into the listener's awareness. The listener's degree of congruence influences the extent of the communication understood; increased incongruence means less understanding of the speaker's covert and overt content and meaning. Likewise, the closer a listener's awareness of the experienced external stimuli, the closer the listener will come to an accurate understanding of what was said. In other words, the listener hears only what is allowed into awareness. This is one view of how two people communicate in an interpersonal relationship.

High levels of congruence enable the listener to accurately perceive the speaker's communications and, ideally, signal when clarifying statements and requests are necessary because the listener either did not understand something or senses that there may be more to the message. Likewise, a speaker's high levels of congruence assist in accurately communicating to the listener the speaker's internal and external experience.

Congruence is the stream upon which accurate and therapeutic communication travel. In this way, a therapist can strive to move as freely as possible in an interpersonal encounter. The therapist is restricted by only the amount of experiential stimuli not perceived into awareness. Therefore, the degree to which a therapist can unerringly perceive a subjective world will play an essential part in attempting to accurately understand the world of a combat veteran in particular. As discussed later in this article, a combat veteran who is expressing symptoms of PTSD will tend to block a great deal of experience from awareness. In my experience, to enter into a veteran's lived world - as a companion, as congruently as possible - means to facilitate a safe opening to further awareness of the veteran's experience.

Carl Rogers's person-centered approach, developed and practiced by numerous others, is mistakenly absent from combat PTSD therapeutic practice, but as was Rogers's nondirective approach for World War II veterans, this therapy may be most healing for our past soldiers and our current ones coming home (Kirschenbaum, 1979; Rogers & Wallen, 1946).

Rogers's Conditions: A Framework from Which Effective Congruence Emerges

Carl Rogers's necessary and sufficient conditions (1957) of therapeutic personality change include the following conditions:

1. Two persons are in psychological contact.
2. The first, whom we shall term the client, is in a state of incongruence, being vulnerable or anxious.
3. The second person, whom we shall term the therapist, is congruent or integrated in the relationship.
4. The therapist experiences unconditional positive regard for the client.

5. The therapist experiences an empathic understanding of the client's internal frame of reference and endeavors to communicate this experience to the client.
6. The communication to the client of the therapist's empathic understanding and unconditional positive regard is to a minimal degree achieved.

No other conditions are necessary. If these six conditions exist, and continue over a period of time, this is sufficient. (p. 96)

Conditions 3 through 5 are typically referred to as the core conditions, and all six were rigorously tested in the 1950s through the early 1970s. In addition, despite ongoing research trends and standards that only minimally value therapeutic orientations lacking a "specific effective treatments for specific problems" paradigm (Freire, 2006, p. 324), these conditions still evidence strong efficacy, thanks in part to the rigorous person-centered studies done in Germany, Belgium, and the United Kingdom (Bozarth et al., 2002; Levant & Shlien, 1984; Lietaer, Rombauts, & van Balen, 1990). Although these conditions - in particular, the three core conditions - were dismissed for lacking sufficiency for successful therapy, their necessity is accepted by most therapy orientations (Beck, Rush, Shaw, & Emery, 1979; Horvath & Symonds, 1991).

Congruence, in part the subject of this article, is regarded by some as a useful tool in building rapport with a client to pave the way for the therapeutic work to take place. Likewise, congruence from a perspective of person-centered therapy is viewed as a precursor to what occurs in therapy. However, I believe that crucial differences exist between the presence of congruence in therapists who view Rogers's conditions as being sufficient and therapists who hold the conviction that purposeful, technical interventions provide the sufficiency that they believe Rogers's conditions lack. In other words, can these six conditions exclusively possess sufficient therapeutic efficacy? Unfortunately, this question is difficult, if not impossible, to answer because of the subjective nature of the philosophy and the approach, the difficulty in measuring the operant variables of a relationship, and the cultural forces (Van Dusen, 1967; Watson, 1984). However, in spite of restrictions placed on person-centered research by diagnostic and empirically biased language, a strong and supportive evidence base exists. Meta-analyses of effective therapeutic ingredients tend to contraindicate the helpfulness of the specific-treatments-for-specific-problems approach, finding more positive therapeutic effects in the common factors of psychotherapy (e.g., the quality of the relationship; Messer & Wampold, 2002; Wampold et al., 1997). These studies do in fact point to possible sufficiency in Rogers's conditions.

Next, can person-centered therapy be helpful to combat veterans with PTSD? Joseph (2004) supports this premise by examining Rogers's theory of personality through the lens of a "breakdown and disorganization of the self-structure" (p. 104), which is in line with the sociocognitive view of PTSD advanced by Horowitz (1986, as cited in

Joseph, 2004) and Janoff-Bulman (1992). Predominantly excluded from the literature on the treatment of combat veterans with PTSD, person-centered therapy - the orientation that strives to achieve high levels of Rogers's conditions of therapeutic growth (Patterson, 1990) - is an underutilized resource in the reintegration of combat veterans' lives. Specifically, a person-centered classification of congruence may be the starting point for therapeutic reintegration of a combat veteran's broken self-structure. In accord with the previous statement, I assert that the notion of how a therapist is congruent varies among therapeutic orientations. Therefore, an essential question involves whether one classification of therapeutic congruence is more essential and respectful than another in the treatment of the men and women who have risked their lives in the service of this country.

The Dual Life of Congruence: Utilitarian or Genuine?

As stated earlier, I contend that two types of congruence exist in the therapy world: utilitarian congruence and genuine congruence. These types exist at the ends of a continuum that I perceive as being directly related to the degree to which a therapist believes Rogers's conditions are necessary and, more important, sufficient. Moreover, these types of congruence may be differentiated in one way based on the values that a therapist holds toward the process and outcome of therapy. One caveat is that some orientations (e.g., psychoanalytic) argue that Rogers's conditions are not novel and that therapists have been and continue to use these attitudes of respect, acceptance, and empathy despite Rogers's contributions (Truax & Carkhuff, 1967). What follows is an explanation of why a utilitarian approach is substantially and therapeutically different from a genuine way of being.

Utilitarian congruence

The first type of congruence, utilitarian, might be understood as a means to an end, with the goal being a strong-enough trust from the client in the therapeutic relationship to allow for a therapist's intervention to successfully take place (i.e., the client trusts in the therapist's abilities and prescribed treatments). This type of congruence is more likely to be described in the literature as a combination of a therapist's transparency and self-disclosure (Beck et al., 1979). Whereas the relationship facilitated in genuine congruence is the therapy, utilitarian congruence is operationalized and constructed as a technique or client variable that precedes a direct, active therapeutic intervention, with the result being a forced or insincere presentation of the therapist, most likely regarded by the client as a means of coercion to do what the therapist subjectively deems as being right for the client. In terms of this type of congruence with combat veterans, they tend to possess a very sensitive "bullshit meter," as a supervisor once stated, and I agree. In other words, the means through which trauma reorganizes individuals' perceptions of the world tend to reduce their tolerance for façades and false intentions.

Genuine congruence

The second type of congruence, genuine, is held as a means to facilitate the other two core conditions of a therapeutic relationship: unconditional positive regard and empathic understanding. However, this does not imply that both conditions are therapeutic ends. From the starting point of being in congruence, once the necessary and sufficient conditions are established in a manner that is real for the therapist (i.e., the therapist is aware of genuine feelings toward the client, in the client's world) and if the client can perceive these conditions as being real, then the so-called end - the getting down to brass tacks, as it were - evaporates.

Genuine congruence is consequently the means to a process where the end is the process itself. The client begins to test the water in what might be his or her first attempt at moving toward a life with no ends and with less reliance on external conditions of worth - in short, a life of continual "becomings." Put another way, as a whole person, "I am as good enough now as I was earlier and will be in the future; there is no happy ending or cathartic, life-changing moment." Part of the outcome of person-centered therapy is a client's "felt sense" (Gendlin, 1984, p. 76) that "you are who you are" despite outside judgments. Likewise, can the therapist be genuine now, as opposed to putting up a façade as a means to procure the client's adherence to a recommended course of treatment with the promise of a reduction in one's symptoms? (Is existence a symptom?) Furthermore, as the philosopher Alan Watts (1961) phrased it, individuals follow their assumptions about the linear course of life to their logical conclusions, only to discover that the assumptions were false and that there was no conclusion in the first place.

Genuine congruence, explained scientifically, facilitates a means by which a person can test hypotheses regarding the accuracy of one's awareness of experience, discovering the introjected values that have informed decision making toward certain choices and not others. Furthermore, if a person determines that the awareness of experience was inaccurate, that it was influenced by undesirable external values, then that person may experience change in which he or she makes choices that more closely match his or her self-experience. Through this shedding of external values, a person comes to trust one's inner values, and consequently, one's accuracy of awareness and communication of awareness become closer to the experiencing of reality.

Some implications of choosing utilitarian versus genuine congruence

Arguably, a theory of personality change or a theory of symptom reduction that fails to emphasize congruence as an existential and genuine way of living will subsequently discourage practitioners of their respective therapeutic orientations from valuing this type of genuine congruence in themselves and their clients - combat veterans in particular. Instead, congruence will be viewed as a small fragment of what constitutes the pathway toward the reduction of symptom criteria and, therefore, successful treatment. That is, utilitarian congruence will mirror in the client how it is valued in the therapist - as a necessary but insignificant part of oneself and the relationship.

Thus, the choice of utilitarian congruence versus genuine congruence is boiled down to a question of whether the relationship alone is enough to produce positive outcomes in therapy. For the therapist who chooses a technique or a utilitarian approach to congruence, studies indicate that interventions must be included in this type of therapy to avoid damage to clients; that is, a utilitarian approach to congruence cannot build and sustain the therapeutic conditions necessary to facilitate growth in the sense that Rogers and his colleagues discussed. Furthermore, utilitarian congruence may actually obstruct unconditional positive regard and empathic understanding from existing in the therapist's lived experience of the client (Rogers et al., 1967). As such, when congruence is viewed as a means to an intervention, the therapist leads the way as an expert. Consequently, for the client's sake, the therapist who uses a methodical, utilitarian approach to being congruent must fulfill the expert role and direct the session to avoid psychological damage owing to inherent lower levels of unconditional positive regard and empathic understanding, which, I assert, occur with techniques.

In contrast, genuine congruence - an authentic realness - allows for the other two of Rogers's conditions to thrive in the therapist. Hence, the therapist experiences the tools (i.e., Rogers's core conditions) to move freely in the client's world and facilitate change from within the client, thereby no longer needing an externalized intervention strategy. These tools differ from the techniques described above because of their experiential nature, existing in the therapist's way of being. In this way, congruence has become the precondition through which the therapist facilitates change from within the client (Vanaerschot, 1990). When congruence is the means and the end - or the illusion of an end - the therapist accompanies the client, trusting that the client will generate internal interventions as needed. The therapist does not instruct the client about the value, logic, or relevance of experience but attends to and facilitates the client's process of becoming a person.

Finally, Lambers (2000) warns that clinicians who lack the ability to experience and internally process incongruent stimuli and awareness may be susceptible to regarding congruence in therapy as a means to express misunderstood feelings to the client. Furthermore, there is a danger that a therapist who tends toward a utilitarian approach to congruence may use misinterpreted expressions of feeling as a means to be transparent with the client but may instead impose personal and subjective values and beliefs onto the client.

The therapeutic process

As a primary point of this article, genuine congruence facilitates in a therapist the quality of trusting the process, endeavoring to make the leap across the vast boundary that distinguishes a "wooden imitation" (Rogers et al., 1967, p. 10) from a therapy that undertakes the risk and uncertainty of entering into an ambiguous swamp of being person-to-person in a therapy relationship. To continue this imagery, the client, a PTSD combat veteran, arrives in the therapist's office living in this swamp, at times impulsively attempting to flee. The therapist, informed by philosophical values of personal growth as well as clinical training, chooses to remain in the safety of the therapeutic boat floating atop the swamp or to step down into the muck of living - in this case, the veteran's life. If the therapist, informed by person-centered values, believes that the veteran already possesses the resources necessary to become a person, then the therapist will choose the difficult but rewarding role as a companion/guide in helping the veteran navigate through the swamp.

The implication is twofold: first, empathy and unconditional positive regard will not come to fruition without a therapist being in congruence; second, for this genuine congruence to exist, a therapist must have developed the aforementioned experiential tools and way of being by becoming his or her own person through the process of self-growth.

A Humanistic Approach to Understanding and Treating Combat PTSD

According to the American Psychiatric Association (2000),

PTSD can be understood as developing after (post-) a life-threatening (traumatic) experience. As a result, anxiety (stress) is experienced by a person to the extent that it becomes a problem (disorder). The traumatic event "involves actual or threatened death or serious injury [. . .] or witnessing an event that involves death, injury, or a threat to the physical integrity of another person" (p. 463). Furthermore, three clusters of symptoms differentiate the signs of a person's experiencing this type of problem: reexperiencing, hyperarousal, and avoidance (American Psychiatric Association, 2000).

Briefly, the reexperiencing symptoms refer to perceptual phenomena of the traumatic content. These symptoms include nightmares, unwanted thoughts and images, flashbacks, and other physical and emotional reactions to reminders of the trauma.

Next, the hyperarousal symptoms indicate that a person is experiencing physiological reactions at varying levels of intensities. These symptoms include hypervigilance and feeling on guard, panic attacks, insomnia, anger and irritability, and other problems that stem from feeling in a state of fight or flight. A common report of hyperarousal symptoms might include experiencing an adrenaline rush for extended periods.

The third symptom cluster, avoidance, can be conceptualized as a set of broken-down coping strategies as a means by which a person who is experiencing hyperarousal and reexperiencing can retreat from the perceptual and physiological intensity of these symptoms. The methods by which one copes with such intense reexperiencing and hyperarousal symptoms include isolation; emotional numbing; withdrawal from previously enjoyed activities, people, and places; and drug and alcohol abuse. Much of the time, withdrawal from family members and close friends becomes the catalyst for a person who is experiencing PTSD to seek assistance. In other words, the person will subjectively know that something has changed at a core level, but he or she may go for years without seeking help.

The breakdown of the combat veteran's self-structure

A shedding of external conditions of worth becomes especially important in understanding how to work with combat veterans with PTSD. There is general agreement that a veteran's common psychological reaction to trauma is a shattering of a sense of invulnerability to harm (Janoff-Bulman, 1992). That is, the trauma splinters the veteran's illusion of a safe, benevolent world, as well as one's self-perceptions as a caring, protective person who is incapable of acts of violence and killing. Because of the traumatic experience of combat, the veteran has had experiences forced into consciousness that would have otherwise, before the trauma, been filtered from awareness to fit with an overall organized self-structure. In contrast to a civilian client, who is given wide berth in learning to integrate inconsistent experiences into a self-structure or schema, the veteran is forced to become aware of inconsistent experiences in an immediate, shocking way.

According to Rogers's theory of personality (1959), a person who possesses external conditions of worth may deny to his or her awareness experiences inconsistent with one's view of the self. For a simplified example, an individual may have a sense of being a nice person (i.e., the frame through which the individual's self-perception is nice, or nice is a value positively regarded by others of importance). Consequently, the individual may not accurately symbolize or become aware of the organismic experience of anger, an unacceptable emotion according to external evaluators. Others, however, may observe this anger, despite the person's subjective denial, because the individual may be unknowingly communicating this emotion, as evidenced by a flushed and expressive face or a raised voice. If this person enters therapy, it would most likely be due to this person's incongruence in self-perception, which is causing anxiety and problems. Through therapy - in particular, a therapy possessing high levels of Rogers's core conditions - the individual gradually begins to see the nice person self-concept as a façade or an illusion. Moreover, this façade, the person comes to realize, was just a vehicle by which to preserve the good will and positive regard of others.

As the individual comes to accept the parts of oneself that are not always nice - that is, an accurate awareness of experiencing anger and a degree of accepting this anger - and gradually allows into awareness anger-related experiences, he or she experiences (in sharp contrast to the past) a sense of not having to deny the experience of anger from self-perception to preserve positive self-regard. This sense is due in part to the person's no longer attaching external values to internal positive regard. Said slightly different, despite experiences that others may value negatively, the client perceives these experiences from an internal locus of control. Thus, the person's defensive denial of the threat of not being nice all the time gradually dissipates (possibly over months or years) as he or she becomes open to new and more congruent conceptualizations of an internal, phenomenological life (Rogers, 1961). In contrast, the veteran in combat is flooded with sharp, inconsistent, and unacceptable experiences that contradict the self-structure and assumptions of oneself and the world.

Because of the extreme nature of the combat trauma, the combat soldier's defenses, by which threat to conscious awareness is avoided, were brought to task and failed to protect the pretrauma understandings of oneself and the world. If psychological defenses could not keep the combat trauma at bay, the soldier fully perceives into awareness the hell subjectively observed on the battlefield. As a result, "the self-structure is broken by this experience of the incongruence [the death and dismemberment of war] in awareness. A state of disorganization results" (Rogers, 1959, p. 229). In other words, the combat soldier has not had sufficient time to restructure core assumptions to accommodate this intrusively inconsistent information of oneself and the world (Piaget, 1952, as cited in Janoff-Bulman, 1992).

Combat trauma

Combat trauma, like all trauma, forces a person to question previous belief systems. For the soldier, the real self and the ideal self become incongruent as a result of a destruction of meaning from the experience of trauma. Following the soldier's return home and the process of transformation from soldier to veteran, the meaning in life that the veteran once had before the combat trauma may be lost. Furthermore, some veterans have reported that living among civilians is almost intolerable. Many combat veterans perceive civilians as being naïve, superficial, and infantile. Veterans believe that they possess a sophisticated understanding of existence - as a result of facing death - that civilians cannot comprehend. Combat veterans may regard the meaning and purpose that they experienced on the battlefield during combat as never to be matched in intensity and purpose again.

This meaning and purpose result from a camaraderie with fellow soldiers forged in the fires of basic training and fed by the shared goals of defeating (if not obliterating) the enemy in combat situations. Combat veterans report complex motivations while in combat, driven by their military training. The core of these motivations is built on the learned use and control of the fight/flight/freeze survival response. Veterans tend to agree that their military training teaches them to override a normal, "civilian" response to threat. Through their training, veterans learn to control the natural flight response to danger and, as their job description dictates, remain in the war zone and fight.

There are caveats to how a soldier's military training alters the response to threat. At times, a soldier must flee or freeze to preserve one's life and, in so doing, the lives of fellow soldiers. In other words, military training does not absolutely revoke the soldier's survival response; rather, it alters the response in such a way as to promote the primary motivation in military combat: defeat the enemy.

To accomplish this primary goal, the soldier must remain alive to fight, as well as to protect fellow soldiers so they can also fight. A soldier must strategically and reflexively choose when survival warrants a fight, flight, or freeze response. Experienced clinicians working with PTSD combat veterans refer to the military modification of the survival response as teaching soldiers combat mode: an instinctual but learned and controlled response to threat. Moreover, the differentiation between a civilian's survival mode and the soldier's combat mode lies in the ability of the soldier to control and direct these innate reactions to threat. As discussed below, a soldier enters basic training with the inborn survival mode of responding to danger (fight, flight, or freeze) and graduates to a combat mode of encountering threat (strategic fight, flight, or freeze). Subsequently, the soldier returns home in combat mode - a valuable modality of operation in the combat zone that becomes a collection of exaggerated reactions to the relatively safe civilian environment, described earlier as the hyperarousal and reexperiencing symptom clusters of PTSD.

The transformation of a soldier into a PTSD combat veteran

This section may clarify the distinction between (a) a soldier who learns combat mode but does not enter battle or does not develop PTSD following combat, and (b) a soldier who experiences one or more traumatic events in battle and develops PTSD. The noncombat veterans honorably serve their country and will usually return home able to reintegrate pre- and post-service selves. Veterans who see combat and subsequently develop PTSD report that a transformation occurs between the time of entering the military and the time of their discharge. The stages that I have heard commonly described in this transformation consist of the following:

> *Civilian self, old self*: Before military training.

> *Breakdown of old self*: Combat training and breakdown of the civilian self, which following training becomes the old self.

> *Military self, new self*: Integration of the new self into a unit of soldiers (an army of one, if you will).

> *New self finds new purpose*: The feelings of purpose arise as the new self and the soldier's unit are trained to accomplish a common goal - win in combat.

> *New self shattered*: Combat happens, during which the new self's combat training more or less overrides the old self's civilian-based fight, flight, and freeze instincts as they would naturally

occur.

Shattered self survives: The combat training may save the soldier's life, and the soldier consequently comes to regard combat mode as a necessary and continuous way to stay alive.

Shattered self returns home: The soldier survives combat and returns home but cannot turn combat mode off.

Combat mode at home: The veteran acts in ways consistent with combat training - that is, maintaining a safe perimeter around the house, sleeping sporadically, being on guard at all times, being unable to leave the perceived safety of home, constantly looking over the shoulder, and so on.

New self and old life: The veteran is unable to integrate the new self into his or her old life and thus becomes at odds with the naïve, civilian way of life.

PTSD: PTSD sets in. The veteran exhibits behaviors deemed appropriate for the preservation of life on the battlefield but considered eccentric, inappropriate, and threatening to family and civilians in the civilian environment. The veteran is diagnosed with PTSD and begins treatment.

Further conceptualizations of combat PTSD

Decker (2007) suggests that the meaning of combat and the

absence of meaning in civilian life may be bridged through the use of spirituality in PTSD treatment. Decker's interactive self identifies how a veteran constructs a worldview through interactions with a stable, controllable environment. Regardless of the extent to which a veteran experienced congruence in pre-trauma life, combat trauma becomes a force through which one's interactive self becomes out of congruence: "The basis of the veteran's belief systems that provided meaning, predictability, and control has been seriously challenged" (p. 33). More important, disregarding the self-structure of a veteran's pre-trauma life runs the risk of negating earlier traumas and personality development that predisposed the veteran to developing a more complex version of PTSD. Likewise, a veteran may experience noncombat trauma during his or her tour of duty, such as rape, severe hazing, or bullying at the hands of fellow soldiers (Polusny & Murdoch, 2005).

In a similar vein, Linley (2003) poses a dialectic theory of posttraumatic growth, suggesting that dimensions of wisdom may account for positive adaptation to trauma. Following trauma, the survivor may perceive positive and negative changes in self-perception. For a combat veteran, this perception may be consistent with their experiences, as described earlier. Furthermore, the combat veteran has experienced a shattering of the belief regarding an invulnerability to harm. In this way, the veteran has moved from life before trauma to life following trauma, from the world as a relatively safe place to the world as an unsafe place. Linley holds that positive adaptation occurs when the veteran can attain wisdom from synthesizing pre- and post-trauma lives. Linley describes the characteristics of posttraumatic wisdom attainment through the recognition and management of uncertainty, the integration of affect and cognition, and the recognition and acceptance of human limitation. In other words, the combat veteran learns to again live in an uncertain world by developing openness to experience, or a congruent self. The veteran also develops a sense of control over thoughts and feelings and can subsequently create a new life narrative that integrates the old self and the new. Finally, the combat veteran begins to see both the good parts and the bad of the self as a gestalt, and by examining and accepting personal limitations, as well as the limitations of others, the veteran develops a sense of altruism. This is consistent with Rogers's process of reintegration (1959), where following the breakdown of oneself, a veteran may begin to move toward congruence between self and experience because of the presence of a relationship that possesses high amounts of congruence, unconditional positive regard, and empathic understanding.

The beginning of the healing process

Subjectively, combat veterans enter into relationships as do most other people: They have their uncertainties about themselves and their fears that they will be rooted out as fakes or imposters. They may wish but have lost all hope that a person whom they encounter in relationship - possibly, a therapist - might see them with as little preconception as possible, that this person could lift their heavy burden and support at least part of it. Of course, these feelings may be outside their conscious awareness as they begin to enter into a relationship. Their tears, which have not been shed in years, seem cosmically distant from flowing but paradoxically exist in close proximity to their awareness - just outside the fringes. Even if these tears have been shed in the past - possibly in empathic response to a fellow soldier's demise or to the melody of the "Star-Spangled Banner" or to the unconditional regard of a child - for many combat veterans, the sensation of crying is foreign. If the tears do run - that is, if the other in the relationship can understand who a veteran is with as little preconception as possible - I imagine that a veteran would experience this sensation as an inviolable, foreign, and yet vaguely familiar one likened to an emotional release permitted to happen as only a small child.

Furthermore, veterans may have feelings and regrets hidden deep but that are accessible under certain conditions: immediate or past memories of physical and verbal acts of hurtfulness toward those close to them; distancing themselves from those whom they love; failing to be psychologically present with loved ones; always distracted by their burgeoning and engulfing addiction to safety; never feeling grounded in themselves because they perpetually exist between the plain of wakefulness and slumber, the combat memories jolting them awake at night and continually running through their minds during the waking hours.

The importance of a real relationship

Unfortunately, the current cognitive treatments for PTSD deemed evidence based fail to sufficiently emphasize, in my opinion, the importance of genuine congruence in the therapeutic relationship (Bradley, Greene, Russ, Dutra, & Westen, 2005). The therapeutic alliance - which has become a convenient method to boil down the broadly accepted therapeutic conditions of genuineness, warmth, and empathy - does not adequately highlight the requisite that a therapist must authentically experience these conditions so that the client can perceive these qualities as being real and not a wooden imitation (Horvath & Symonds, 1991; Truax & Carkhuff, 1967).

Another difficulty exists in that research indicates that therapists tend to be imprecise when rating the degrees to which they provide these conditions in a therapy session. Furthermore, a distinct positive association exists between an inexperienced outsider's ratings and the client's ratings of condition levels. Paradoxically, an outside observer and the client are more accurate than the therapist in judging the amount of therapeutic conditions in the room, which leads to the deposition that the quality of the therapeutic relationship exists only in the eye of the beholder. In other words, in addition to the therapeutic conditions being held as necessary but insufficient by most orientations, without external feedback (e.g., the Barrett-Lennard Relationship Inventory), the therapist is unable to discern the degree to which these conditions are facilitated (Rogers, 1975).

Conclusion

Therapists and clinicians have a choice while a veteran attempts to make sense of life after war: exist in the combat veteran's world or stand back as an observer. This choice starts with the differentiation between two conceptualizations of therapist congruence.

Utilitarian congruence and genuine congruence are contrasted in this article as creating divergent modalities of a therapeutic relationship. I argue that genuine congruence, the starting point to Rogers's conditions of therapeutic personality change, is most effective with combat veterans. Combat trauma creates in the soldier turned veteran an extreme state of incongruence within a short amount of time. A therapist must be able to enter into the veteran's subjective world and act as a companion/guide who can assist the veteran in making sense of the shattering experiences of combat and consequently help him or her move forward toward reintegrating into life.

References

American Psychiatric Association. (2000). *Diagnostic and statistical manual of mental disorders* (4th ed., text rev.). Washington, DC: Author.

Beck, A. T., Rush, A. J., Shaw, B. F., & Emery, G. (1979). *Cognitive therapy of depression*. New York: Guilford Press.

Bozarth, J. D., Zimring, F. M., & Tausch, R. (2002). Client-centered therapy: The evolution of a revolution. In D. J. Cain & J.

Seeman (Eds.), *Humanistic psychotherapies: Handbook of research and practice* (pp. 147-188). Washington, DC: American Psychological Association.

Bradley, R., Greene, J., Russ, E., Dutra, L., & Westen, D. (2005). A multidimensional metaanalysis of psychotherapy for PTSD. *American Journal of Psychiatry, 162*(2), 214-227.

Decker, L. R. (2007). Combat trauma: Treatment from a mystical/spiritual perspective. *Journal of Humanistic Psychology, 47*(1), 30-53.

Freire, E. S. (2006). Randomized controlled clinical trial in psychotherapy research: An epistemological controversy. *Journal of Humanistic Psychology, 46*(3), 323-335.

Gendlin, E. T. (1984). The client's client: The edge of awareness. In R. F. Levant & J. M. Shlien (Eds.), *Client-centered therapy and the person-centered approach: New directions in theory, research and practice* (pp. 76-107). New York: Praeger.

Horvath, A. O., & Symonds, B. D. (1991). Relation between working alliance and outcome in psychotherapy: A meta-analysis. *Journal of Counseling Psychology, 38*(2), 139-149.

Janoff-Bulman, R. (1992). *Shattered assumptions: Towards a new psychology of trauma.* New York: Free Press.

Joseph, S. (2004). Client-centred therapy, post-traumatic stress disorder and posttraumatic growth: Theoretical perspectives and practical implications. *Psychology and Psychotherapy: Theory, Research, and*

Practice, 77(1), 101-119.

Kirschenbaum, H. (1979). *On becoming Carl Rogers*. New York: Delacorte Press.

Lambers, E. (2000). Supervision in person-centred therapy. In D. Mearns & B. Thorne (Eds.), *Person centred therapy today: New frontiers in theory and practice* (pp. 196-211). London: Sage.

Levant, R. F., & Shlien, J. M. (Eds.). (1984). *Client-centered therapy and the person-centered approach: New directions in theory, research and practice*. New York: Praeger.

Lietaer, G., Rombauts, J., & van Balen, R. (1990). *Client-centered and experiential psychotherapy in the Nineties*. Leuven, Belgium: Leuven University Press.

Linley, P. A. (2003). Positive adaptation to trauma: Wisdom as both process and outcome. *Journal of Traumatic Stress, 16*(6), 601-610.

Messer, S. B., & Wampold, B. E. (2002). Let's face facts: Common factors are more potent than specific therapy ingredients. *Clinical Psychology: Science and Practice, 9*(1), 21-25.

National Center for Posttraumatic Stress Disorder. (2007a). *Epidemiological facts about PTSD*. Retrieved December 23, 2007 from http://www.ncptsd.va.gov/ncmain/ncdocs/fact_shts/fs_epidemiological.html

National Center for Posttraumatic Stress Disorder. (2007b). *How common is PTSD?* Retrieved December 23, 2007, from http://www.ncptsd.va.gov/ncmain/ncdocs/fact_shts/fs_how_com mon_is_ptsd.html

Patterson, C. H. (1990). On being client-centered. *Person–Centered Review, 5,* 428-432.

Polusny, M. A., & Murdoch, M. (2005). Sexual assault among male veterans. *Psychiatric Times, 22*(4), 34-37.

Rogers, C. R. (1957). The necessary and sufficient conditions of therapeutic personality change. *Journal of Consulting Psychology, 21*(2), 95-103.

Rogers, C. R. (1959). A theory of therapy, personality, and interpersonal relationships, as developed in the client-centered framework. In S. Koch (Ed.), *Psychology: A study of a science* (pp. 184-256). New York: McGraw-Hill.

Rogers, C. R. (1961). *On becoming a person.* Boston: Houghton Mifflin.

Rogers, C. R. (1975). Empathic: An unappreciated way of being. *The Counseling Psychologist, 5*(2), 2-10.

Rogers, C. R., Gendlin, E. T., Kiesler, D. J., & Truax, C. B. (1967). *The therapeutic relationship and its impact: A study of psychotherapy with schizophrenics.* Madison: University of Wisconsin Press.

Rogers, C. R., & Wallen, J. L. (1946). *Counseling with returned servicemen.* New York: McGraw-Hill.

Truax, C. B., & Carkhuff, R. R. (1967). *Toward effective counseling and psychotherapy: Training and practice.* Chicago: Aldine.

Vanaerschot, G. (1990). The process of empathy: Holding and letting go. In G. Lietaer, J. Rombauts, & R. van Balen (Eds.), *Client-centered and experiential psychotherapy in the Nineties* (pp. 267-293). Leuven, Belgium: Leuven University Press.

Van Dusen, W. (1967). The natural depth in man. In C. R. Rogers & B. Stevens (Eds.), *Person to person: The problem of being human, a new trend in psychology* (pp. 211-234). Walnut Creek, CA: Real People Press.

Wampold, B. E., Mondlin, G. W., Moody, M., Stich, F., Benson, K., & Ahn, H. (1997). A meta-analysis of outcome studies comparing bona fide psychotherapies: Empirically, "all must have prizes." *Psychological Bulletin, 122*(3), 203-215.

Watson, N. (1984). The empirical status of Rogers' hypotheses of the necessary and sufficient conditions of effective psychotherapy. In R. F. Levant & J. M. Shlien (Eds.), *Client-centered therapy and the person-centered approach: New directions in theory, research, and practice* (pp. 17-40). New York: Praeger.

Watts, A. (1961). *Psychotherapy, East and West*. New York: Pantheon Books.

About the Typeface

This book was printed using the *Adobe Caslon* font. This font was derived from the Caslon typeface, originally created by the British gunsmith and typeface designer William Caslon in 1722. This typeface has a remarkable history in that the first printings of the American Declaration of Independence and the Constitution were set in Caslon, a favorite typeface of Benjamin Franklin. Caslon's types were based on seventeenth-century Dutch old-style designs, which were then used extensively in England. Designer Carol Twombly developed *Adobe Caslon* by studying specimen pages printed by William Caslon between 1734 and 1770. In modern times, the well-known publication *The New Yorker* uses this font.

www.ingramcontent.com/pod-product-compliance
Lightning Source LLC
Chambersburg PA
CBHW061957280526
45787CB00005B/1894